Rethinking Library Technical Services

Rethinking Library Technical Services

Redefining Our Profession for the Future

Edited by
Mary Beth Weber

ROWMAN & LITTLEFIELD
Lanham • Boulder • New York • London

Published by Rowman & Littlefield
A wholly owned subsidiary of The Rowman & Littlefield Publishing Group, Inc.
4501 Forbes Boulevard, Suite 200, Lanham, Maryland 20706
www.rowman.com

Unit A, Whitacre Mews, 26-34 Stannary Street, London SE11 4AB

British Library Cataloguing in Publication Information Available

Library of Congress Cataloging-in-Publication Data

Rethinking library technical services : redefining our profession for the future / edited by Mary Beth Weber.
p. cm.
Includes bibliographical references and index.
ISBN 978-1-4422-4871-7 (cloth : alk. paper) – ISBN 978-1-4422-3863-3 (pbk. : alk. paper) – ISBN 978-1-4422-3864-0 (ebook)
1. Technical services (Libraries) I. Weber, Mary Beth, editor.
Z688.5.R48 2015
025'.02–dc23
2014044983

∞™ The paper used in this publication meets the minimum requirements of American National Standard for Information Sciences Permanence of Paper for Printed Library Materials, ANSI/NISO Z39.48-1992.

Printed in the United States of America

Contents

Acknowledgments

I'd like to acknowledge the following individuals:

- All the contributors who wrote chapters. Thank you for agreeing to be part of this book and for your hard work. Some of you were strangers to me before this project, and I'm glad to have made your acquaintance.
- My Rutgers colleague Melissa De Fino for providing feedback regarding my ideas and my chapters. Thank you also for agreeing to be interviewed.
- My ALCTS colleagues Karen E. K. Brown, Erica Findley, Norm Medeiros, Sarah Peterson, and Ginger Williams. Thank you for agreeing to be interviewed.
- My unit director Grace Agnew for her support and encouragement during the writing process.
- My Rutgers colleague Fay Austin for agreeing to be interviewed and for sharing her vision of the future.
- My daughters Christina and Nicole for their encouragement during the long process of researching, writing, and editing.

Introduction

What Is Technical Services?

Mary Beth Weber

DEFINING "TECHNICAL SERVICES"

Any discussion of technical services begins with how it is defined and what work or departments it includes. *Technical services* holds a different meaning for each individual or institution. For some, technical services is a category of work that might include resource acquisition or description, and it could also include end processing, bindery operations, or preservation. This can include responsibilities not traditionally associated with technical services, such as reference or library instruction. An institution might not have a specific "technical services" department, and resource description, acquisitions, and electronic resources management might report to systems, public services, or another department. There is not a single answer for what constitutes technical services as it is unique to each library or institution and is shaped by factors including the library or institution's mission, available staffing, financial considerations, and interaction with other departments or operations within the organization. Gorman in *Technical Services Today and Tomorrow* defines technical services as "All the tasks carried on in a library that are concerned with the processing of library materials . . . to make them accessible to the users of the library. Such processes include: ordering and claiming; cataloguing and classification; serials control; database and catalogue maintenance; marking of processed materials; shelving, housing and retrieval; . . . binding and preservation; [and] budgeting and planning for these activities."[1] See table 0.1 for an illustration of the diversity that exists among libraries regarding technical services configurations and functions.

WHAT ASPECTS OF TECHNICAL SERVICES HAVE CHANGED?

Technical services operations have changed dramatically over the last ten to fifteen years, much of this fueled by technological advances. How resources are acquired and made available to users has drastically changed. Print, once the predominant format, is still collected and cataloged, but the balance has shifted in favor of electronic resources, which can serve more users and simultaneously. Electronic resources have added features such as the ability to highlight or bookmark passages online, generate citations, or create annotations. Gone is the need to acquire multiple copies of a title, borrow a title by interlibrary loan (ILL), or limit the loan period for a title. New publication models enable readers to view, download, or print just the content of interest to them. Acquisitions and cataloging, for the most part, have transitioned from operations that required many labor-intensive manual processes and paper forms, frequently handled by a large staff, to operations that conduct much of their business virtually using email and the Internet. Orders are placed, received, and paid electronically. Cataloging has evolved to become "resource description" and encompasses descriptions created using schemas in addition to MARC and is used to describe born-digital resources or nontraditional resources for which MARC is not a good fit. Metadata may include crowd-sourced descriptive information or resource description provided by external partners, as in the case of research data or digital projects. Resource description has progressed from elaborate AACR2 note-laden bibliographic records to detail-laden description that includes links to authority files, websites, and supplemental resources as well as technical, rights, and preservation information. All of this has led to downsizing of staff, shifting work to staff, moving work out of technical services in some cases, or revising position descriptions so that new hires can handle what administrators deem important.

Collection development has moved into the electronic realm. Slips and review plans have electronic counterparts that include reviews, author affiliations, and the ability to filter searches and orders by format. Typical of the electronic information overload, slips may be saved for future use or sent to colleagues. The evolution of collection development and management is reflected in this quote by Horava: "Traditionally, pride and prestige were imbued in the hundreds of individual daily actions of building a permanent collection that would serve our community's present and future needs with reasonable effectiveness."[2] As Horava points out, the bulk of collection development and management focused on print books. This is no longer the case, as a variety of resources compete for their share of the budget. Electronic resources, particularly packages, databases, and PDA programs, have taken center stage, with streaming media not far behind. In addition, an institution's scholarly output must be captured, described, and made avail-

Table 0.1.

Institution	Configuration	Website
Cornell University	Acquisitions and E-Resources Licensing Issues; Automation; Cataloging and Metadata Services; Post-Cataloging Services	http://lts.library.cornell.edu/
Georgetown University	Acquisitions; Electronic Resources and Serials; Metadata Services; Preservation	http://www.library.georgetown.edu/tech-services
University of Minnesota	Monographs Acquisitions and Cataloging 1; Electronic and Print Serials; Specialized Cataloging; Monographs Acquisitions and Cataloging 2; Health Sciences Libraries Tech Services	https://wiki.lib.umn.edu/TS/HomePage/
SUNY Buffalo	Vocabulary Control and BISON Database Management; Continuing Resources Division; Funds Management and Technical Services Support; Monographs Division; Preservation	http://library.buffalo.edu/aboutus/contactus/cts.html
Princeton University	Acquisitions Services; Cataloging and Metadata Services; Circulation; Holdings Management and Shelving Services	http://library.princeton.edu/departments/tsd/tech/
University of Illinois at Urbana-Champaign	Acquisitions; Content Access Management; Digital Content Creation; Collection Management Services; Preservation and Conservation	http://www.library.illinois.edu/tsd/index.html
University of North Carolina–Chapel Hill	Resource Description and Management; Monographic Services; E-Resources and Serials Management; Preservation Department	http://library.unc.edu/about/dept/university-libraries/technical-services-and-systems/
Stanford University	Access Services; Acquisitions; Metadata; Preservation	http://www-sul.stanford.edu/depts/ts/

University of Chicago	Continuing Resources Cataloging; Continuing Resources Orders; Data Management Services; Monographic Cataloging; Monographic Orders; Piece Processing; Receiving	http://www.lib.uchicago.edu/e/about/departments/
University of Texas at San Antonio	No department specifically named Technical Services; Metadata and Collections Support report to Systems; Acquisitions and Serials Control and Electronic Resources report to Collections and Curriculum Support	http://lib.utsa.edu/files/default/About/orgchart.pdf
University of Montana	Bibliographic Management Services includes Cataloging and Metadata Services; Acquisitions Services; Electronic Resources and Rights Management Services; Digitization Services	http://www.lib.umt.edu/BMS

able to users. Having adequate shelving space and weeding are not as relevant in the predominantly electronic environment. Weeding takes a different twist in the electronic environment. Collection development, too, has moved to a more user-centered model. Chadwell notes, "As we move forward and make more progress in the transition from print to digital, it is clear that it is going to be easier and easier to determine the impact that our collection building has on our users' daily lives. It is also going to be imperative that we keep our users' developmental, education and entertainment needs in mind—more than we ever did in the print realm. . . . We may risk losing relevancy in our users' daily lives if we do not."[3]

Preservation continues to be an important component of technical services, and has shifted its focus to preserving rare and fragile materials through digitization. It may seem that the inclination to preserve print has been reduced when so much content is now available electronically, can be acquired almost instantaneously (except in cases where license negotiation is required), and can serve multiple users, including remote users. This is only partly true, since the need to preserve an institution or community's unique cultural artifacts is extremely important, and the push to do so is evidenced by the popularity of initiatives such as Preservation Week, which began in 2010 because 630 million items in collecting institutions require immediate attention and care.[4] Print preservation may be deemed less critical due to reliance on JSTOR or Portico. Some work, such as the need to bind materials (paperbacks, back issues of print periodicals, or scores, for example), has greatly been reduced due to lack of funding or the transfer of funding to emerging areas of need. Digital preservation is a very real and important need for institutions and organizations that produce or archive content. The move to digital and reliance on vendor-supplied services introduces new considerations. Born-digital resources, including websites, are particularly at risk since consideration is often not given to preserving and archiving this material, ensuring access into the future. Technological obsolescence and data decay are two concerns associated with digital preservation. Schottlaender notes, "The most immediate and significant consequence of the dynamic nature of digital information resources is that their preservation calls for a much more active process than that required for analog resources. Passive preservation ('put it someplace cold and dark and throw away the key') simply will not work in the digital environment."[5]

Technical services work has switched to a user-centered model in which librarians do not necessarily acquire and preserve what they anticipate users might want and use or decide how resources are described. Choice has been transferred to users. A recent example of this is exemplified by patron-driven acquisitions (PDA), which have been implemented by libraries in a number of ways and primarily for e-book purchases (there are also models for both print and streaming media). However, this is not a case in which users select whatever they want but instead access titles from a list compiled from a profile based on collection areas and needs. Changes in patron behavior and delivery of public services have driven collection development to acquire more digital collections. The focus on the user has impacted resource description with initiatives like self-tagging in the public catalog and crowd-sourced metadata. These initiatives introduce quality assurance (QA) considerations since they lack authority control or other controls that librarians have painstakingly implemented to ensure that users can find, identify, select, and obtain the correct resources, and not have to choose between split files of names or subject headings.

The role of the technical services librarian has evolved from someone whose primary concentration was within the technical services department, who might have supervised support staff, who perhaps had limited interactions with public services personnel. Technical services librarians were often the only people who created orders, handled vendor negotiations, or provided cataloging. In contrast to what was formerly considered a backroom operation for the meek, technical services librarians now negotiate licenses for databases, serials packages, and e-book platforms. They partner with public services operations to provide optimal access to resources. They advise on displays in the public catalog and accommodate requests from public services librarians that will enhance search and retrieval of resources for users. Resource Description and Access (RDA) has transformed the level of knowledge catalogers possess to enable them to provide resource description for a range of materials using a schema-agnostic code that will enable sharing with information communities beyond libraries. Some technical services work has been transferred to high-level staff members due to factors including increased reliance on vendor-supplied services and emerging needs like institutional repositories and preserving an institution's unique intellectual and scholarly output. The economy and dismal job market has led to an increase in highly educated individuals applying for entry-level support staff positions. Support staff positions and the requirements for these positions have become increasingly sophisticated and in some cases have enabled librarians to focus on new initiatives and challenges. In other cases, this has led to a reduction in the number of librarians in a technical services operation, compromising access and other important functions that are at the core of any library's suite of services.

THE EVOLUTION OF TECHNICAL SERVICES

What, then, *is* technical services? What does it mean? How do we remain relevant and avoid the fear of being eliminated or marginalized due to the perception that some, if not all, of our work can be automated or outsourced, can be handled by well-trained support staff, or, worse yet, is no longer necessary? Change is an evolutionary process, and changes to technical services operations and their work are necessarily bad. To illustrate this point, it is useful to look at some of the critical areas of need and resulting changes that took place in the last ten to fifteen years. Pressing issues in technical services circa 1999–2004, which may now seem trivial, included relocation of technical services (within a library or offsite), perceived deprofessionalism of technical services, automating technical services processes, lack of a website to document technical services workflows and procedures, macros for technical services workstations, and "false dualism" (us versus them between public and technical services). These issues are epitomized in this quote from Margaret Bing in 1999: "Suddenly, and without much warning, cataloging is no longer considered a 'public service,' and is no longer worthy of being considered a 'core' or necessary subject for study in our library and information science schools. How could this have happened? Where and how did cataloging suddenly become such a stepchild? How did the so-called 'technical services' suddenly become 'non-public services'?"[6]

Cost and quality of technical services has been a constant concern, evidenced by this quote from Jane Padham Ouderkirk's 1999 paper "Technical Services Task Assignment: From Macros to Collection Management Intelligent Agents": "During the past five years, there has been a surge of agitation about the cost and quality of technical services. Published opinions tend toward either extreme—either that traditional technical services are sacrosanct and that the very survival of libraries is dependent on in-house staff performing the work, or that technical services are no longer a core service and should be contracted out in their entirety."[7] Outsourcing was a thorny issue as far back as 1999: "Outsourcing has been used selectively in libraries for years. . . . Recently, it seems to be the panacea that could possibly eliminate the need for an expensive technical services department."[8] Some of this sentiment continues to prevail. There are individuals who are confident that the library will fail to provide services or build collections without technical services, those who want to maintain technical services operations in their current configuration, retain staffing levels, and maintain established ways of working. To them, the current organization and workflows are effective, and they question the need to change them. They fail to consider the future and how it may change their work as well as the mission and role of libraries. This is in sharp contrast to those who declare MARC dead, RDA useless, who state that no one uses the integrated library system since they can use databases, discovery layers, or Google, and who are ready to embrace new modes of working without hesitation and might even consider switching to public services. While technical services provides the infrastructure to enable public services, libraries have downsized or decentralized technical services while maintaining technical services functions, and have thrived. Nadler stresses that the lines between traditional library roles are blurring and that the library's mission may more aptly be described by a circle illustration than the component parts.[9]

NEW ROLES FOR TECHNICAL SERVICES LIBRARIANS

A review of position descriptions posted to the Autocat discussion list in the early 2000s reveals the beginning of a shift from traditional technical services responsibilities to increasingly sophisticated endeavors. Positions posted to Autocat in 2002 include Head of Database Development, Head of Serials Cataloging, and Head of Technical Services/Webmaster. These are for the most part traditional, and the last title hints at emerging needs. The Head of Database Development handled catalog maintenance, original cataloging of print and nonprint resources, and authority work. The Head of Serials Cataloging position required cataloging serials in all formats, maintaining currency in emerging issues in bibliographic control, and performing original and complex cataloging. Positions posted in 2003 show a shift toward new technologies and the expertise required to handle them: Metadata Librarian and E-Resources Librarian. In addition to original cataloging, the Metadata Librarian position required expertise in projects that used XML, EAD, FGDC, and Dublin Core. The E-Resources Librarian position stated that the successful individual's responsibilities would include developing and implementing an e-resource management database and registering and activating new e-resource titles for the library.

Rogers-Collins and Fowler are researching the evolution of technical services job titles and responsibilities. They presented their findings at the 2013 ALA Annual Conference at the ALCTS Role of the Professional Librarian in Technical Services Interest Group meeting. Their goal was to determine whether new "flashy" position titles included new or broader responsibilities as compared to some mainstream and traditional positions. What they discovered is that there has been a change in job responsibilities to match the new job titles and current environment. Other types of positions (Digital Applications Librarian, for example) did not exist five or ten years ago. New roles for technical services librarians include data management services, increasing responsibility for institutional repositories, a greater role in supporting and enabling public services, and increased collaboration with catalogs, purchases, and provision of resource description.[10] Some of this collaboration has been realized through Cornell and Columbia's 2CUL, the Greater Western Library Alliance's shared e-books initiative, and a collaborative cataloging project between CIC member libraries to share language expertise.

PREPARING FOR AN UNCERTAIN FUTURE

Creative Solutions to Challenges

Creative solutions for challenging problems often are developed by technical services librarians. Terry Reese created MarcEdit, Eric Lease Morgan developed the now defunct Mr. Serials, and Deborah Fritz created Metadata in Many Metadata Formats (RIMMF) to aid catalogers with learning and using RDA. Other examples include virtual teams that provide triage to cooperatively solve problems, and using a LibGuide to communicate technical services policies to public services colleagues.[11] Do technical services librarians have the ability to visualize the future and what role they might play? Are they proactive and forwarding thinking? Or are they short-sighted and reactive, not responding to change until it is upon them? They can set the tone for change, influence vendor offerings, and vow not to take a passive role within their profession. There will also be trade-offs, and they must accept these changes to prepare for a future in which funding for education, including libraries, is threatened. For example, full-level, "Cadillac" cataloging with numerous elaborate descriptive notes may no longer be practical given staffing constraints and competing priorities. Approval plans and standing/recurring orders and the expertise and time required to manage them may no longer be needed in light of Patron Driven Acquisitions and other collection development models.

Determining New Skills for an Uncertain Future

The final consideration for technical services librarians is to determine what new skills are needed. How can technical services librarians prepare for an uncertain future? What should library science programs do to train new librarians? Many master's programs do not require cataloging or technical services courses. This is a source of concern with technical services librarians and was an issue as far back as 1999, as evidenced by this quote from Bing: "I have not heard of any school suggesting that its general reference courses be eliminated, yet how can it be that something so vital to the organization of libraries as the development of its catalog be considered a nonessential discipline?"[12] Rogers-Collins and Fowler are considering the following questions for the next steps of their research, which addresses future technical services librarians: Are master's-level library science programs preparing graduates for professional responsibilities? Are students interested in technical services as a career? If the work/skills that technical services librarians have acquired in library school are being shifted to support staff, what is the value of the MLS for technical services librarians?[13]

The chapters in this book cover a variety of issues relevant to technical services as we face an uncertain future and constant change. These issues include the current state of technical services and how we might influence the outcome of vendor-provided offerings, the future of "traditional" cataloging work, MARC and RDA, weeding and inventory control in an electronic environment, research data and its role, and the skills needed for the future of technical services. These chapters are written by a diverse and talented group of technical services librarians who bring a wealth of knowledge and expertise to their chapters. This book also includes interviews with technical services librarians who are leaders in the profession regarding issues that surround the future of technical services and our work.

NOTES

1. Michael Gorman, *Technical Services Today and Tomorrow* (Westport, CT: Libraries Unlimited, 1998), 3–4.

2. Tony Horava, "Challenges and Possibilities for Collection Management in a Digital Age," *Library Resources & Technical Services* 54, no. 3 (2014): 143.

3. Faye A. Chadwell, "What's Next for Collection Management and Managers? User-Centered Collection Management," *Collection Management* 34, no. 2 (2009): 76–77.

4. "Preservation Week: Pass It On," Association for Library Collections and Technical Services, American Library Association, http://www.ala.org/alcts/confevents/preswk.

5. Brian E. C. Schottlaender, "Guest Editorial: The Digital Preservation Imperative: An Ecosystem View," *Library Resources & Technical Services* 58, no. 1 (2014): 2.

6. Margaret Bing, "The False Dualism," *Journal of Library Administration* 29, no. 2 (2000): 24.

7. Jane Padham Ouderkirk, "Technical Services Task Assignment: From Macros to Collection Management Intelligent Agents," *Journal of Academic Librarianship* 25, no. 5 (1999): 397.

8. Bing, "False Dualism," 27.

9. Judith Nadler, "The Transformation of Research Libraries," University of Chicago Libraries, 2013, http://www.lib.uchicago.edu/e/about/LibraryTransformation_2page.pdf.

10. ACRL Research Planning and Review Committee, "Environmental Scan 2013," Association of College and Research Libraries, 2013, http://www.ala.org/acrl/sites/ala.org.acrl/files/content/publications/whitepapers/EnvironmentalScan13.pdf.

11. Mary Beth Weber and Gracemary Smulewitz, "Triage in the Digital Age," paper presented at the Charleston Conference on Library Acquisitions, November 9, 2011, Charleston, SC; Jennifer W. Bazeley and Becky Yoose, "Technical Services Transparency," *Library Resources & Technical Services* 57, no. 2 (2013): 118–27.

12. Bing, "False Dualism," 28.

13. Karen Rogers-Collins and Rhonda Fowler, "Do 'Traditional' Technical Services Librarians Still Exist in Academic Libraries?," presentation at the ALCTS Role of the Professional in Technical Services Interest Group, American Library Association Annual Conference, Chicago, June 29, 2013.

Chapter One

The Future of Traditional Technical Services

Julie Renee Moore and James L. Weinheimer

We are at a point in technical services librarianship where many of us acknowledge that with so many changes happening, with ideas flying, and new standards swirling around us without any real assurance that any of them will work or will help us to do a better and more efficient job, as staffing and budgets are shrinking and resources are becoming more complex, it feels as though the sky is falling. In this chapter, we share our thoughts and views on the future of traditional technical services and discuss whether there is a future for traditional cataloging, acquisitions, and technical services functions.

PURPOSE OF TECHNICAL SERVICES

We first consider the purpose and functions of traditional technical services. The main purpose of traditional technical services is to provide levels of quality assurance for:

- the resources themselves (selection);
- ensuring that those resources can be found today as efficiently and effectively as possible (with a high level of precision and recall) in various ways: by browsing, author, title, or subject;
- making certain that those materials will be findable in the future by enabling quick payment, providing appropriate shelving accommodation, archiving rare materials, conserving fragile and damaged resources, etc. (conservation, acquisitions, shelving).

TECHNICAL SERVICES FUNCTIONS

What are the traditional functions of technical services? Certainly, *cataloging* plays a central role in technical services and is at the heart of the library. What service do catalogers provide that is central to the library's core mission? In its most basic form, they help people to locate resources. The role of the catalog librarian[1] remains the same as it historically has been; namely, to describe resources so that users can fulfill the basic FRBR tasks (Functional Requirements for Bibliographic Records, http://www.ifla.org/publications/functional-requirements-for-bibliographic-records) and find, identify, select, and obtain those relevant resources. The tools, rules, and metadata schemas will continue to evolve, but the purpose remains the same.

There is a tendency to consider only current users, but we must also think about the users who will seek human knowledge many years into the future. (Note: Author Julie Moore's background is in anthropology, and she views her work as a catalog librarian as an extension of her passion for anthropology.) Catalog librarians play a vital role in preserving the human record. In 2010, Michael Gorman wrote, "Civilization and learning require the human record to be organized, accessible, and preserved. Cataloguers play an important role in that great enterprise—an enterprise that is dedicated to no less a purpose than ensuring the people of the future know what we know, thus enabling them to add to that ever-expanding record."[2]

THE FUTURE IS LONGER THAN THE PAST

This phrase was included in a speaker's slides for a program offered by the Association for Library Collections and Technical Services (ALCTS). The speaker continued by stating:

> Our work is situated in time. This implies that, first, while it is of course necessary to act on the basis of present expectations and resources, policy and practice decisions have multiple ripple effects extending further forward in time than we are able to imagine. Second, remembering the continuity of actions in time will help us to explore new ideas for improving access to information resources, while continuing to understand and value the best of our accomplishments to date.[3]

From an anthropologist cataloger's perspective, this resonates. We are organizing, making accessible, and preserving resources both for people in the present and for people in the future. As catalogers, we must stay focused on the future while acknowledging our past. We continually encounter bibliographic records from earlier times. This is a fact of life as standards have evolved over time or as substandard records were added to our catalogs for inventory projects or other short-term needs. It is critical to have an understanding of prior cataloging codes as well as the current code. We have a very long history in cataloging, but the future is even longer.

Technical services and cataloging have been evolving from the beginning, something that seems to be a misconception among noncatalogers, particularly administrators who fail to understand the need for cataloging. For consistency's sake, catalogers require "rules" (AACR) or now "instructions" (RDA: Resource Description and Access) and standards as guidelines to inform their work. This consistency is important in moving into the future. Machines can process data effectively only if it is consistent. It has been our experience that noncatalogers fail to appreciate how much the rules (and now instructions) have evolved over time. This has been impacted by the emergence of new formats and has been shaped by new access concerns prompted by electronic resources. In addition, staffing (or lack thereof) has led to a greater reliance on batchloading processes or vendor offerings. All of this in turn has changed our work as catalogers. Much is left to "cataloger's judgment," which requires a great understanding of the rules and an even greater knowledge and understanding of the history of how the rules have developed. As Weitz wrote,

> Those conjoined twins of the AACR rules and the MARC data structure, both of which have persisted over more than four decades, have appeared to be stable. But those who use the standards on a daily basis have an acute awareness of how much AACR and MARC have continued to evolve. In other words, to an extent that non-catalogers are generally unaware, catalogers have dealt with change constantly. As it turns out, catalogers have proven themselves to be as resilient and adaptable as either AACR or MARC. That resilience and adaptability will stand catalogers in good stead as we move from the world of AACR to the world of *RDA, Resource Description and Access.* Those qualities will come in just as handy as we also begin to evolve from MARC toward a post-MARC data structure, whatever it may turn out to be.[4]

Weitz eloquently continues:

> When done conscientiously, cataloging has always been more art than science. We catalog real-world resources that may or may not conform to the theories that our rules try to codify. As I wrote in the introduction to my *Cataloger's Judgment,* "the world of stuff to catalog is so vast, so slippery, so surprising that individual judgment will always enter into our decisions. . . . Catalogers are thoughtful judges concerning matters of description and access."[5] It is that judgment leavened with imagination that has carried catalogers through these decades of change. That same judgment and imagination will continue to stand them in good stead through the era of Resource Description and Access (RDA), and post-MARC data structure, and whatever future marvels the world sends them to catalog.[6]

Cataloging does not stand alone as a function in technical services. It is midstream in an intertwining process that neither begins nor ends with cataloging. Whether it resides in technical services or public services, the beginning of this stream begins with selection and collection development. To acquire what librarians (and others) have requested, resources pass through the acquisitions functions to be ordered, purchased, delivered, and, for invoices, to be encumbered. Resources are then cataloged and provided with a description and subject analysis (subject access points), and may include a classification number. One of the most vital pieces of cataloging is what one might call "quality control," a large part of which is authority control. These traditional functions look very different from how they looked twenty-five years ago, or even five or ten years ago. They will continue to evolve as we move into the future.

Looking into a future that includes primarily digital materials, we believe that these traditional functions of technical services will continue to evolve; however, these traditional functions will continue to exist in some form. Even in the digital world, there will be a continued need to catalog and for catalogers to provide description and access to the user, both the library user of today and the library user in years to come. Library resources will continue to be selected, collected, and acquired, even if they are digital or electronic. As we move to the linked data environment, there will still be some form of authority control (although it will likely be called something else), even if the mechanism is pointing to an identifier rather than an actual Library of Congress (LC) Name Authority File Record or Subject Authority File Record, the concept will remain. Users will rediscover that they can find materials more efficiently when the terms or names used are controlled. While these functions might look very different, the authors are convinced that these functions will continue to exist as we move into the future, into the age of the MARC 21's replacement (likely BIBFRAME), and while using linked data.

THE NEED FOR COOPERATION

In the past, various methods and industries developed that helped libraries with technical services functions (publishers and book jobbers for selection; different standards for cataloging and access; standards for archives, conservation, and even shelving). All these methods involved *cooperation* among libraries and the various industries. With the advent of the Internet, normal (traditional) methods have broken down. For instance, publishers and libraries, once respected business associates, seem to have become bitter enemies. This has been fueled in part by economic problems. Vendors are struggling to maintain their share of the market, develop new services, and satisfy investors. Librarians have seen their budgets continue to shrink, leading to the elimination of critical resources that are important to their work (such as authority control) and loss of staffing. Additionally (and perhaps most importantly), library core values and ethics have evolved to help ensure that librarians used their choices for the good of their communities and not their own gain.

THE CHALLENGES

There are more materials than ever, or, perhaps more accurately, libraries believe that they must provide a "single search box" that finds "everything." This is not an entirely new concept. In the nineteenth century, libraries tried cataloging each article in every journal they collected (or, in other words, providing a "single search" for everything through the catalog) but failed because the workload could not be realistically sustained. That is when Poole devised his index, and separate journal indexes were begun. In the past (and currently), catalogers created *in analytics* for select book chapters or journal articles to enable discovery of important pieces that reside in a larger work. Another related circumstance is the "bound-with," where one single-part monograph is bound with another. Creating a bound-with binds together separately published works into a single volume and may be used for monographs as well as serials. Therefore, we need to "link together several bibliographic records representing individual titles that physically exist in a single container (i.e., a printed volume, microform, etc.). These titles have been brought together locally or by a publisher. While some of these records could represent analyzed titles, their defining feature is that they are bound together, and not kept separately on the shelves."[7] When author Moore worked at an academic law library in the late 1990s, the first legal monographic series with many different titles was issued electronically on CD-ROM. The law library purchased a giant CD-ROM tower. Moore created "parent" and "children" (or "host" and "guest") bibliographic records for the catalog, so that the public could still find the resources with the same efficiency and effectiveness as when locating them in print format. In current times, this may sound ludicrous, but at the time (about fifteen years ago), it was a huge innovative leap. Over time, there were new titles on the CD-ROMs every month. New titles were added and old ones were deleted just as is seen with contemporary e-book and e-journal packages.

Regarding the Internet, those were also revolutionary times in librarianship. It was an amazing stroke of genius in cataloging to create a MARC field and subfield (856 $u) that could handle a URL so that the user could directly access the electronic resource. Cataloging Internet resources was a source of an even greater challenge with many new debates. Catalogers began debating the "content versus carrier" issue, which considered one of the first decisions that a cataloger makes: determining what is being cataloged—the content or the carrier? This was also the beginning of the demise of the GMD (General Material Designation), an early warning indicator to show the nature of the material being cataloged (videorecording, sound recording, etc.). The content versus carrier debate grew heated with the advent of playaways, prerecorded audio player devices for audiobooks that first entered the market in 2005.

The emergence of the Internet also led catalogers to consider whether a resource is "published" when it is made available on the Internet. There was further debate about when a work was issued in print and was simultaneously available on the Internet. This was an especially hot topic in the realm of theses and dissertations, which, when issued in print, are not considered to be "published," per se, yet if they are on the Internet, they are considered published. There is slightly different treatment for them when they are accessible on the Internet. This differs from the former situation, when dissertation were issued in print and later made available on microfilm or microfiche, and are handled like a reproduction. There was a great deal of talk about "born-digital" materials versus a reprinting of sorts to the Internet. Once the Internet came into general use by librarians, there were many very exciting debates. Tim Berners-Lee invented the World Wide Web (WWW) in 1989 at CERN (Conseil Européen pour la Recherche Nucléaire, or European Council for Nuclear Research). It was only in 1993 that the WWW technology was made available by CERN in the public domain.[8] It took about ten years for the technology to become widespread and embraced by the general public. In reality, it has only been available for about ten to fifteen years, which is a relatively short period of time, considering that it is now so ubiquitous.

It seems that human beings are determined to repeat the past, except in an even bigger way. We are not collecting fewer resources or cataloging simpler resources. Instead, we are collecting *more* resources, and they are providing greater challenges to catalog. While we *can* search them in one box, just linking them all together causes problems with different standards, different forms of names and subjects, and so on. Just because we *can* do something via the technology, we must now always ask, "Is this really in the best interest of the user?"

THE ELEPHANT IN THE ROOM

The authors had a fascinating email discussion with an information technology (IT) specialist at an academic library who estimates that his library receives over 2,000,000 bibliographic records annually that have to be handled and loaded into the catalog. These records comply with standards other than AACR/RDA and MARC, or follow no standards at all. This is the proverbial elephant in the room. The authors question how anyone can realistically be expected to retain *any* level of quality assurance for 2,000,000 bibliographic records per year. We need to ask, "*Should* we be dumping everything into the catalog?" Technology has made it possible, but is it in the user's best interest?

A Water Quality Analogy

The above situation is analogous to a stream that empties into a lake that people endeavor to keep clean. If at the same time, a mighty river that is polluted is also emptying into the same lake, the labor to clean the water in the stream is wasted when the public, who takes their water from the lake, find it increasingly polluted. In such a situation, it makes little sense to continue to attempt to keep the water in the stream clean. Ultimately, the polluted lake becomes unusable.

Technical services librarians face other challenges. Technical services budgets and staffing are declining. The new cataloging instructions and standards (e.g., RDA, BIBFRAME, and FRBR) are *not* simpler and do not promise greater cataloging efficiencies. Nonetheless, many libraries have implemented RDA, which was designed to replace AACR2 and is the first step toward the post-MARC environment (most likely BIBFRAME). All of this requires a steep learning curve. The end goal is to deliver the bibliographic universe that is currently housed in our library catalogs onto a global platform of the greater semantic web via linked data. This is a noble goal and one that is worth the fuss *if* we can get ourselves onto the onramp of the semantic web fast enough and before libraries are completely left in the dust.

The library catalog has traditionally focused on making materials "findable," and that has not necessarily meant that they are "easy to find." The future finding tool, however, must be "easy to use" and require no training of the public (thus, the single search box). As searching technology advances, entirely new searches can be created; as a result, people will come to expect new capabilities through searching and may have unrealistic expectations regarding what technology can provide. Russell's blog discussed how to find things that were impossible to find before (and not that long ago). He showed as an example a photo of a nondescript building in an unknown city taken from a room high in another building across the street. The question he asks (and answers) is: "What is the phone number of the office where this photo was taken?" Quite remarkably, such questions *can* be answered today, and as people start to understand this, they will begin to ask more and more such questions. And their expectations for finding quick and easy access to answers will rise.[9]

In comparing this to our history, we expect to be able to type in a few words (e.g., twain finn) and get what we want. When card catalogs were the norm, this would have seemed like the wildest science fiction. Not only is it possible today, it is considered fundamental and even ho-hum. Searching will continue to change, and technical services must be able to change along with it. Possibly in ten years' time, things that are considered impossible today will become reality. Libraries must stay agile to be able to respond to evolving needs. This is the perfect sort of research for OCLC and research libraries to do: to keep up with these quickly evolving technologies so that we know enough to be able to respond to them. This is part of the responsibility of being a "think tank."

Individuals are becoming increasingly tired of wading through the mountains of irrelevant information that they find on the web. There are serious concerns with privacy and a greater awareness that search engine optimization is being used to manipulate the results to favor companies (that are in business to make a profit) over the individual user searching for information. In a 2012 blog entry, Sullivan questions Google's ability to provide relevant search results and questions whether the company has lost sight of its original core mission. [10] Kidman, in a 2014 post to his blog, *Lifehacker*, states that he believes Google's search results are useless. [11] Keeping our core values in mind, we must consider that the information provided by Google and others is manipulated with a profit in mind. This flies in the face of our core values, such as intellectual freedom, privacy, equity of access to information, and democracy.

THE OPPORTUNITIES

During this transition period and beyond, there are many opportunities. *Collaboration* will be vital, not only to the survival of technical services but to the survival of libraries themselves. Libraries simply need more help. Today, it is possible to collaborate with groups with whom we did not previously collaborate, such as taking records created in a foreign country in a radically different format (e.g., ONIX or some other format) and including them in the library catalog. Linked data offers many advantages. It is, however, very much in its infancy. The linked data movement promises to help catalogers with authority control issues, although there are a lot of unresolved problems. For more information, visit the WorldCat Linked Data Explorer website (http://experiment.worldcat.org/entity/work/data/12477503), which provides an example of linked data being used to describe *Zen and the Art of Motorcycle Maintenance.*

Various application programming interfaces (APIs) can be incorporated into catalogs, many for free (e.g., the Google Translate widget provides a quick view of your catalog and its records in a different language). It is not perfect, but it is quick, easy, and inexpensive. It is also a fact that almost every organization is facing the same challenges as libraries. They may be more eager to collaborate than before, and the technology exists to allow them to do so.

THOUGHTS ABOUT THE LIBRARY OF THE FUTURE

The future of technical services is dependent, in large part, on what is to become of the library of the future. Will the library of the future be limited to a virtual library? Only time will tell, but we certainly think and hope not. We believe that there is room enough for both physical objects (even books) *and* digital objects to coexist in our collections. Our users have different learning styles and preferences. While there is evidence that some users prefer materials delivered virtually, there are also users who prefer print. Some people appreciate the visceral activity of reading a print book. There are also studies that show that readers absorb less when reading an e-book as compared to reading the same story in print, at least regarding the sequence of events. [12]

There are many library resources that simply cannot be made available in a digital format. Some resources are meant to be discovered in three-dimensions. Consider the many curriculum materials (manipulatives, kits, three-dimensional resources, realia, models, games) in our libraries whose sole purpose is to enable a three-dimensional and/or tactile experience. Braille resources also come to mind. While it is true that one can take a photograph of these materials, the experience of discovering them digitally is simply not the same as being able to see (and in some cases touch) the material in the manner in which it was intended to be experienced. While the content is the same, even reading a print book, compared to reading an e-book, is a slightly different experience. When we consider library resources, we need to keep in mind *all* resources, not just books/e-books or journals/e-journals, and not only resources with the highest circulation statistics, but *all* of the special format materials and special collections cataloging that takes place in a library.

Special collections make one library's collection distinct from all others. They house "hidden treasures," and it behooves us, as catalogers, to expose these treasures to the world. Special collections materials should rank as the top priority of work for catalog librarians. These collections certainly distinguish us from any other library. Within traditional special collections, one finds rare books, and thus, the whole realm of rare book cataloging. Again, we are beginning to see some very exciting developments in rare book cataloging with rare books being made available digitally. This also enables one of our core values: stewardship. By limiting the handling of these books, the actual books will last for many more years into the future, while yet providing the content to users via the Internet. However, just as with any e-book, the content may be the same, but there is a vast difference between viewing the book digitally and being able to read the actual book, which may have been written by hand with calligraphy on vellum. It might be an illuminated manuscript, where one can see the strokes of gold leaf and the details of the brush hairs. These details might not matter to the general user. However, there is a difference between viewing the actual manuscript versus the digital object. In rare book cataloging, the cataloger takes special care to describe the particular manifestation of the book, almost as describing a museum artifact. Do these details have meaning to general collections? To a special collection, these details are important. Most libraries have special collections that house the gems, the unique, the special formats, and the rare materials of our libraries.[13] The library catalog, however, should not promote any particular format over another; all formats should be treated so that they are presented equally to the public.

WHAT IS A LIBRARY, REALLY?

To state that librarians, technical services librarians in particular, are standing on shifting sands is an understatement. It would seem that librarians are racing to grasp at every new technological fad and gadget possible to appear more relevant in our current Google- and smartphone-obsessed society. Today's librarians are engaging their users via tweets, texting, and gaming. Librarians are "embedding" themselves into instructor's online lessons. Librarians are reexamining "the library as place." Librarians are providing places and spaces to create. Libraries are serving as publishers. Libraries are serving as recording studios. Libraries provide printing support. Libraries provide a technical support station for every technological gadget the user might own, in an attempt to duplicate Apple's Genius Bar. In many university settings, the library is becoming more like a student union where the students congregate, armed with fast food and lattes. Libraries provide wonderful spaces for exhibits, programs, lectures, community organization meetings, and classes. Libraries are changing dramatically to accommodate these new activities and services. Many of the "traditional" services are being dismantled or repurposed. Some libraries are recycling their print books as quickly as possible, while others are completely paperless. There are librarians who pride themselves by saying that the library that they envision needs no more space than a desktop. Some libraries are eliminating their reference desks altogether. Additionally, some libraries are abolishing their technical services departments. Because so many of the new functions of a library are dependent upon information technology expertise to work, the library IT department has become an important, if not the dominating, department. While we desperately need the cooperation of IT to help us move forward into this brave new technological world, we must also keep in mind that the IT mindset is very different from the generalist librarian mindset. In our opinions, it is an unfortunate turn of events when library administrators place IT in charge of the entire library. Borrowing from the Oldsmobile's advertising slogan, this is not your father's library. It is also not even the library that many catalogers used when they were students. The future of technical services functions is dependent, in large part, upon what is to become of the library of the future.

LIBRARIAN ETHICS AND CORE VALUES

One of the most important things for librarians to do is to consider what it is to be a librarian. Our profession has developed certain ethics and core values. When we keep these core values in mind as we plan ahead, they will guide us well into the future. We are absolutely convinced that these core values must stay intact as we move into the future.

After focusing his studies on the important writings about values in librarianship of four great twentieth-century librarians (namely, Shiyali Ramamrita Ranganathan [1892–1972], Jesse Hauck Shera [1903–1922], Samuel Rothstein [1921–2014], and Lee W. Finks), Gorman wrote his own book entitled *Our Enduring Values: Librarianship in the 21st Century*, in which he outlined a list (and explanations) of what he found to be the eight core values of librarianship. Gorman's core values (with concise explanations) follow:

- *stewardship* (preserving the human record to ensure that future generations know what we know);
- *service* (ensuring that all our policies and procedures are animated by the ethic of service to individuals, communities, society, and posterity);
- *intellectual freedom* (maintaining a commitment to the idea that all people in a free society should be able to read and see whatever they wish to read and see);
- *rationalism* (organizing and managing library services in a rational manner);
- *literacy and learning* (encouraging literacy and the love of learning);
- *equity of access to recorded knowledge and information* (ensuring that all library resources and programs are accessible to all, overcoming technological and monetary barriers to access);
- *privacy* (ensuring the confidentiality of records of library user; overcoming technological invasions of library use);
- *democracy* (playing our part in maintaining the values of a democratic society; participating in the educational process to ensure the educated citizenry that is vital to democracy). [14]

While librarians are pursuing new technology and gadgets to appear more relevant to today's society, we desperately need to hold true to the core values that Gorman advocates.

SOLUTIONS

It must be recognized that there are multiple solutions to almost any problem, but the solutions may not be easy to implement and may be expensive. Solutions may demand tremendous changes from many groups as they actually begin to work together or as new tools are created and used. Whether people decide to adopt and pay for these solutions depends on their perception of the importance of the problems. Of the challenges we have examined, no single library can solve all of them, but many libraries nevertheless are facing exactly the same problems. If solutions are to exist, librarians need new tools that are much more powerful, and just as important, they need a new way of seeing things.

There are many organizations worldwide that want to provide access to *exactly the same materials* that are at *exactly the same locations* (i.e., using the same URLs). There are tools to find and communicate with almost anyone in the world, and these tools are inexpensive (some are even free) and easy to use. Therefore, there are almost unlimited opportunities to work with new partners. The tools for information capture and to transform that information are also far more powerful than at any time in history.

There are major and wide-ranging consequences to accepting the "single search box" option, and these consequences are not being discussed, although they are being felt everywhere. If people are going to accept the single search box, the consequences for libraries are the same as the analogy we provided of a lake being filled with water from the clean stream versus the huge, polluted river. In such a case, why continue with efforts to maintain a tiny stream that is clean?

DECISIONS AND DECISION MAKERS

Who should make the decision whether traditional technical services should continue? Is it selectors or reference librarians? Should it be the catalogers? Perhaps it should be the library administration: the library director or dean? Perhaps it should be the director's or dean's supervisor—should it be decided by the provost, the mayor of a city, the governor, or maybe the head of the entire organization? The library's user community should have a major voice. Compare this to the analogy of the water quality of the lake and who should make the decision on it. Should it be the people polluting the river? The people in charge of the stream? The people in charge of the lake (who have already allowed the lake to become polluted)? Or should it be the people who drink the water from the lake?

The answer is to engage the community who actually uses the resources to make the decision, and not to leave it in the hands of the polluters, or even in our hands. A major part of this decision is whether the catalog will continue to be a tool for information discovery or if it will become merely a tool for inventory purposes (i.e., if the catalog will be used to find something mentioned in a citation found through completely other means). If the catalog will become an inventory to find known items and serve no other purpose, then perhaps our methods are no longer necessary. Who will decide? Again, we think the user community should decide. It must be recognized that there are solutions to the problems we face, but those solutions will require major changes from everyone concerned. It will also require money. If libraries think that their only tools are relational databases, MARC records, ISO2709 format and communications, and they are looking at these issues alone, then they will absolutely fail. We do believe that it will happen, and in fact, we think it is inevitable because the algorithms and SEO (search engine optimization) used in search engines outside of the library are unsustainable for purposes other than marketing. New methods will be developed and adopted that will look very similar to what libraries have been doing all along (traditional technical services). We think that these are the important issues facing technical services.

A Practical Example

How could something like this work? Let us start with a hypothetical academic library in Fresno, California, that has been given 500,000 "free" metadata records for digitized U.S. government documents. (Note: This is an actual example and is typical of what catalogers are faced with handling on an increasingly frequent basis.) These records are not in MARC format, and the access points number well over one million. These records do not follow any discernible rules, and the names used differ from the library's authorized access points (this library uses the LC Name Authority File). For example, the records might use the access point "U.S. House of Representatives" while the authorized access point in the catalog is "United States. Congress. House." There are at least a million access points. What can the library do?

If catalogers are expected to change all of the records to AACR2 or RDA and change all the access points to authorized LC Name Authority File forms, and add LC Subject Headings, it would constitute a massive multiyear or multidecade project. But that would not be sufficient: new government documents appear constantly, and a library that continues to accept these records will discover that the conversions will continue in perpetuity. First, the library needs to understand that other organizations are looking at the same resources and records and struggling with identical problems. Although the other organizations may not be libraries and may follow the same rules, the same forms of access points, or even the same formats, they still need to edit the records to fit into their finding tools. If your library could establish a project with these other organizations to update the records—potentially with many other agencies—each could organize the workload and make the work more manageable. What would be needed for this to work?

It would require lots of new tools, including those to help the other organizations struggling with the same problems to find one another. It would require other tools to allow these organizations to work together on the same records in an organized fashion, and still other tools that allow participants to collaborate and coordinate their work. The business world uses these kinds of tools, which could be adapted for library purposes. Instead of changing an access point from "U.S. House of Representatives" to "United States. Congress. House," the focus could be to add a URI that links to the Virtual International Authority File (VIAF), DBpedia, or some newly created tool that will include everyone's access point. In this way, everyone could benefit from edits to an individual record. This is the promise of linked data, and it could be extended in a variety of ways.

However, if a library decides to convert the records to MARC using MarcEdit and deposit them in the local catalog, other kinds of collaboration are not possible, because to collaborate, the other organizations would have to be given permission to access your catalog to make changes. No one would grant this level of permission. Even then, any updates would be limited to your library's users, and there would be no reason for other organizations to participate. In order for a collaboration like this to succeed, the records need to reside outside of the library's catalog in another database. Then the database would *not* need to be populated with MARC records and could be set up in various ways. Organizations could work on the records in the database, which could remain separate. Local catalogs could be set to search multiple databases seamlessly (federated searching) while the users would never have to know that they are simultaneously searching multiple databases. Finally, if the original organization that created these records for the U.S. government documents was made aware of the issues and given the tools, they could add the URIs themselves, thereby eliminating a massive amount of after-the-fact labor at each individual organization. Therefore, any solution involves not only new tools but new collaborations.

The problem of selecting Open Access materials is very similar. If the task is seen as the responsibility of a single library that selects materials that will then be cataloged individually by local catalogers, the task is obviously impossible. However, if the task is seen differently, and many organizations are considering the same materials on the web and are trying to make decisions regarding which materials are worthwhile, the task becomes primarily one of *coordination* and *sharing of effort*. For instance, an art history selector at Emory University may select an Open Access resource and make a request to the cataloging department, resulting in a record that people at Emory University can find and use. Can a tool be made that will allow everyone to benefit from the selector's decision at Emory University? Yes, and it could be included in the database described above that would enable catalogers to work together more closely on government documents. Instead of the records coming just from the organization creating original records for government documents, it could include other requests to catalog specific resources from selectors in all topics who could then work together from anywhere. Catalogers could collaborate to update these records for each community. From a technical point of view, this can be done. The result would be a catalog in a real sense: a collection of materials selected by experts based on ethical considerations and described and organized by other experts, also based on ethical considerations.

To create a tool like this would not be cheap. It would require resources for hardware; software would need to be developed, adapted, and adopted; and staff and training would be required, plus it would demand major changes from almost everyone concerned. Nevertheless, it is also something that very definitely *can* be done and is being done in other fields of work. If there is a chance for the values of traditional technical services to continue, it is our opinion that something like this must be done. The question is will it be done.

CONCLUSION

Technical services needs substantial help to survive and to get the necessary resources to accomplish its work. While many of the traditional methods continue to break down, we may still be able to provide the public with the traditional technical services offerings, and there is evidence that people still want what the traditional purposes were designed to provide. To do that, libraries would need to become more open and focus on the final products rather than on the methods used (which will probably evolve at an ever increasing rate). Looking into the future with the entirety of resources that we need to catalog and run through the entire technical services stream in view, we believe that the traditional functions of technical services will continue to evolve and will look very different from contemporary functions; however, we hope these traditional functions will continue to exist in some form. Resources will continue to need to be selected, collected, acquired, and cataloged, and there will be a continued need for authority control, even more in the future than there is right now.

NOTES

1. We acknowledge that the job titles "cataloger" or "catalog librarian" have fallen out of fashion among some, being replaced by job titles such as "metadata specialist" or "information scientist with a specialty in metadata," "metadata strategist," "information architecture engineer," "access and description professional," "resource description and access librarian," "structured knowledge organizer," "resource alchemist," "database sanitation engineer" (due to the fact that one spends most of the time cleaning up databases), or "semantic engineer" as per the Autocat discussion list (July 2014). We have decided, at least for this chapter, to continue to name this title what it really is, namely, "cataloger" or "catalog librarian." We find it to be clearer, less ambiguous, and more honest than the other terms.

2. Michael Gorman, foreword to *Conversations with Catalogers in the 21st Century*, ed. Elaine R. Sanchez (Santa Barbara, CA: Libraries Unlimited, 2010), viii–ix.

3. David Miller, "Basic Values and the Future of Cataloging," paper presented at the Association for Library Collections and Technical Services, Cataloging and Classification Section Forum, American Library Association Midwinter Meeting, Seattle, WA, January 21, 2007, http://www.ala.org/alcts/ianda/bibcontrol/07futcat.

4. Jay Weitz, "Judgement and Imagination: Carrying Cataloging Through Times of Change," in Sanchez, *Conversations with Catalogers*, 171.

5. Jay Weitz, *Cataloger's Judgment: Music Cataloging Questions and Answers from the Music OCLC Users Group Newsletter* (Westport, CT: Libraries Unlimited, 2014), xix–xx.

6. Weitz, "Judgement and Imagination," 174.

7. Yale University Library, "Bound-Withs," MFHD Policies and Procedures, 8th ed., http://www.library.yale.edu/cataloging/ccc/Bound-withs%20revised8.doc.

8. "The Birth of the Web," CERN, http://home.web.cern.ch/topics/birth-web.

9. Daniel M. Russell, "What Does It Mean to Be Literate in the Age of Google?," Louis Clark Vanuxem Lecture, Princeton University, February 28, 2012, published on *SearchReSearch* (blog), November 4, 2012, http://searchresearch1.blogspot.ca/2012/11/presentation-on-what-does-it-mean-to-be.html.

10. Danny Sullivan, "Dear Google: Crappy Results Like This Don't Give the Impression You Care about Search," *Search Engine Land* (blog), January 26, 2012, http://searchengineland.com/dear-google-crappy-santorum-results-dont-give-the-impression-you-care-about-search-109388.

11. Angus Kidman, "Why Google's Search Results Are Useless Right Now," *Lifehacker* (blog), February 11, 2014, http://www.lifehacker.com.au/2014/02/why-googles-search-results-are-useless-right-now/.

12. Alison Flood, "Readers Absorb Less on Kindles Than on Paper, Study Finds," *Guardian*, August 19, 2014, http://www.theguardian.com/books/2014/aug/19/readers-absorb-less-kindles-paper-study-plot-ereader-digitisation.

13. Julie Renee Moore, "Cataloging at the Opposite Ends of the Cataloging Continuum: From Rare Books to Digitized Manuscripts," sabbatical report, California State University–Fresno, 2014, 5.

14. Michael Gorman, *Our Enduring Values: Librarianship in the 21st Century* (Chicago: American Library Association, 2000), 26–27.

Chapter Two

The State of Technical Services Today

Mary Beth Weber

This chapter discusses the current state of technical services in regard to its relationship with vendor-supplied products and services, taking into consideration how library professionals can influence the outcome of vendor offerings such as e-books, licensing, record sets, or authority control. It also discusses technical services advocacy and how to promote the value of our work to our colleagues, administrators, and users. This is particularly important during difficult economic times when funding is being cut and vacant positions are eliminated.

VENDOR-PROVIDED PRODUCTS AND SERVICES

The current state of technical services includes many vendor-provided products and services. Most catalogers use OCLC's website or the Library of Congress (LC) to obtain cataloging copy, whether to upgrade vendor-supplied acquisitions records or to create an original bibliographic record. Many technical services functions are reliant on an integrated library system (ILS), which is typically a vendor product. Collection development relies on resource vendors, as do acquisitions and cataloging to some extent. Serials librarians frequently use vendors for services like A-to-Z lists to aggregate their serials titles from databases and to provide access. Vendors are integral to technical services functions. The relationship between vendors and librarians can be tense, as in dissatisfaction with so-called Big Deals or costly journal subscriptions. OCLC services like Connexion are available by subscription with little room for negotiation or customization of services. Open source can be an alternative, yet it requires a substantial commitment of time since there is no vendor support to coordinate upgrades or solve problems.

However, technical services librarians do have options when dealing with vendors, including the ability to influence pricing for their offerings and the opportunity to provide feedback so that vendors may develop products and services that more closely match libraries' needs.

It is understandable that technical services librarians may be dissatisfied with vendor offerings and services. Library users request e-books that they can easily purchase from Amazon themselves. Public services librarians may be hindered by an inability to find materials due to poor-quality vendor-supplied bibliographic records, licenses that take weeks to negotiate, or clunky OPAC interfaces. Rather than becoming frustrated when vendors do not provide what libraries want and need, technical services librarians should focus on partnering with vendors to influence how their processes and products are offered to libraries. Although many processes in technical services are reliant on vendors, there is still room for negotiation. Libraries are consumers and should feel free to express specific needs, dissatisfaction with service or products, requests for enhancements or new services, and the like. Technical services librarians also act as agents of the library, serving as both the advocate of the library and its users. Rather than feeling overpowered, sidetracked, or ignored, technical services librarians can instead position themselves to negotiate with vendors.

THE ROLE OF VENDORS

The question is not whether technical services librarians can influence vendors, but *how* they can influence the outcome of vendor-provided offerings such as e-books, licenses, record sets, or authority control. They can begin by considering that vendors are businesses that are in competition with other businesses, all seeking a share of the library's budget. Vendors need to pay salaries and bills, turn a profit to encourage continued investment, support products sufficiently to satisfy current customers, and develop current or new products and services to attract customers. Improving and developing products and services is in the vendor's best interest; this is how they retain and increase market share and make profits.

Vendors take risks every time they choose to invest resources in developing a product or service. They contemplate whether the resources invested in a particular improvement pay off in terms of

- increased customer use of their products
- customers paying for a new module for the ILS or ERM
- customers purchasing enhanced record sets, buying more e-books on a vendor's platform, or outsourcing authority control to a vendor

- customers making the difficult decision to switch to a new ILS, advocating to their governing bodies for additional funding, and investing their own staff time to make the change

Are enough customers willing to pay for a particular product that will enable the vendor to repay its investment? Vendors do respond to customer requests, but they also weigh the cost of satisfying an individual customer request against the cost of doing so and its potential for helping them earn a profit. They must determine whether honoring a particular customer's requests will benefit their product and also appeal to other customers.

Vendors use the information gathered from customers and prospective customers to identify and evaluate potential improvements to existing products and services plus explore possibilities for new products and services. They also use customer input to assess potential profits and to refine new products that are being developed before they are released for sale. Technical services librarians can influence product development by communicating with vendors through many channels.

Collaborating to Develop Standards

Another means to make vendors more accountable and to negotiate with them for the best products and services is to develop standards and to make vendors adhere to them. An even better approach is to enlist the vendors as partners in the development of standards. This will help guarantee their buy-in and willingness to apply standards. Standards are documents that provide advice to the profession "on various aspects of library service."[1] Calls are frequently issued by standards organizations or professional organizations to enable library professionals to comment on a proposed standard. Their informed input helps to shape the final guidelines put forth in the standard. Standards are developed by organizations such as the National Information Standards Organization (NISO) (http://www.niso.org/home/) and the American National Standards Institute (ANSI) (http://www.ansi.org/). Some examples of standards include the ANSI/NISO document *Guidelines for the Construction, Format, and Management of Monolingual Controlled Vocabularies*[2] or the ANSI/NISO/LBI Library Binding standard.[3]

Developing a new standard or revising an existing one takes time because it requires reaching a broad consensus that the standard is needed and agreeing on which elements to include. Although time consuming, standards development is a powerful way to influence vendors because the process involves collecting data from many individuals about what libraries need and want, then analyzing that data to agree on the essential elements that are needed by many libraries. The standards development process gives vendors some assurance of a return on the investment they make in developing products based on that standard. For example, most major electronic resource management systems have implemented ANSI/NISO Z39.93, commonly known as SUSHI, for harvesting usage statistics.

Guidelines and Codes of Practice

Guidelines and codes of practice are similar to standards but are typically less technical. The COUNTER (Counting Online Usage of Networked Electronic Resources) Code of Practice[4] is one example that is familiar to many technical services librarians. Guidelines and codes are typically developed by groups formed to address a specific issue, such as the need for consistent usage statistic reporting. Like standards, they are useful in communicating a widespread need and broad consensus to vendors on how to meet that need.

There are numerous opportunities for librarians to participate in developing standards and guidelines. They can articulate a need for new standards and guidelines. They can volunteer to serve as liaisons between library associations and standards development organizations, or on teams developing or revising a specific standard. They can be alert to requests for comments on proposed standards, which are often distributed via discussion lists such as ACQNET-L, COLLDV-L, and AUTOCAT, and invest the time to study the draft and submit comments. They can attend webinars and conference sessions related to standards development, participating in the discussion of needs. Librarians can also discuss draft standards with vendor representatives, encouraging the vendor to pay attention and consider the standard as products and services are developed. They can partner with vendors to co-develop and lead efforts to develop guidelines, as in the case of the *Recommended Practices for the Presentation and Identification of E-Journals*, more commonly know as PIE-J.[5] Other examples include the *MARC Record Guide for Monograph Aggregator Vendors*[6] and the Shared Electronic Resource Understanding (SERU).[7]

Engaging in Dialogue

Conversations with vendor representatives are a less formal but still important way to influence product development. Vendor representatives frequently have multiple objectives when they schedule visits to libraries, including introducing new products, selling new products and services, educating librarians about features that make their products more valuable than competitors' products, checking on satisfaction with existing products, and learning about library needs that could contribute to product enhancements or new product development. Librarians should prepare for vendor visits by reviewing existing products and services. In preparation for those visits, they may consider: What works well? Which recent enhancements is the library using?

Where does the product fall short? What does a related product do that this vendor's product does not do? The librarian should also consider emerging needs, issues, and problems that a vendor might be able to assist in solving.

While meeting with the vendor representative, the librarian should discuss how existing products are performing and any desired improvements. Whenever possible, the meeting should start on a positive note by discussing what is viewed as the product's helpful features. Representatives are interested in how libraries are using new features, as this validates the company's decision to invest in developing those features, and provides the representative with examples to use with other customers, particularly since the vendor might ask the library to serve as a reference for other customers or potential customers regarding a specific service or function. Desired improvements should be next introduced to the vendor, and librarians are advised to give a specific example of how the feature would improve workflow or solve a problem. Written documentation and examples provide specific concrete information for vendors and also serve to document the conversation and what was conveyed to the vendor. Librarians should realize that the representative is likely to ask questions, both to gain a better understanding of the desired feature and to gauge whether this feature is a need that is likely to be shared by many libraries. The vendor's representative may also be aware that a similar feature is being discussed in the company as a possible fee-based addition to existing products; if so, the representative may ask questions aimed at gauging whether this feature is something that the library might be interested in purchasing. While it may be tempting to exaggerate the importance of a desired improvement, libraries and vendors are best served by realistic conversations about needs versus wants. Librarians should bear in mind that for the vendor to stay in business and provide products and services that the library needs, the vendor has to correctly judge the risk and rewards of investing in product development.

Librarians have opportunities to meet with vendors at conferences and trade shows. While impromptu conversations are helpful in building good relationships, scheduling an appointment is best for discussing specific ideas for product and service development. Scheduling an appointment is preferable to dropping by the vendor's booth when a particular issue must be discussed. When scheduling appointments to meet at large conferences, librarians should briefly mention that they hope to discuss an idea for improving a specific product as the librarian's usual representative may want to invite a product manager to participate in the meeting. It is helpful when possible to submit a list of questions or needs in advance so that the vendor can fully prepare for the meeting and make the best-qualified representative available for the meeting.

Another means for librarians to influence vendor offerings is to participate in focus groups and product development forums, which may be offered at conferences and trade shows or virtually through online conferencing or discussion lists. These events may be advertised on electronic mailing lists, or vendors may invite current customers to participate. Typically, the vendor will give a brief presentation introducing a proposed product or demonstrating an early version of a product in development. The presentation may be followed by the presenter initiating a group discussion eliciting feedback on desirable features, although larger sessions may include breakout tables with vendor representatives prompting discussion and taking notes in small groups. Participating in product focus groups and development forums is not only a good way to influence product development, but it is also an opportunity to network and learn from other librarians with similar needs and to share common concerns.

Librarians can influence vendor offerings by subscribing to and participating in discussions on targeted discussion lists. The list may be related to a specific topic (acquisitions, collection development, cataloging, etc.) or may be hosted by a vendor, such as OCLC-CAT, Music OCLC Users Group (MOUG), or the Ex Libris Users of North America Law Library Interest Group. When a vendor implements an update that does not work as anticipated and may contain a bug, or when a vendor has instituted an unfavorable policy (such as OCLC withdrawing credit for original cataloging contributed to its database), the community of library professionals can have an impact on making the vendor reconsider. At the very least, the vendor will be aware of customer feelings and be prepared to lose business. Vendor-hosted discussion lists are also a good place for vendors and librarians to develop a rapport and working relationship as opposed to an adversarial "us versus them" situation. Each party must realize that neither side will get 100 percent of what it wants and everyone will benefit from some negotiation.

Service and Enhancement Requests

Librarians can play a role in product and service development by submitting service and enhancement requests for current products. Service requests are submitted when a product does not perform as expected or a new need has emerged and the current product is unable to accommodate it. An example of such a case was when Resource Description and Access (RDA) was formally adopted by the three U.S. national libraries. Many ILS vendors were not fully RDA compliant, and customers who imported RDA records found that their systems were unable to accommodate new fields such as the 3XX fields for content, media, and carrier type. When a service request has been submitted, the vendor may respond directly to the library, correcting a problem related to a specific installation of an ILS, for example. When a vendor receives several service requests related to the same issue, they may release a software patch or update a knowledge base. Enhancement requests are submitted when products perform as expected but not as desired. For example, early electronic resource management systems were often designed to store a single payment record per title per fiscal year, while some resources required multiple payments during the fiscal year.

Librarians may partner with vendors to develop new services. Advisory groups may be general, such as an ILS vendor's advisory group, or an approvals/firm order vendor advisory group. Examples of targeted vendor advisory groups include the YBP Medical Library Advisory Group and the American Association of Law Libraries' Vendor-Supplied Records Advisory Working Group. Joining an advisory group and attending its meetings enables librarians to get firsthand knowledge about changes to an organization (mergers, new hires), an overview of improvements, product and marketing updates, information on emerging trends, and also the ability to provide feedback and have a stake in the group's products and services.

When problems or feedback are provided to vendors, be very specific and provide examples so that they can clearly see the problem or determine its cause. Regardless of how much planning and alpha testing go into a product, there will be unanticipated problems, and these are usually discovered when a product or service goes live and is available to customers. User documentation may be nonexistent, lacking in specificity, or cumbersome to navigate. Again, this is the librarian's opportunity to provide input, as they are paying for the products and services the vendor has developed. Libraries may choose to reduce their level of service with a vendor to indicate that they are not happy with the service; if a vendor is losing business, they should also be informed as to why this has happened.[8] It is in the vendor's best interest to acknowledge this feedback and act upon it. Otherwise, this gives the library reason to believe they have received poor service and are likely to share this information with other libraries, particularly if they start the search for a new vendor. Form a united front with other libraries, possibly through your consortia or professional organization.

NEGOTIATE FOR SERVICES AND PRICING

Negotiation is a critical skill for technical services librarians. They negotiate license agreements to access resources, to support cataloging functions, and so on. This is a skill that is not typically taught in library science programs, and librarians are often unprepared to engage in negotiation.[9] Ashmore and Grogg published "The Art of the Deal: Negotation Advice from Library Leaders and Vendors" in 2009, and some of the issues they raise in their article in regard to electronic resources are still problematic: interlibrary loan or document delivery for electronic resources; long-term access since there is no mechanism to facilitate perpetual access, which both librarians and vendors acknowledge; and price, over which vendors may lack flexibility. [10] Libraries may be able to negotiate better pricing and terms through a consortium, yet this is also a complex area of negotiation, requiring a different skill set and an understanding of how to accommodate multiple interests. [11]

NASIG offers both a beginner's guide for working with vendors and a licensing guide to help those new to the process. [12] Have a specific agenda for any meeting with vendors, and take charge of the meeting. Additionally, make sure that you are fully informed about the company, particularly its current status and any changes in products. It is important to know if a company has been acquired by another, will enter into a merger, or will acquire a competitor, as all these factors influence the type of product and service you receive, including pricing and customer service responsiveness. Flowers notes that "Negotiations with library materials vendors can have a significant impact on a library's success in terms of service to its users and effective use of its financial resources." [13] Some of the things that technical services librarians can do to prepare for negotiations with vendors are to prepare a negotiations position paper; conduct a bidder's conference; select vendors with deliverables that most closely meet your library's needs; establish procedures to monitor, document, and control vendor performance; and develop strategies to use when vendors do not perform as expected or promised. [14] Librarians also need to bear in mind that they have tactics that they may exploit during the negotiation process, such as the ability to take their business elsewhere if not satisfied or if a better offer is made by another vendor. In the current economy, vendors need to fight for every account, and some companies will take a customer at a loss under the belief they will eventually recoup their losses rather than see business go to a competitor. [15] Libraries may use volume of business or size of account or their reputation as negotiating tools. [16] Membership in an academic consortia or some other prestige might appeal to vendors, who may value your library as a customer and add your name to their marketing materials. [17]

TECHNICAL SERVICES ADVOCACY: HOW TO PROMOTE THE VALUE OF ONE'S WORK TO COLLEAGUES, ADMINISTRATORS, AND USERS

The first part of this chapter has focused on working with vendors, but the current state of technical services also includes advocating for one's work and its significance to the library's operations. Technical services librarians often feel that their work is not valued in the same way as that of their colleagues who are in more public positions and work directly with users. Reporting the number of copy, complex, and original cataloging records created monthly may lack the impact of reporting how many reference questions were answered on-site and virtually. Since many technical services librarians manage staff and functions, their work may be viewed more as a production management function and therefore less professional than that of a subject specialist or public services librarian. This is not to say that technical services librarians do not work with the public, as their role has changed due to factors that include the emergence of non-MARC metadata and institutional repositories and the ability for users to submit queries or error reports that are directly routed to technical services. However, since the work of technical services librarians is very specialized and may require many detailed processes, its significance or impact on overall library operations may be overlooked or misunderstood by administrators. Catalogers frequently note how administrators want to cut authority control since they do not understand the purpose it serves. Administrators may also incorrectly believe that vendor-supplied cataloging is fine as is and is ready to use as soon as those records are loaded in the library's catalog. What they fail to realize is that there are different types of vendor-supplied cataloging. There are basic "placeholder" records frequently used for approval books or other large-scale purchases, such as a PDA program. Vendor-supplied cataloging *can* be ready to use if it is purchased and the library has a detailed profile with the vendor. Acquisitions may be overlooked by administrators who feel PDA answers all the library's collection needs or that what the library acquires is so mainstream that entry-level staff can handle all ordering and related processes. Their lack of understanding fails to recognize that acquisitions encompasses more than placing orders and loading records. It also requires correctly identifying the item that has been requested; negotiating the best price for that resource; possibly negotiating a license, rights, and ongoing access; dealing with currency conversions and other matters related to foreign orders; and the time-consuming return of resources to obtain a refund.

At a time when library budgets are being severely cut and vacancies are not being filled, and when "traditional" positions compete with emerging trends that lead to positions such as Metadata Strategist, Digital User Experience Librarian, Undergraduate Experience Librarian, and Instructional Design Librarian, the need to advocate for one's work has taken on added importance. What are some of the ways that technical services librarians can advocate for their work? A first step is to promote their work so that others fully understand what they contribute to the library overall and the implications of what would happen should that work cease to be provided. When others understand a process and its outcome, they are better prepared to support that work, particularly when that work has a direct influence on the outcome and success of their work. A public service librarian's ability to help users locate appropriate resources will be severely hampered by an OPAC that has split files for name and subject headings because it lacks authority control. Collection development librarians may overlook the fact that their library does indeed own a particular resource since the brief record used to represent that resource in the OPAC is very minimal and substandard.

ALCTS's Role in the Advocacy Movement

In February 2012, the ALCTS Advocacy Task Force hosted an electronic forum (e-forum) titled "Advocacy: What Does It Mean for Technical Services?" Advocacy, when used in reference to libraries, does not immediately bring to mind technical services. Instead, the usual reaction is about public service offers and resources. The e-forum moderators compiled the following questions to generate discussion:

- How do you define advocacy? What does it mean to you?
- Do you have an "elevator speech" about technical services? Do you have individual speeches for each department within technical services or one for technical services as a whole?
- If you're a library educator or work closely with a library school, what is your program doing to advocate to new professionals/librarians-in-training (students) about the field of technical services?
- What can ALCTS do for you or for our profession in terms of advocacy?
- Establishing standards and serving as advocates to publishers and vendors to convey our needs (cost, licensing agreements, standards for record sets and metadata) is a form of advocacy. What do you see as the critical areas of need?
- ALCTS can provide publications and documentation to enable our members to meet the needs at their institutions and to facilitate collaborative problem solving. What do you see as the critical areas of need?
- Education is critical for new professionals as well as established technical services professionals. What do you consider to be core competencies? What areas could ALCTS address in terms of offerings?

In response to the first question, participants agreed that promoting the work and visibility of technical services is vital to our survival in the face of continuing budget cuts and staffing shortages. They acknowledged that administrators may be aware of technical services costs but not necessarily of the benefits of technical services. Participants reported that they promoted their departments through tours and orientations, newsletters, outreach to different departments/ branches, permitting non–technical services personnel to shadow technical services staff, and teaching courses.

The idea of an elevator speech for technical services librarians is a novel concept. E-forum participants responded that such a pitch focused on conveying what they do and their work's value to their colleagues and users. The importance and impact of statistics (number of items ordered, cataloged, etc.)

was noted. Tours, blogs, participating in student orientation, and working at the reference desk were also cited as ways to promote the work of technical services.

In regard to the MLS and education, participants addressed the lack of emphasis on technical services courses. A question was raised as to whether certain courses should be required to earn an MLS or if ALA should accredit programs that do not require technical services courses.[18]

The ALCTS Advocacy Task Force also issued a report that contained recommendations regarding technical services advocacy. The group was charged to "to identify what ALCTS members mean by 'advocacy,' define ALCTS' role in advocating for our functions or for libraries, and recommend what steps, if any, ALCTS should take to strengthen its advocacy efforts."[19] The report addressed different types of advocacy: backroom advocacy, which is what takes place at one's job, institution, and community, and advocating for the profession "through recruitment and training of our next generation of librarians, and also by educating people on how technical services enables the primary functions of libraries."[20]

The Technical Services Librarian Advocate

While advocacy has not typically been a role that technical services librarians have played, the time has come for them to think differently. Current technical services librarians often work closely with their public services and collection development colleagues with the common goal of the users and their needs in mind. Without technical services, the most basic library services, such as reference, are not possible. Technical services librarians need to advocate for adequate funding and staffing so that they may in turn enable other library operations. They must be advocates for their work since there is little possibility others will take up their cause. Promoting one's work can be done in a number of ways. One way is to serve on public services committees and groups that will benefit from your knowledge and how it enables their work. Consider hosting an open house where your staff and you demonstrate some of your work processes and provide a tour of technical services. Be willing to answer questions, regardless of how trivial or annoying they may seem. The goal is to establish common ground with your colleagues and to form alliances. The greater an understanding they have of your work, the more likely you are to garner their support. Having a presence on your library's website is essential, and your page should include a listing of services you provide, a staff directory with contact information, an organization chart, and policies and documentation. The term *transparency* is a contemporary buzzword, but is very important in this respect. Your work should be understood by others in the library and not viewed as a shadowy backroom practice reserved for the socially inept. If volunteers are solicited to work with the public, consider participating or asking your staff to participate. This will also help to promote your department and its work.

NOTES

1. American Library Association, "ALA Standards and Guidelines," May 12, 2014, http://www.ala.org/tools/guidelines/standardsguidelines.

2. Available at http://www.niso.org/apps/group_public/download.php/12591/z39-19-2005 r2010.pdf.

3. Available at http://www.niso.org/apps/group_public/download.php/6565/Library Binding.pdf.

4. Available at http://www.projectcounter.org/code_practice.html.

5. Available at http://www.niso.org/workrooms/piej.

6. Available at http://www.loc.gov/aba/pcc/sca/documents/FinalVendorGuide.pdf.

7. Available at http://www.niso.org/publications/rp/RP-7-2012_SERU.pdf.

8. Janet L. Flowers, "Negotiations with Library Material Vendors: Preparation and Tips," *Bottom Line: Managing Library Finances* 16, no. 3 (2003): 100.

9. Beth Ashmore and Jill E. Grogg, "The Art of the Deal: Negotiation Advice from Library Leaders and Vendors," *Searcher* 17, no. 1 (2009): 18.

10. Ibid., 23.

11. Ibid., 24.

12. William Joseph Thomas, "NASIGuide: A Beginner's Guide to Working with Vendors," NASIG, http://www.nasig.org/uploaded_files/92/files/Publications/WorkingVendors.pdf; Rick Anderson, "NASIGuide: License Negotiation 101," NASIG, http://www.nasig.org/uploaded_files/92/files/Publications/anderson_nasigguide.pdf.

13. Flowers, "Negotiations with Library Material Vendors," 100.

14. Joe Auer, "Negotiating a Better Deal with Vendors: Tips on Managing the Acquisitions Process," *Information Systems Management* 10, no. 4 (1993): 68.

15. Sharon Srodin, "Let's Make a Deal! Tips and Tricks for Negotiating Content Purchases," *Online* 28, no. 4 (2004): 17.

16. Flowers, "Negotiations with Library Materials Vendors," 101–2.

17. Srodin, "Let's Make a Deal!," 19.

18. A summary of the e-forum discussion on advocacy is available at http://www.ala.org/alcts/ano/v23/n1/e-forums.

19. Advocacy Task Force, Association for Library Collections and Technical Services, "Final Report," American Library Association, June 15, 2012, p. 1, http://connect.ala.org/files/2145/finalreport_advocacytf_june2012.pdf.

20. Ibid, 2.

Chapter Three

The Current State of Bibliographic Description

Sylvia Hall-Ellis

Discovering and sharing knowledge in a dynamic environment of print, electronic, and digital assets impacts and changes the ways catalogers and metadata specialists provide resource descriptions. Emerging technologies coupled with the expansion of information, the availability of new writings for researchers and scholars, and increased access to digital assets such as textual content, images, and multimedia converge to reinvigorate library services in communities, specialized collections, and academic commons across the country.

Catalogers, technical services librarians, and metadata specialists design, implement, enhance, and maintain digital asset management systems. They are integral managers of comprehensive systems designed to facilitate the ingestion, annotation, cataloguing, storage, retrieval, and distribution of organized, discoverable resources. They devote effort to acquiring author rights, resolving copyright issues, protecting intellectual property, building institutional and collaborative repositories, and facilitating access to open-access collections. During the last two decades, user and market demands have driven the information discovery environment and forced a reexamination of traditional bibliographic description and have led to the incorporation of metadata schemas into the workflow and daily operations of technical services workflows in libraries and information centers.

The rapid expansion of non-MARC schemas and digital resources, the dynamic expansion of assets born on the Internet, uneven quality and authority control of web-resident resources, and the need for human intervention to organize these has prompted catalogers and information professionals to address metadata issues. Online catalogs and information seekers' use patterns were changing; demands for natural language searching and one-stop tools were becoming dominant among users.

Building on their role of managing bibliographic data, catalogers were the individuals responsible for creating metadata. Yet, parallel to increasing demands for professionals with the education, knowledge, and technical skills required for working with non-MARC metadata schemas, libraries were reconfiguring or disbanding technical services departments and outsourcing cataloging tasks. Professional cataloging positions were being collapsed into paraprofessional jobs. New library school graduates seeking positions as catalogers competed in a shrinking labor market and feared losing jobs to paraprofessionals. Differentiating the knowledge of professionals from paraprofessionals became increasingly critical; employers differentiated between the two different levels of library employees. Position descriptions for entry-level professionals began to evolve from traditional cataloging to metadata specialists in 2001–2002. By the end of the decade, two-thirds of the position descriptions required familiarity, knowledge, or experience working with traditional MARC and emerging non-MARC metadata schemas. [1]

Managers of technical services departments recognized the importance of training staff members to work with metadata and the benefits of hiring new catalogers who had the education and experience to handle digitization projects. Since 1998, a growing number of academic libraries planning and undertaking digitization projects increased the need to create metadata to support their identification, discovery, assessment, and management. [2] In 2008, an Association for Library Collections and Technical Services (ALCTS) Task Force and heads of cataloging reported the impact on their departments. [3]

Leaders of the community of catalogers and library and information science (LIS) educators continued to discuss metadata, the role of catalogers, which non-MARC schemas to adopt, digitization projects, and the building of repositories at conferences over the next years. [4] Ellero attempted to determine the extent to which metadata knowledge, skills, and competencies appeared in cataloger position descriptions. [5] She reported the presence of metadata knowledge in 18 percent of position descriptions. A review of digitization projects revealed that catalogers participated actively by creating metadata, integrating digital assets into the host library's catalog, building crosswalks among various schemas, collaborating with partner institutions (e.g., museums, historical societies), drafting dictionaries and taxonomies, and training staff. [6] DeZelar-Tiedman reported that catalogers possessed the credentials and technical skills needed for successful digital projects. [7] She found that experience in designing databases, constructing taxonomies, analyzing data and its behavior, and understanding the importance of standards in an interoperability environment served catalogers well as contributors to digital projects.

THE ARRAY OF METADATA SCHEMAS THAT CATALOGERS AND METADATA SPECIALISTS USE

The contemporary library or information center purchases information packages and assets for its permanent collection in print, online, and as digital assets. Cataloging or bibliographic description is routinely referred to as the process of describing an information resource, choosing name and title access points, conducting subject analysis, assigning subject headings, and constructing a classification number. As information professionals move toward a global framework for bibliographic description, catalogers and metadata specialists refer to an information package as the manifestation of a work, focusing on the physical object, as distinct from its intellectual content.

Building on the fundamentals articulated in the four Functional Requirements for Bibliographic Records (FRBR), Boydston and Leysen observed that catalogers have experience analyzing bibliographic data and differentiating among works, expressions, manifestations, and items.[8] They identified four domains in which catalogers work (knowledge of standards, cooperative environment, management and supervisory skills, user knowledge) and three factors (cost, supply of catalogers, education and training) that influence their participation in digital projects. From the cataloger's perspective, a new resource in the collection is an instance of recorded information (called a *work*) that needs to be described bibliographically so that users can identify, retrieve, locate, and use it. The informational content of a work is recorded available in an *expression* that is made available in a manifestation that is exemplified as an *item*.[9]

Preserving and providing access to documents, photographs, maps, and other archival materials prompted libraries and consortia to undertake digitization projects. The Internet connects millions of websites and serves as an easily accessible framework for the publication and sharing of knowledge and information. Primary cultural heritage organizations in communities, libraries, historical societies, and archives harnessed digitization to make available resources that had been available only to visiting researchers and scholars. Preserving and providing access to digitized and born-digital material required the construction of bibliographic descriptions for these surrogates.[10] In their roles as primary information providers, libraries were early users of digital technology, yet the processing, cataloging, and building of databases with bibliographic descriptions did not fit easily into the structured framework used in traditional library catalogs. The use of metadata schemas provided reasonable, affordable frameworks into which these bibliographic descriptions could be entered, indexed, accessed, and maintained.

An examination of the websites and the position descriptions for the individuals who build and maintain them reveals the array of metadata schemas used by libraries, historical societies, archives, and organizations providing access to digital assets. Initially, the technical skills for catalogers and metadata specialists included competencies in programming and scripting languages.[11] Writing the XML markup language used for creating websites was a commonly demanded skill during the first ten years of the study (September 2000 through August 2010). In a 2014 research study conducted by Hall-Ellis of 146 representative position descriptions for catalogers and metadata specialists requiring work with metadata schemas during a twelve-year period (2000–2013),[12] this competency appeared in approximately one-third (n=42; 28.8 percent) of the descriptions, followed by HyperText Mark-up Language (HTML) (n=13; 8.9 percent) and MySQL, the second most used open-source relational database management system[13] (structured query language) (n=7; 4.8 percent).

Providing timely access to digital assets prompted library administrators and digitization project managers to consider the adoption of metadata sche-mas. Overcoming resistance to using nontraditional metadata schemas chal-lenged the community of catalogers. However, in direct response to meeting users' needs, catalogers and metadata specialists began to favor descriptive metadata schemas.[14] The ease of creation, modest investment for software, and training requirements contributed to the selection of specific metadata schemas for discreet applications. In Hall-Ellis' 2014 research study noted in the preceding paragraph, the most commonly identified metadata schema was Dublin Core (n=79; 54.1percent).[15] This was followed by EAD (En-coded Archival Description) (n=43; 29.5 percent),[16] MODS (Metadata Ob-ject Description Schema) (n=27; 18.5 percent),[17] CONTENTdm (n=26; 13.7 percent),[18] and METS (Metadata Encoding and Transmission Standard) (n=22; 15.1 percent).[19]

DEMANDS FOR INCREASED SPECIFICITY REGARDING ACCESS TO CULTURAL AND SCIENTIFIC ASSETS

Created to facilitate the discovery of information and resources, metadata provides a standardized set of descriptive elements that can be used to sup-port discovery by organizing electronic resources, providing digital identifi-cation, supporting access to born-digital assets, and preserving surrogates of items previously available as print and visual images. The term refers to three types of metadata:

- *structural metadata* describes the design and specification of data struc-tures;
- *descriptive metadata* refers to the unique instances of data content; and,
- *administrative metadata* contains information about the creation, file types, access, rights, and preservation of the resource.[20]

Communities of practice develop and adopt metadata schemas to meet users' needs. Through a collaborative effort, members of a discipline evaluate the resources to be described, the affordability and availability of tools and software, and ease of use for patrons to deliver the desired outcomes. Consideration is given to the time, effort, and cost of training, the functional capabilities of the selected schema, the ease of crosswalking metadata between schemas, and the investment of resources to maintain data integrity and database quality.

As a result of the global accessibility of resources via the Internet, a demand for increasing specificity among practitioners and users has resulted in the proliferation of metadata schemas. Catalogers have historically established themselves as the organizers of metadata that are used to identify, retrieve, and deliver information resources to users. The development of metadata schemas changed the traditional library environment. The work of catalogers and later metadata specialists moved away from the traditional catalog card through a period of retrospective conversion to machine-readable descriptive bibliographic data to the creation of metadata in unique schemas to provide global access through the Internet and in preparation for an evolving semantic web.[21] Technical skills and cataloging competencies that technical services staff had to learn and master expanded proportionately to the number of metadata schemas that an institution adopted to meet users' needs.

CONTINUOUS LEARNING FOR CATALOGERS AND METADATA SPECIALISTS

The education and training of catalogers and classifiers can be traced to the days when Melvil Dewey demanded that students in his two-year preliminary class in the Columbia College Library achieve technical excellence.[22] The integration of theoretical considerations into cataloging practices began with the animated discussions of Sir Anthony Panizzi at the British Museum, moved to the innovative work of Charles Ammi Cutter, evolved with Seymour Lubetsky's visionary leadership, combined with the development of MARC and online public access catalogs, and currently resides in challenges driven by the Internet, metadata schemas, and cataloging tools.

Catalogers and metadata specialists invest years of professional experience and continuous learning to master the technical skills, proficiencies, and competencies required in their daily work. Employers expect them to possess broad-based theoretical knowledge, extensive hands-on experience, and mastery of computer-based tools and system-specific familiarity that appear to exceed the requirements and preferences stated in position announcements for new hires. The professional development, continuing education, and practical experiences for catalog librarians and metadata specialists remain critically important in librarianship.

Academic preparation; the theoretical basis for the organization of print, online, and digital assets; communication competencies; and collegial working relationships are applicable to each member of the cataloging, technical services, and bibliographic control teams. Upon completion of graduate school with an accredited library degree, these individuals require the time and support of administrators and managers to continue their professional growth to gain a comprehensive understanding of the cataloging code, classification, subject analysis, authority control, MARC formats, metadata schemas, database quality assurance processes, and integrated library system operations. Additionally, the professional cataloger and metadata specialist need to communicate effectively in writing and verbally; train and supervise paraprofessional staff, student workers, and volunteers; work independently and collaboratively; and remain current with technological and bibliographic changes in the field.

Continuous learning is available both in formal and informal formats. Professional organizations, the Library of Congress (LC), and library consortia are leaders in professional development opportunities for catalogers and metadata specialists. LC participates in the writing, field-testing, and dissemination of training materials for catalogers and metadata specialists. As part of its commitment of excellence in service to the profession, LC offers training materials, learning modules and webcasts and hosts the official standards documents for cataloging and metadata schemas. [23]

Through webinars, workshops, electronic forums (e-forums), conference presentations, and official publications, ALCTS offers an array of learning experiences for practitioners at all levels in libraries and information centers. [24] ALCTS's Cataloging and Metadata Management Section (CaMMS) promotes learning through the Continuing Education Committee, the Continuing Education Training Materials Committee, research and publications, the Resource Description and Access (RDA) Planning and Training Task Force, and ten interest groups. [25] Library associations across the United States and professional associations offer cataloging, metadata, and related topic workshops, seminars, and conferences for their members.

Research study findings suggest that the community of catalogers is responsible for identifying, preparing, delivering, and evaluating these learning opportunities. The evidence indicates that work remains to be done by everyone concerned about the recruitment, education, and careers of catalogers and metadata specialists.

MARC: A FRAMEWORK FOR LIBRARY METADATA

The history of MARC cataloging began in the 1950s when LC investigated the possibility of using automated techniques for its internal operations.[26] The acronym for MAchine-Readable Cataloging, MARC, defines a data format that emerged from the LC-led initiative. MARC formats provide the mechanisms by which computers exchange, use, and interpret bibliographic information, and its data elements form the foundation of online library catalogs. The Council of the British National Bibliography organized a similar development in the United Kingdom. In 1966, LC initiated a pilot project for the MARC format. Participants in the pilot included the Argonne National Laboratory, Harvard University, the University of California at Los Angeles's Institute of Library Research, the University of Chicago, the University of Florida, and Yale University. In 1968, these efforts came together as MARC II.

The Purpose of MARC

Since its inception, MARC's designers envisioned a framework for data representing library materials in a variety of formats and languages that could be used in automated systems with flexibility to support related applications (e.g., circulation, cataloging, acquisitions, inventory, and collection analysis). The successful pilot broadened in 1971 to provide online capability, and the types of bibliographic records in the MARC format expanded to include languages in addition to English, serials, maps, films, manuscripts, and other materials. By 1974, the MARC system represented in LC's catalog totaled approximately 500,000 records.[27]

Differing requirements promulgated by their controlling bodies led to the development of USMARC and UK MARC in the 1980s. By the late 1990s, nearly fifty different versions of MARC existed around the world. Catalogers and their colleagues in systems development recognized the benefits of unifying the differing versions of MARC. Long, thoughtful deliberations and consultation between LC and the British Library (BL) led to the discontinuation of UK MARC, the adoption of USMARC in the UK, and renaming the LC version MARC 21 in 1998 to reflect its universal applicability.

The LC Network Development and MARC Standards Office (NDMSO)[28] maintains and publishes the official versions of the MARC 21 formats and associated documentation[29] and issues annual updates. The MARC 21 suite of documentation includes the bibliographic format (including eight types of materials), the authority format, the holdings format, the classification format, and the community information format. In addition to these formats, NDMSO publishes official documentation for country codes, language codes, geographic codes, organization codes, and relator, sources, and description conventions codes. Catalogers may access MARC from LC's website free of charge or purchase the documentation from a bibliographic utility, integrated library system (ILS) vendor, or external supplier of cataloging data.

Development for Increased Capabilities in ILSs

State-of-the-art library catalogs contain the local bibliographic database and provide successful integration between the patron and the computer-based system. The ILS's technical capabilities enable users to query, search, and interact with the local online public access catalog (OPAC) and comparable systems that are geographically remote. Because these activities are technologically feasible and efficient, the goal to consider information resources, regardless of format or geographic location, is the cornerstone of the multitype resource sharing and interlibrary loan (ILL) environments.

Libraries have not progressed uniformly toward the goal of integrated systems. The presence of fragmented bibliographic data about library materials in brief and incomplete surrogate records continues to complicate the process of identifying the exact status of items. Library staff must search the catalog, on-order files, shelf lists, officials,[30] binding files, circulation files, overdue materials files, continuing resources (serials) files, and departmental activity-specific files. Until libraries build, access, and maintain a comprehensive integrated system reflecting the intellectual qualities of all resources, the lack of cohesion and incomplete bibliographic records will frustrate staff members and patrons alike. They will continue to expend significant resources (human, capital, and time) to compensate for incorrect, incomplete data. The planning, implementation, and evaluation required to achieve this goal requires the appropriate attention from librarians and their staff in the twenty-first century.

Understanding the cataloging process requires familiarity with and ease of use of the cataloging rules, authority records and files, classification schemes, subject heading lists, MARC documentation, and local practices. The cataloging process enables the cataloger to construct bibliographic records that support several functions in the library's integrated library system. Access points in the bibliographic record facilitate the searches that librarians conduct as part of reference, readers' advisory, and collection development processes. Patrons query the OPAC to determine if the library owns specific titles, identify resources, and determine owning locations.

Limitations (Current and Potential for the Future)

The development of new types of print and digital resources challenged technical services staff to describe them using the cataloging rules within the structured MARC framework. Written for use on mainframe computers, the MARC structure relied on the identification and assignment of coded metadata in fixed- and variable-length fields. Indices were constructed through disassembling MARC data into a series of pointers that came together to provide structured screen displays. The conversion of information from card catalogs to machine-readable databases of MARC records served to facilitate access to the historical collections in libraries and information centers. However, the advent of newer physical formats and packaging could not be easily transcribed within the confines of the cataloging rules and MARC structure.

Catalogers and technical services staff recognized the acceleration of change. Observations, experience, and research convinced them that traditional cataloging rules within a MARC framework could not continue to meet the growing demands of users with increasing expectations and technology sophistication without changes.

THE WAR OF THE "CATALOGING RULES"

Librarians have collaborated to develop a cataloging code for use in the United States and the United Kingdom since 1904. Following dedicated correspondence and negotiations, the first international cataloging code appeared as *Catalog Rules, Author and Title Entries*[31] in the United States and *Cataloguing Rules, Author and Title Entries* in England.[32] Both the American and the British editions contained the 174 rules for entry and headings for authors, titles, and bibliographic descriptions. Disagreements regarding usage appeared with notes to explain the differences and interpretations for catalogers. These cataloging codes did not contain rules for descriptive cataloging. Therefore, when the committee members identified an area that would benefit from further explanation, they included supplementary rules prepared by librarians at LC. Revisions and expansions to the cataloging code appeared in 1941 and 1949. The Library Association and the American Library Association (ALA) continued to publish editions of their respective cataloging codes for domestic use. In 1949, ALA published the descriptive cataloging rules for monographs, serials, and some nonbook materials developed at LC.[33] Supplemental publications contained rules for nonbook materials.

Attention to the development of a cataloging code continued after the 1949 revision. In 1951 ALA commissioned Seymour Lubetsky to analyze the cataloging code and prepare a report. Issued two years later, *Cataloging Rules and Principles*[34] advocated a transition for the cataloging code from a case-based to a principle-based perspective. In 1956 Lubetsky was appointed the editor of the anticipated cataloging code. The ALA published this draft cataloging code, *Code of Cataloging Rules: Author and Title Entry*, in 1960. [35]

Sponsored by the International Federation of Library Associations (IFLA), the International Conference on Cataloguing Principles was held in Paris in 1961. Conference participants examined the choice and form of headings in author/title catalogs. They published a statement of twelve principles (commonly called the Paris Principles) [36] and envisioned this document would serve as the framework for the future standardization of cataloging internationally.

Development through AACR2rev

Work to update the next revision of the cataloging code continued. The ALA and the Library Association continued to work collaboratively on a new cataloging code. Members of their respective committees exchanged minutes and working papers and attended each other's meetings. In support of their work, LC assisted with revision of the descriptive cataloguing rules, and the representatives of the Canadian Library Association (CLA) participated in the review of drafts of the rules. In 1966, ALA and the British Library Association signed a memorandum of agreement for continued revision of the cataloging rules. Because of the importance of their involvement, LC and the CLA agreed to participate formally in the revision process.

Anglo-American Cataloguing Rules (AACR)

The combined efforts of ALA and the BLA culminated in 1967 with the publication of two versions of the *Anglo-American Cataloguing Rules* (AACR), a North American text [37] and a British text. [38] The long-awaited AACR text contained four sections: Part I, "Entry and Heading" (based on the Paris Principles, the 1949 ALA Rules, and Lubetzky's 1960 draft); Part II, "Description" (consisted of revised rules from the 1949 Library of Congress Rules); Part III, "Non-book Materials" (contained rules for both entry and description of nonbook materials and revised rules from the 1949 LC Rules with supplementary LC rules); and an appendix that listed rules for entry and heading that differed in the other version. Between 1969 and 1975, amendments for the North American text appeared in LC's *Cataloging Service Bulletin* and for the British text in the Library Association's *Anglo-American Cataloguing Rules Amendment Bulletin*.

International Standard Bibliographic Description (ISBD)

Attendees of the International Meeting of Cataloguing Experts in Copenhagen in 1969 developed a program of International Standard Bibliographic Description (ISBD). Designed for international adoption, ISBD standards were made to identify components in a bibliographic description, a preferred order of information, and necessary punctuation. The first ISBD standard for monographs (ISBD(M)) was published in 1971.[39] By 1974, cataloging experts completed a revision of AACR chapter 6 following the ISBD(M) that was available in two versions.[40] The chapter 6 revision included rules for printed monographs and reproductions of printed monographs (including microform reproductions). Revisions to AACR chapter 12 (AV and Special Instruction Materials)[41] and AACR chapter 14 (Sound Recordings)[42] soon followed. The wide acceptance of these three ISBD standards led to the development of a general framework for standard bibliographic description known as ISBD(G).[43]

Joint Steering Committee for the Revision of AACR

Representatives from five professional library associations worked together as members of the Joint Steering Committee for Revision of AACR (JSC). Established in 1974, the JSC includes members representing ALA, the BL, the CLA (represented by the Canadian Committee on Cataloguing), the Library Association, and LC. An Australian Committee on Cataloguing (ACOC) representative attended JSC meetings from 1981, and ACOC became a full JSC member five years later. Assigned the task of aligning the North American and British texts into a single version, the JSC appointed two editors for the revised code, Michael Gorman of the BL and Paul W. Winkler of LC.

In 1978, the JSC published a version of the *Anglo-American Cataloguing Rules*.[44] Best known as AACR2, the cataloging code was divided into two parts. Part I, "Description," was based on the ISBD(G) framework and included a general chapter (chapter 1) and chapters for individual formats, including new chapters for machine-readable data files (MRDF) (chapter 9) and three-dimensional artifacts and realia (chapter 10). Titled "Entry and Heading," Part II contained rules for descriptive cataloging that were more closely aligned with the Paris Principles. LC, the NLC, the BL, and the Australian National Library (ANL) adopted AACR2 in January 1981. The *Concise AACR2*,[45] an abridged version of the cataloging code, was published later that year. The JSC released revisions to AACR2 in 1982, 1983 (published in 1984), and 1985 (published in 1986). By 1987, the JSC completed a draft revision of AACR2 chapter 9 ("Computer Files").[46]

The substantive changes to AACR2 were sufficient in number and extent for the JSC to incorporate the 1982, 1983, and 1985 revisions along with unpublished modifications into a new edition. Published in 1988, catalogers could purchase book and loose-leaf editions of AACR second edition, 1988 revision.[47] In 1993, the JSC released a set of amendments. Further amendments that the JSC approved between 1992 and 1996 were incorporated into a second revision of *Anglo-American Cataloguing Rules*, second edition. [48] Catalogers had a choice between print and CD-ROM formats. The JSC released two sets of amendments, in 1999 and in 2001, which included a revision of chapter 9 ("Electronic Resources"). By 2002, the JSC adopted a new edition of AACR2 that incorporated the amendments issued to date and revisions to chapter 3 ("Cartographic Materials") and chapter 12 ("Continuing Resources"). [49] A recommendation by the International Conference on the Principles and Future Development of AACR and IFLA-led efforts to harmonize ISBD(CR), ISSN practice, and AACR2 resulted in the revision of chapter 12. The second revision (2002) of AACR was available in a loose-leaf format. Amendments were published in 2003, 2004, and 2005 and could be easily integrated into the loose-leaf format. The ALA, CLA, and the Chartered Institute of Library and Information Professionals (CILIP) published the cataloging code.

Anglo-American Cataloging Rules, Second Edition, Revised with Amendments (AACR2r)

The authoritative guide to descriptive cataloging, catalogers used AACR2r to construct bibliographic records that would be added to an ILS and an OPAC, or potentially contributed to a bibliographic utility for reuse by other libraries. The rules covered the bibliographic description and the provision of access points for library materials collected in an array of formats and languages. Part I provided information and guidance for the bibliographic description of the resource being cataloged. Part II provided guidance and examples for the identification and establishment of access points and references to them. In both parts, the rules proceed from the general to the specific. [50] In order to catalog materials in multiple formats, catalogers had to purchase AACR2r from ALA or subscribe to Cataloger's Desktop, a compilation of resources available through an institutional subscription from LC's Cataloging Distribution Service (CDS) that was first available in 1994. The introduction of this tool began the eventual shift away from print tools to a multiuser tool that could be updated more quickly.

SHORTCOMINGS RESULTING FROM THE CHALLENGES DESCRIBING EMERGING FORMATS AND ASSETS

Technical services staff and their reference librarian colleagues identified a number of limitations and challenges in the integrated library system environment at the end of the twentieth century. The rules dictating the transcription of bibliographic data were inflexible; select data elements had to be repeated to adhere to cataloging rules, indexing algorithms, and display requirements. The established terms to describe physical formats were not updated routinely and did not keep pace with the increasing diversity found in library collections. Different physical packaging for the same intellectual content mandated the construction of a separate MARC record. Catalogers had to review the metadata in MARC records representing different formats of the same intellectual content to ensure that the access points were consistent. Integrating older, brief bibliographic records with newer ones could result in a database of inconsistent quality. Maintaining authority control for the access points needed for efficient searching required significant time and effort that had the potential to exceed resources available. The introduction of icons to facilitate patron use did not uniformly parallel the metadata contained in the MARC record.

ATTEMPTS TO UPDATE AACR2R

Recognizing the perceived shortcomings of the cataloging rules, the JSC began working in December 2004. The cataloging community envisioned a new edition of the rules that would articulate the framework for improved user access through increased access in an online environment.[51] Compatibility with other standards for resource description and retrieval that could be used globally influenced the formation of a revised set of cataloging rules that catalogers could use and interpret easily and efficiently for print, online, and electronic formats.

Professional associations and organizations representing all facets of libraries and information centers participated in a review of the cataloging rules document, terminology, the order and drafts of the chapters, general material designations, content carriers, and specific guidance with an increased focus on bibliographic description, unpublished and serial publications, assembled collections, early print resources, and related technical transcriptions of physical packaging for all types of materials. Following consideration of the proposed framework for a new edition of the cataloging rules, the community of catalogers determined that further revisions of AACR2 into another edition (identified as AACR3) did not allow for the comprehensive modifications or new framework that accommodated international standards required to achieve a set of content standards for all types of materials that could be adopted globally in increasingly powerful integrated library systems or on the Internet.[52] The consensus of catalogers suggested that although the proposed AACR3 structure aligned loosely with FRBR and the ISBD rules, the document was deemed awkward, was not ideally metadata friendly, provided insufficient guidance regarding authority control for points of access, and was not responsive to future needs while allowing cohabitation with AACR2 bibliographic records in existing database environments.

EMERGENCE AND PROMISES OF RESOURCE DESCRIPTION AND ACCESS (RDA)

The preparation and adoption of a cataloging code is a major accomplishment for the community of catalogers, metadata specialists, and technical services librarians. Professional librarians lead teams of colleagues in all types and sizes of libraries, serving diverse clienteles and building print, online, and electronic collections, complimented by digital assets. In 2004, catalogers, metadata specialists, librarians, researchers, system designers, vendors, and interested representatives from the information industry worked individually and collaboratively through professional associations to draft the Resource Description and Access (RDA) cataloging code.[53]

THE COLLABORATIVE DEVELOPMENT PROCESS

Committees representing professional organizations, individual practitioners, and libraries invest significant time and effort into the drafting, revision, and preparation of the manuals, guidebooks, and other documentation that catalogers use. These committees represent the constituencies of librarians, library staff members, and vendors who use the manuals, guidebooks, and other documentation (commonly called tools). The tools used to catalog and classify information packages have evolved over more than one hundred years.

Charged with the responsibility to review and update the cataloging rules, committee members take their assignments seriously, devoting countless hours over months and years to drafting an updated version that will serve the community of catalogers well for an extended period of time. Joining with LC, the National Library of Agriculture (NAL), the National Library of Medicine (NLM), the Machine-Readable Bibliographic Information Committee (MARBI), the National Information Standards Organization (NISO), and representatives from the professional library associations formed the JSC.

MARBI was an interdivisional group of representatives from three divisions within ALA. The nine voting MARBI members included representatives from ALCTS (http://www.ala.org/alcts/), the Library and Information Technology Association (LITA) (http://www.ala.org/lita/), and the Reference and User Services Association (RUSA) (http://www.ala.org/rusa/). MARBI members were responsible for drafting official ALA positions regarding the standards for the representation of bibliographic information. Comprehensive information and an introduction to MARBI and its work are available in the *USMARC Formats: Background and Principles*.[54] MARBI encouraged the creation of needed standards for the representation in machine-readable form of bibliographic information; to review and evaluate proposed standards; to recommend approval of standards in conformity with ALA policy (especially the ALA Standards Committee); to establish a mechanism for continuing review of standards (including the monitoring of further development); to provide commentary on the content of various implementations of standards to concerned agencies; and to maintain liaison with concerned units within ALA and relevant outside agencies. MARBI was disbanded on July 1, 2013, and replaced by the ALCTS/LITA Metadata Standards Committee. The new committee's charge, as taken from their website is to "play a leadership role in the creation and development of metadata standards for bibliographic information."[55]

NISO (http://www.niso.org/home/) is a nonprofit association credited by the American National Standards Institute (ANSI) (http://www.ansi.org/). The leaders of more than seventy publishers, information technological corporations, libraries, and organizations serve as NISO representatives and voting members. The association's members identify, develop, maintain, and publish technical standards to manage information in print, electronic, online, and digital formats. The NISO standards apply to traditional and emerging technologies and include the full range of information-related needs, including retrieval, repurposing, storage, metadata, and preservation. NISO standards are developed through consensus and identify model methods, materials, or practices for libraries, bibliographic and information services, and publishers.

CONSTITUENCIES AND CONSIDERATIONS

Libraries and information centers work in an environment that blends traditional collections, online resources, digital assets, and web-based links to cultural heritage institutions around the world. The global vision of exchanging metadata for use in multiple schemas is contingent upon the use of RDA for the creation of records by catalogers and information specialists. Therefore, the development of RDA has an inherent requirement for adoption by groups within and outside the library community. During the drafting and refinement of RDA, the JSC worked with the Dublin Core Metadata Initiative (DCMI) (http://dublincore.org/) and other semantic web communities to compare the conceptual models and standards used by each; the LC Network Development Office and MARC Standards Office to ensure compatibility of RDA with MARC 21; the IFLA Meeting of Experts on an International Cataloguing Code (IME ICC), which is responsible for revising and updating the Paris Principles for the twenty-first century; and the publishing community, which has developed a list of carrier terminology based on its ONIX standard for use in the publisher and library communities.[56]

Library associations and organizations participate in the collaborative process through the ALCTS Committee on Cataloging: Description and Access (CC:DA). CC:DA consists of nine voting members, twelve nonvoting ALA liaisons, fifteen nonvoting non-ALA liaisons, two interns, one webmaster, and six nonvoting ex-officio representatives from the JSC, LC, MARBI, OCLC, and ALCTS (appointed from CaMMS) serving two-year terms and led by a chair. [57]

EMERGENCE OF THE NEED FOR A NEW SET OF RULES

By 2005, the collaborating constituencies concluded that the new cataloging rules would be titled *RDA: Resource Description and Access*. The JSC developed and released a strategic plan to guide its work and the collaborative, parallel efforts of professional association and library organizations. [58] Drafts of Part I and chapters were released for review and comment until October 2007. The JSC adopted a new organization for the cataloging rules that featured closer alignment with FRBR and the Functional Requirements for Authority Data (FRAD) models, and direct reference to the FRBR entities and user tasks so that catalogers could easily understand and learn RDA concepts and system designers could create powerful applications to support resource discovery. No specific record structure permeated the document, and library and information communities could apply the rules to a range of database structures. RDA's goal was a future-oriented, flexible set of content description rules that provided an adaptable framework defined by object-oriented models and relational structures. [59]

Issued in late 2008, the JSC discussed the full draft of RDA and responses from the community of catalogers at its April 2009 meeting. Based on a set of recommendations from the LC Working Group on the Future of Bibliographic Control in January 2008, leaders of the community of catalogers slowed work on RDA and planned a test of its feasibility for adoption and benefits to users in the library and patron communities. In May 2008, at LC's request, NLM, NAL, and the U.S. RDA Test Coordinating Committee devised and conducted a national test of RDA. The process to select test sites began in late 2008 and concluded with announcements in mid-2009. A revised text was delivered to the publishers in June 2009. In June 2010, RDA was published in the RDA Toolkit. [60] Preparation continued through June 2010. Phase One (July 1 through September 30, 2010) provided a learning curve for test participants. During Phase Two (October 1 through December 31, 2010), participants submitted test records for review and analysis. Test participants submitted questionnaires and met in an open forum hosted by ALCTS at the 2011 ALA Midwinter Meeting. LC, NLM, and NAL released a report describing the test and evaluation in May 2011 and released a revised document to the public in June 2011.[61]

Twenty-six sites in the library and information environment tested RDA to evaluate the technical, operational, and financial implications. The assessment included an articulation of the business case for the new cataloging rules, benefits to libraries and end users, cost analyses for retraining staff, and reengineering of cataloging processes.[62] The evaluators concluded that *RDA* fully met two goals: (1) to provide a consistent, flexible and extensible framework for all types of resources and all types of content, and (2) to be independent of the format, medium, or system used to store or communicate the data. RDA mostly or partially met the following three goals: (1) compatible with internationally established principles and standards; (2) compatible with descriptions and access points in existing catalogs and databases; and (3) enable users to find, identify, select, and obtain resources appropriate to their information needs. They concluded that RDA did not meet three goals: optimization for use as an online tool; written in plain English and able to be used in other language communities; and easy and efficient to use, both as a working tool and for training purposes. RDA did not directly address two additional goals: readily adaptable to newly emerging database structures, and usable primarily within the library community but able to be used by other communities.

Contingent on satisfactory progress and the completion of eight tasks, the Coordinating Committee recommended that RDA should be implemented by the national libraries no sooner than January 2013 and that they should commit resources to ensure progress was made because of the significant effort required from many in and beyond the library community. The specific tasks included rewriting RDA in clear, unambiguous, plain English; defining a process for updating RDA in the online environment; improving functionality of the *RDA Toolkit*; developing full RDA record examples in MARC and other encoding schemas; announcing completion of the Registered RDA Element Sets and Vocabularies; demonstrating credible progress toward a replacement for MARC; ensuring and facilitating community involvement; leading and coordinating RDA training; and soliciting demonstrations of prototype input and discovery systems that use the RDA element set (including relationships).[63]

Dreams and Promises

The community of catalogers envisioned a new set of cataloging rules that would increase technical capabilities for the international exchange of bibliographic and related metadata, position them to respond to increasingly sophisticated user demands, and resolve the frustrations of the revisions and interpretations of AACR2. Catalogers and a growing number of metadata specialist colleagues wondered whether RDA was sufficiently robust and practical enough to provide the fundamental shift needed to support library metadata and resource discovery. A transitional tool between those scenarios, RDA established a framework and used widely accepted database and metadata practices to accommodate future growth and interaction with other metadata schemes. RDA contained the building tools that appealed to catalogers and metadata specialists, stored the data in a coded form, and allowed systems to create displays with clear meanings for users in a multiplicity of contexts. The goal to achieve an international exchange of data required that records could be presented in different languages. Visionary leaders of the cataloging community anticipated that the basic object was to provide in RDA the schema and guidance elements of a metadata system that would use FRBR/FRAD as its model and RDF with XML as its encoding system.

Technical services librarians anticipated that the business model provided in the report of the RDA test would contain sufficient specificity to persuade managers, administrators, and board members that the transition to the new cataloging rules would be a prudent, affordable, one-time investment. Catalogers, metadata specialists, and their department leaders anticipated that training and support would be incorporated into their annual budgets.

Designed to be used as an online resource, RDA required catalogers to learn both old and new rules through the availability of online resources and training. Significant new capabilities and features for the creation and use of descriptive bibliographic metadata encouraged an eagerly awaiting community of catalogers. The element-set approach provided greater specificity and granularity designed to make cataloging data easier to share and control. RDA elements were mapped into a semantic web and linked data registry.[64] The establishment of proper entities, attributes, and relationships was considered easier to expand than the versions prescribed in AACR2. The development of specific MARC 3XX fields to record relationships was welcomed as a standardized approach to record much-needed data that could not be placed within the existing MARC framework. The new cataloging rules offered the potential to use the metadata in the vocabularies specifically in the revolution they represented for the future. New authority records reflected RDA conventions. It seemed that problems with general material designations and icons in integrated library systems were resolved.[65]

Selected changes in RDA were not uniformly embraced. These proposed promises included six major changes, as well as others: spelling out abbreviations (which will remain in pre-RDA or legacy records); removing corrections of errors at the point of the error (which could deprive users of needed information and create additional work for catalogers in notes fields); removing the supplying of missing imprint place justifications; accepting nonstandard transcription capitalization (creating a confusing mix in hit lists); removing correspondence between the transcription or description and added entries (creating patron confusion concerning why a particular search key produced a particular record); discontinuing ISBD inclusions (which will remain in legacy records, reducing the ease of international records exchange and the use of records in multilingual catalogs); removing "O.T." and "N.T." from between "Bible" and name of book, spelling out if no name of book; substituting *Qur'an* for *Koran*; standardizing a treaty entry under first country mentioned or a single country when between one country and a group of countries (e.g., no rule of three for treaties); combining the transcription of noncast movie credits in a credit note; increasing use of added entries for additional author entries; and dropping rule of three conflicts with 2010 citation practice.

Changes in the 2010 version of RDA did not include the following seven areas: using a main entry under name of the editor or compiler for works by different authors to achieve conformance with scholarly practice; removing the alternate title as part of the title proper transcription; establishing a general material designation for equipment and other items that are increasingly acquired and circulated by libraries; making a specific material designation (SMD or unit name) for carriers of library resources; transcribing the imprint jurisdiction if lacking on the piece; substituting "B.C.E." and "C.E." for "B.C." and "A.D."; and improving the imprint transcription for reproductions and having a compound imprint with original publisher and reproduction publisher to avoid placing either in a note. [66]

Challenging Implementation and Testing

The decision by LC, NAL, and NLM followed the public release of the U.S. RDA Test Coordinating Committee's report with recommendations. [67] The three national libraries and twenty-three partner institutions sought to gain insights into benefits for libraries and their patrons that would be derived from the adoption of the new cataloging code. Test participants had an opportunity to determine staff training needs, review technical services and cataloging workflows for different formats and languages of materials, calculate the financial requirements and commitments required to fully adopt and implement RDA, and solicit opinions from their catalog users, including non–technical services staff.

During the RDA test period, the twenty-six participating institutions generated 10,570 bibliographic records, 12,800 authority records, and 8,000 survey responses. The representative group of participating sites included libraries, archives, museums, book vendors, systems developers, library schools, and consortia. Comments from catalogers and metadata specialists focused on the RDA documents, the code's usability, the potential workflow and financial impacts on local operations, the RDA-compliant bibliographic and authority records, requirements for modifications to ILS software, and the challenges inherent in continuing to use an aging MARC format. Despite negative comments and lingering hesitation from individual catalogers, metadata specialists, and support staff involved in technical services, the full implementation of RDA moved forward. To delay the implementation would have negatively impacted the ability of libraries, information centers, archives, and museums to participate fully in the information industry of the twenty-first century.

Although numerous leaders in the cataloging and metadata community generally supported the implementation decision, the RDA test revealed several problems, including (but not limited to) the benefits for library staff and users. However, the increasing demand for a robust metadata framework compelled the library community to move ahead with the national implementation of RDA. The economic impact and financial requirements to adopt RDA locally remained a challenge as materials vendors and ILS providers scrambled to meet the demands that the new cataloging code placed on their business and support operations. Their eventual solutions to the technical requirements to realize the full benefits of RDA had the potential to empower libraries as they continued to share data with other organizations and institutions, transitioned to an updated and compatible cataloging framework that better accounts for nonprint resources, and provided accurate, rapid access to information using emerging database technologies, such as the Semantic Web, cloud computing, and the eXtensible Catalog (XC) (http://www.extensiblecatalog.org).

Adoption of RDA

After more than a decade of effort, on June 13, 2011, the three U.S. national libraries announced that they would adopt RDA (with certain conditions) no earlier than January 1, 2013.[68] The decision to adopt a new cataloging code was based on the content and not the economic needs of the sponsoring organizations. On March 2, 2012, LC announced its long-range training plan and a March 31, 2013, implementation date.[69]

ROLE OF METADATA

Benefits of a Schema-Agnostic Environment

A schema-agnostic environment refers to the ability of something—such as software, hardware, or metadata—to work with various systems rather than being customized for a single system. To realize RDA's goal to create a framework with the tools necessary to create metadata that can be used in widely accepted databases and schemas, an agnostic environment was ideal. As the number of libraries, institutions, and organizations creating metadata and data sets created for use locally and sharing globally increases, the potential for conflicting metadata schemas grows. Adopting a set of cataloging rules that are not dependent on a specific format or schema creates an environment in which the databases and discovery schemas can be developed for a specific user group without impinging on the integrity of the data or impacting its potential use elsewhere.

The adoption of a set of metadata fields supports resource discovery. Technical services librarians can work with systems developers, vendors, and publishers to determine a comprehensive set of metadata for a bibliographic record, recognizing that a select group of users will require the entire record while others will use a small part of the data for searching and discovery. New carriers and formats that contain information will continue to be developed; others will fall out of daily use and eventually retire. An agnostic set of rules to use when describing resources preserves the consistent use of metadata and eliminates the need to make modifications in response to changing packages and carriers.

An open-access agnostic environment promotes a mechanism to transfer and share metadata among the library and information user community with minimal restrictions and crosswalking difficulties. The creation, use, and storage of metadata can occur in an open-architecture environment. Entering metadata into a schema equates to a global contribution to the information community for future use without the need for additional transcription or editing. The costs for repurposing metadata can be minimized to exporting, transporting, and loading into a different schema for another user group.

The Move to Decommission MARC

The expanded capabilities envisioned as part of RDA could not be fully realized within the confines of the MARC structure. When MARC was developed, moving data elements into and out of it did not seem appropriate or necessary. Using the data to produce printed catalog cards, proof slips, and bibliographies was revolutionary in 1968. Although the data that can be transcribed into MARC has continued to evolve, the MARC framework has remained static with limited additions of fields and subfields while deauthorizing the use of others and modifying the use of code designations and values.

RDA testers and early adopters recognized that the MARC format could not serve future needs for hosting and sharing metadata. RDA provides guidance for the transcription and changing of metadata representing a unique bibliographic record. Yet the relationships and linkages that the community of catalogers and representatives of collaborating organizations identified as significant advances for the transporting and sharing of metadata could not be accommodated in MARC. Without a new framework, the anticipated benefits for technical services staff and system developers would remain unrealized. Library users would continue to encounter problems driven by the database structure rather than the intellectual content representing the collection.

Libraries continued to feel a need to deliver a powerful, comprehensive gateway to resources within the local institution while maintaining a connection to neighboring institutions and disparate collections around the world. The pressure to deliver a list of comprehensive, multilingual resources in print, online, and digital formats with a single, federated search prompted librarians to seek a solution. Combining metadata from different schemas with a varied amount of authority control among access points would result in a large number of items, the quality of which would be suspect.

Rather than change the MARC structure (which is not in and of itself problematic), the international standards and protocols for the transfer and use of metadata among different schemas need to be updated. Using the XML format will enable technical services librarians, system developers, and vendors to build and maintain databases that respond to users' demands without the need to re-enter or modify the bibliographic metadata residing in online library catalogs. Metadata can be stored and displayed differently in individual library, information centers, and other organizations to meet user needs. Using a database framework other than MARC empowers the individuality of the gateway to information that the library user community expects and demands.

BIBFRAME: THE NEW MARC?

In response to the need for a different database framework for metadata, LC developed the Bibliographic Framework Initiative (BIBFRAME) to serve as a foundation for the future of bibliographic description on the web and in the broader networked world.[70] Conceptually envisioned as a replacement for MARC, BIBFRAME is a general model for expressing and connecting bibliographic data and determining a transition path for the MARC 21 formats and preserving a robust data exchange for resource sharing and cataloging cost savings. LC announced the initiative in May 2011, hired a contractor to evaluate related initiatives and data modeling in May 2012, published the BIBFRAME document in January 2013, and issued primary-use cases and requirements in August 2013.[71]

The BIBFRAME model consists of four high-level classes of data: creative work, instance, authority, and annotation.[72] Instead of combining data into a surrogate record to represent a resource in a manner similar to that used in MARC, BIBFRAME relies on relationships among data and controlling identifiers. The goals that BIBFRAME developers used to determine its applicability include a clear differentiation between conceptual content and its physical manifestation(s) (e.g., works and instances); a focus on unambiguously identifying information entities (e.g., authorities); and leveraging and exposing relationships between and among entities. The BIBFRAME model remains under discussion and testing. [73]

CONCLUSION AND OBSERVATIONS

The evolution of the cataloging rules for the transcription of bibliographic data and the schemas into which they are placed parallels the development of technologies and the Internet. Moving from a structured, inflexible environment with clearly defined search strategies and results available to users, in the twenty-first century technical services librarians work with system designers, software developers, and information technologists in an environment of multiple metadata schemas and the global potential for transporting, sharing, and displaying metadata in customized formats for specific patron user groups. Together these constituencies are working through the minute details of cataloging rule implementation and adoption. Technical services librarians involved in the cataloging and metadata description processes share comments on discussion lists, blogs, and wikis. Suggestions for modifications originate in response to specific problems and needs, working their way through professional associations to CC:DA for review, consideration, and action.

Changes in the cataloging rules confronted technical services librarians, catalogers, metadata specialists, and administrators. Because "change remains the crucial challenge for organizations," technical services staff in libraries throughout the country were impacted and called upon to respond with flexibility and a positive attitude. [74] The development of RDA demonstrated that the community of catalogers had evolved into an articulate voice dedicated to meeting the technical needs of transcribing accurate bibliographic data for use in a multiplicity of metadata schemas that could be contributed to and shared globally. The isolationist viewpoints reflected in country-specific cataloging rules are being replaced with an international collaborative perspective.

The library community adopted characteristics reflective of a built-to-change organization that strategizes, creates value, and designs for the future. [75] Anticipating the future and positioning the community of libraries and information centers for success in a supportive culture demonstrate that each cataloger, metadata specialist, technical services manager, and administrator has a responsibility to identify and participate in training, resources, opportunities, and other activities that will contribute to a higher level of professional performance for the library user, the individual library, and the global network of cultural heritage guardians and information providers.

NOTES

1. Sylvia D. Hall-Ellis, "Metadata Competencies for Entry-Level Positions: What Employers Expect as Reflected in Position Descriptions, 2000–2013," *Journal of Library Metadata* (forthcoming).

2. Jeanne M. K. Boydston and Joan M. Leysen, "Observations on the Catalogers' Role in Descriptive Metadata Creation in Academic Libraries," *Cataloging & Classification Quarterly* 43, no. 2 (2006): 3–17.

3. Association for Library Collections and Technical Services, Continuing Education Task Force, "Continuing Education for Catalogers: Summary of Survey Responses," March 31, 2003, https://scholarsbank.uoregon.edu/xmlui/bitstream/handle/1794/986/CETFpublic.pdf?sequence=5.

4. Bradford Eden, "Report of the ALCTS Heads of Cataloging Departments Discussion Group, American Library Association Midwinter Conference, Philadelphia, January 2003," *Technical Services Quarterly* 21, no. 2 (2003): 76–79; Ingrid Hsieh-Yee, "Cataloging and Metadata Education: A Proposal for Preparing Cataloging Professionals of the 21st Century: Final Report," December 2002, http://www.loc.gov/catdir/bibcontrol/CatalogingandMetadataEducation.pdf.

5. Nadine P. Ellero, "The Name and Role of the Cataloger in the Twenty-First Century," in *Innovative Redesign and Reorganization of Library Technical Services: Paths for the Future and Case Studies*, ed. Bradford Lee Eden, 119–58 (Westport, CT: Libraries Unlimited, 2004).

6. "Collective Digitization Programs in the United States," LYRASIS, https://www.lyrasis.org/LYRASIS Digital/Pages/Preservation Services/Resources and Publications/Digital Toolbox/History.aspx; Israel Yañez, "Metadata: Implications for Academic Libraries," *Library Philosophy and Practice*, October 2009, http://www.webpages.uidaho.edu/~mbolin/yanez.htm; Laurie Lopatin, "Library Digitization Projects, Issues and Guidelines: A Survey of the Literature," *Library Hi Tech* 24, no. 2 (2006): 273–89.

7. Christine DeZelar-Tiedman, "Crashing the Party: Catalogers as Digital Librarians," *OCLC Systems & Services: International Digital Library Perspectives* 20, no. 4 (2004): 145–47.

8. Boydston and Leysen, "Observations on the Catalogers' Role."

9. IFLA Study Group on the Functional Requirements for Bibliographic Records, "Functional Requirements for Bibliographic Records: Final Report," February 2009, http://www.ifla.org/files/assets/cataloguing/frbr/frbr_2008.pdf.

10. International Federation of Library Associations, *Guidelines for Digitization Projects for Collections and Holdings in the Public Domain*, March 2002, http://www.ifla.org/publications/guidelines-for-digitization-projects-for-collections-and-holdings-in-the-public-domain.

11. Hall-Ellis, "Metadata Competencies for Entry-Level Positions."

12. Ibid.

13. "MySQL," Wikipedia, http://en.wikipedia.org/wiki/MySQL.

14. Hall-Ellis, "Metadata Competencies for Entry-Level Positions."

15. Dublin Core Metadata Initiative, Dublin Core Metadata Element Set, version 1.1, http://dublincore.org/documents/dces/.

16. Library of Congress, EAD—Encoded Archival Description, version 2002, http://www.loc.gov/ead/.

17. Library of Congress, MODS—Metadata Objects Description Schema, http://www.loc.gov/standards/mods/.

18. OCLC, CONTENTdm, http://www.oclc.org/contentdm.en.html.

19. Library of Congress, METS—Metadata Encoding & Transmission Standard, http://www.loc.gov/standards/mets/.

20. NISO, "Understanding Metadata," 2004, http://www.niso.org/publications/press/UnderstandingMetadata.pdf.

21. "Metadata Standards," Wikipedia, http://en.wikipedia.org/wiki/Metadata_standards.

22. Henry Watson Kent, *What I Am Pleased to Call My Education*, ed. Lois Leighton Comings (New York: Grolier Club, 1949), 15–17.

23. See the Library of Congress website for more information: http://www.loc.gov/library/.

24. See the Association of Library Collections and Technical Services website for more: http://www.ala.org/alcts/.

25. Association of Library Collections and Technical Services, "Cataloging and Metadata Management Section (CaMMS)," http://www.ala.org/alcts/mgrps/camms.

26. *Encyclopedia of Library and Information Science*, 2nd ed., ed. Miriam Drake, s.v. "Machine-Readable Cataloging (MARC) Program" (New York: Marcel Dekker, 2003), 1712–30.

27. Henriette D. Avram, *MARC: Its History and Implications* (Washington, DC: Library of Congress, 1975); Henriette D. Avramet et al., "MARC Program Research and Development: A Progress Report," *Journal of Library Automation* 2, no. 4 (December 1969): 242–65.

28. See their website at http://www.loc.gov/marc/ndmso.html.

29. NDMSCO, "MARC Format Overview," http://www.loc.gov/marc/status.html#bib.

30. Officials were maintained in technical services when there were only paper catalogs. They contained more information than a shelf list and were considered to be the authority for classification and subject access.

31. Committees of the American Library Association and the (British) Library Association, comp., *Catalog Rules, Author and Title Entries* (Chicago: American Library Association, 1908).

32. Committees of the Library Association and of the American Library Association, comp., *Cataloguing Rules: Author and Title Entries* (London: Library Association, 1908).

33. *Rules for Descriptive Cataloging in the Library of Congress*, adopted by the American Library Association (Washington, DC: Library of Congress, Descriptive Cataloging Division, 1949).

34. Seymour Lubetzky, *Cataloging Rules and Principles: A Critique of the A.L.A. Rules for Entry and a Proposed Design for Their Revision* (Washington, DC: Processing Department, Library of Congress, 1953).

35. Seymour Lubetzky, *Code of Cataloging Rules: Author and Title Entry* (Chicago: American Library Association, 1960).

36. *Statement of Principles Adopted at the International Conference on Cataloguing Principles, Paris, October 1961*, annotated ed. with commentary and examples by Eva Verona (London: IFLA Committee on Cataloguing, 1971), 91–96.

37. *Anglo-American Cataloging Rules*, prepared by the American Library Association, the Library of Congress, the Library Association, and the Canadian Library Association (Chicago: American Library Association, 1967).

38. *Anglo-American Cataloguing Rules*, prepared by the American Library Association, the Library of Congress, the Library Association and the Canadian Library Association (London: Library Association, 1967).

39. *ISBD(M): International Standard Bibliographic Description for Monographic Publications*, 1st ed. (London: IFLA Committee on Cataloguing, 1974).

40. *Anglo-American Cataloging Rules: North American Text: Chapter 6: Separately Published Monographs, Incorporating Chapter 9, "Photographic and Other Reproductions," and Revised to Accord with the International Standard Bibliographic Description (Monographs)* (Chicago: American Library Association, 1974); *Anglo-American Cataloguing Rules: British Text: Chapter 6 Revised (Including a Revision of Appendix V)* (London: Library Association, 1974).

41. *Anglo-American Cataloging Rules: North American Text: Chapter 12 Revised: Audiovisual Media and Special Instructional Materials* (Chicago: American Library Association, 1975).

42. *Anglo-American Cataloging Rules: North American Text: Chapter 14 Revised: Sound Recordings* (Chicago: American Library Association, 1976).

43. *ISBD(G): General International Standard Bibliographic Description: Annotated Text*, prepared by the Working Group on the General International Standard Bibliographic Description set up by the IFLA Committee on Cataloguing (London: IFLA International Office for UBC, 1977).

44. *Anglo-American Cataloguing Rules*, prepared by the American Library Association, the British Library, the Canadian Committee on Cataloguing, the Library Association, the Library of Congress. 2nd ed., ed. Michael Gorman and Paul W. Winkler (Chicago: American Library Association; Ottawa: Canadian Library Association, 1978; London: Library Association, 1978).

45. Michael Gorman, *The Concise AACR 2: Being a Rewritten and Simplified Version of Anglo-American Cataloguing Rules, Second Edition* (Chicago: American Library Association; Ottawa: Canadian Library Association; London: Library Association, 1981).

46. *Anglo-American Cataloguing Rules Second Edition: Chapter 9: Computer Files: Draft Revision*, ed. for the Joint Steering Committee for the Revision of AACR by Michael Gorman. (Chicago: American Library Association; Ottawa: Canadian Library Association; London: Library Association, 1987).

47. *Anglo-American Cataloguing Rules*, prepared under the direction of the Joint Steering Committee for Revision of AACR, a committee of the American Library Association, the Australian Committee on Cataloguing, the British Library, the Canadian Committee on Cataloguing, the Library Association, Library of Congress, ed. Michael Gorman and Paul W. Winkler, 2nd ed., 1988 rev. (Ottawa: Canadian Library Association; London: Library Association Publishing; Chicago: American Library Association, 1988).

48. *Anglo-American Cataloguing Rules*, prepared under the direction of the Joint Steering Committee for Revision of AACR, a committee of the American Library Association, the Australian Committee on Cataloguing, the British Library, the Canadian Committee on Cataloguing, the Library Association, the Library of Congress, 2nd ed., 1998 rev. (Ottawa: Canadian Library Association; London: Library Association Publishing; Chicago: American Library Association, 1998).

49. *Anglo-American Cataloguing Rules*, prepared under the direction of the Joint Steering Committee for Revision of AACR, a committee of the American Library Association, the Australian Committee on Cataloguing, the British Library, the Canadian Committee on Cataloguing, Chartered Institute of Library and Information Professionals, the Library of Congress, 2nd ed., 2002 rev. (Ottawa: Canadian Library Association; London: Chartered Institute of Library and Information Professionals; Chicago: American Library Association, 2002–2006).

50. "About AACR2," AARC, http://www.aacr2.org/about.html.

51. Joint Steering Committee for the Development of RDA, "Historical Documents: Draft of AACR3 Part I—Background," January 12, 2005, http://www.rda-jsc.org/aacr3draftpt1.html.

52. Barbara Tillett, "AACR3: Resource Description and Access," presentation at the 2004 ALA Annual Conference, Orlando, FL, http://www.ala.org/alcts/sites/ala.org.alcts/files/content/events/pastala/annual/04/tillettch12.pdf; Kathy Glennan, "From AACR2 to RDA: An Evolution," presentation at the Music Library Association, Bibliographic Control Committee Meeting, February 26, 2006, http://bcc.musiclibraryassoc.org/Descriptive/RDA_Evolution.pdf; Deirdre Kiorgaard and Ann Huthwaite, *Authority Control in AACR3* (Canberra: National Library of Australia, 2005).

53. Ibid.

54. *USMARC Formats: Background and Principles*, rev. ed., prepared by MARBI, the American Library Association's ALCTS/LITA/RUSA Machine-Readable Bibliographic Information Committee in conjunction with Network Development and MARC Standards Office (Washington, DC: Library of Congress, 1996).

55. See the committee's website at http://www.ala.org/lita/about/committees/Jnt-meta for additional information.

56. *RDA: The Cataloguing Standard for the 21st Century*, http://www.rda-jsc.org/docs/rdabrochure-eng.pdf.

57. Association of Library Collections and Technical Services, "Committee on Cataloging: Description and Access (CC:DA)," http://www.ala.org/alcts/mgrps/camms/cmtes/ats-ccscat.

58. Joint Steering Committee for the Development of RDA, "Strategic Plan for RDA, 2005–2009," November 1, 2007, http://www.rda-jsc.org/stratplan.html.

59. Joint Steering Committee for the Development of RDA, "Historical Documents: A New Organization for RDA," accessed May 26, 2014, http://www.rda-jsc.org/rda-new-org.html.

60. The *RDA Toolkit* is a browser-based, online product. See http://www.rdatoolkit.org/.

61. *Report and Recommendations of the U.S. RDA Test Coordinating Committee*, May 9, 2011, http://www.loc.gov/bibliographic-future/rda/source/rdatesting-finalreport-20june2011.pdf.

62. Ibid.

63. Ibid.

64. Open Metadata Registry, http://metadataregistry.org/schemaprop/list/schema_id/1.html.

65. Joint Steering Committee for the Development of RDA, "Working Documents," http://www.rda-jsc.org/working2.html#chair-6.

66. John McRee (Mac) Elrod, email communication to the Autocat discussion list, June 20, 2011.

67. *Report and Recommendations of the U.S. RDA Test Coordinating Committee*, May 9, 2011, http://www.loc.gov/bibliographic-future/rda/source/rdatesting-finalreport-20june2011.pdf.

68. "Response of the Library of Congress, the National Agricultural Library, and the National Library of Medicine to the RDA Test Coordinating Committee," June 13, 2011, http://www.nlm.nih.gov/tsd/cataloging/RDA_Executives_statement.pdf; "RDA Adoption Recommended by Three U.S. National Libraries," blog, June 14, 2011, http://www.rdatoolkit.org/blog/184.

69. "Library of Congress Announces Its Long-Range RDA Training Plan ," March 2, 2012, http://www.loc.gov/catdir/cpso/news_rda_implementation_date.html; Library of Congress, "RDA Training Plan for 2012–March 31, 2013," February 27, 2012, http://www.loc.gov/aba/rda/pdf/RDA_Long-Range_Training_Plan.pdf.

70. See the Bibliographic Framework Initiative website at http://www.loc.gov/bibframe/.

71. Kevin Ford, "What Is BIBFRAME?," November 6, 2013, http://www.slis.wisc.edu/documents/2013-uwisc-webinar-1.pdf.

72. Library of Congress, "Overview of the BIBFRAME Model," http://www.loc.gov/bibframe/docs/model.html.

73. A discussion list for BIBFRAME is available at http://www.lsoft.com/scripts/wl.exe?SL1=BIBFRAME&H=LISTSERV.LOC.GOV.

74. Dan S. Cohen, *The Heart of Change Field Guide: Tools and Tactics for Leading Change in Your Organization* (Boston: Harvard Business School Press, 2005), 1.

75. Edward E. Lawler and Christopher G. Worley, *Built to Change: How to Achieve Sustained Organizational Effectiveness* (San Francisco: Jossey-Bass, 2005), 26.

Chapter Four

Restructuring Monograph Acquisitions in Academic Libraries

Innovative Strategies for the Twenty-First Century

Michael Luesebrink

LIBRARY ACQUISITIONS: AN INSTITUTIONAL APPROACH

The invention of the Gutenberg printing press precipitated a transformation in scholarly communication that resulted in the birth of the scholarly monograph. This innovative technology laid the foundation for a print-based culture that would reside at the modern university. In the late nineteenth century, spurred by the modern library industry created by Dewey, came the institutionalization of library practices that gave rise to the professionalization of cataloging and acquisitions.[1] During the twentieth century came the emergence of the modern academic library, which assumed the mantle of supporting the educational and research endeavors of their students and faculty by building and sustaining their library collections. By the twenty-first century the digital revolution created by the Internet produced a paradigm shift that transformed scholarly communication and higher education institutions. In contemporary library technical services, this digital revolution significantly transformed the institutional practices associated with library acquisitions.

Contemporary academic libraries are in the midst of a significant organizational transformation. This chapter explores the transformations associated with restructuring acquisitions units in academic libraries. Grounded in a bureaucratic framework, the traditional academic library is transforming its work into an innovative, market-based approach to serving its parent institution. This model is shifting from a library-centric to a user-centric approach based on innovative practices. The social change precipitated by this shift is driven by technological innovation that is transforming higher education.[2] This technology innovation process has been attributed to demand-driven forces in the marketplace.[3] In supporting the changing roles of academic libraries, acquisition units have transformed their practices by moving from a supply-side approach to a demand-driven approach when building collections. This change is based on the assumption that future academic libraries will shift from acquiring predominantly print materials to predominantly digital resources. Therefore, this raises the question: how can library acquisitions support the mission of contemporary academic libraries? This chapter details how acquisitions is achieving this transformation by restructuring institutional frameworks and practices influenced by demand-driven acquisition methodologies and staffing trends.

This chapter describes library acquisitions in the traditional academic library model, and when referring to library content, it specifically pertains to monographic materials. The examination will begin with a description of the traditional academic library within the context of its support toward the overarching institutional mission. It segues into the role that acquisitions plays within the library organizational framework of collection building, ownership of content, and institutional property rights. It changes gears in the next section and examines the role of academic libraries in the current university institutional environment. It describes the demand-driven methodologies that contemporary acquisition units are using as offered by the scholarly publishing marketplace. It culminates with a consideration of the impact of staffing trends in relation to acquisitions institutional structures, workflows, and practices. The chapter concludes by describing the institutional changes that are restructuring and transforming the acquisitions environment and closes with a discerning glimpse at the future of the acquisitions industry.

TRADITIONAL LIBRARY ACQUISITIONS: SUPPLY-SIDE APPROACH

One of the primary responsibilities of the traditional academic library is to provide access to content that supports the research and scholarship of its academic community.[4] In the modern college or university, the role of the academic library is reflected in the strategic mission, which defines how it will support the institutional goals.[5] The acquisitions department plays a pivotal role in backing the academic library in support of the institutional mission. Its primary objective is to acquire content that supports the library's collection development mission, which in turn enables the institutional research, scholarship, and education in the academic community. Traditionally, library acquisitions is divided into two basic categories: serials and monographs (books). Some libraries have special acquisition units for maps, documents, and nonbook materials or media content that might include microfilm.[6] This organizational structure was functional until the 1990s when the World Wide Web entered the library landscape. More importantly, this division of the acquisitions organization was based almost exclusively on print-formatted materials. Advances in information technology (IT) have changed the library institutional environment. IT studies have shown that when clusters of network technology innovations were introduced into contemporary organizations, they were followed with the predominant adoption of Internet-related services.[7] In the case of academic libraries, technological innovations facilitated Internet access and services for their patrons.

Traditionally, the academic library's primary mission was to provide access to content that supports the educational and research needs of its academic community on campus. The academic library is in the business of building and sustaining its library collections. This is accomplished through funding support by the university administration that the library uses to acquire library resources. The collection-building process directly supports the array of disciplinary cultures that reflect the institution's faculty research interests. By providing the appropriate library content, the academic library, in turn, sponsors faculty research productivity and indirectly supports the tenure-track process.[8] This arguably makes the acquisitions unit the cornerstone for building library collections.

For academic institutions, building library collections is an investment in intellectual property. Library collections are a matter of content ownership or property rights management. The institutionalization of property rights by academic libraries is an example of how institutional actors are responsible for selection processes such as collection building.[9] The role of acquisitions in building collections is to support the library's mission through the purchase of library materials. This comprises an investment in fixed property assets for the parent institution. This ownership of traditional print collections promotes the intellectual property rights paradigm manifested in copyright law. It allows the library to store content in their collections for the purpose of loaning the material, from a community property rights perspective, to its patrons within limitations imposed by copyright law. In short, the parent institution's right to content ownership through building collections reflects its institutional investment in social capital by owning, storing, and providing access to library material for research and scholarship.

Library acquisitions purchases scholarly content that has been vetted through the peer-review process. Refereed scholarly journals and monographs play a vital role in the scholarly communication process because peer review is used to measure their impact, success, and influence with their respective disciplines in higher education. In addition, the peer-review process of faculty publications is pivotal for tenure and promotion.[10] Referees in the peer-review process are responsible for what is accepted into the scholarly publishing literature. The acquisition of literature published by an institution's faculty is directly influenced by the peer-review process and becomes part of the faculty members' research productivity. The peer-review process has been used for centuries as a mechanism for ensuring credibility and reliability in scholarly communications. Peer review and the scholarly publishing industry are important to acquisitions' role through sustaining collection development objectives and building library collections.

The relationship between library acquisitions and the scholarly publishing industry has traditionally been tenuous. This has changed with the explosion of electronic resources due to technological innovations. As a result, publishers have taken a more proactive role when dealing with academic libraries. This is especially apparent with the digital innovations associated with electronic formats, namely, with electronic journals (e-journals) and electronic books (e-books). [11] In recent years, acquisitions librarians and academic vendors have fostered closer working relationships. On a business level, acquisitions librarians are proactively dealing with vendor representatives to negotiate pricing structures and contractual agreements. On an operational level, vendor support groups work closely with acquisitions staff to solve workflow issues and create technological efficiencies that reduce labor and time when processing library content through proprietary software. It is on this level that we are concerned with the machinations of the acquisitions cycle, which is the heart of the organizational unit.

The traditional acquisitions cycle is composed of highly structured library institutional practices and workflows, predicated on a bureaucratic structural framework. The author will use the acquisitions cycle for acquiring monographs at his institution to describe the workflows associated with ordering and processing library content in our unit. The acquisitions cycle (see figure 4.1) illustrates the traditional book ordering process. In academic libraries, the first step in the cycle starts with a request for library materials from faculty or selector librarians. The cycle proceeds, in the second step, when an order is placed with an academic vendor or publisher who fills the order, depending upon availability. In the third step, acquisitions staff initiate the ordering process by creating an acquisitions record in the integrated library management system (ILS), which generates an accession number or some other means to track the acquisitions record. This process includes encumbering funds for purchase of the library material by charging the appropriate fund account allocation. When the vendor ships the library material, it is shipped under the terms of either payment by invoice or through a prepaid account. When the item arrives at the library, the next step is initiated when an acquisitions staff member processes the invoice in the ILS and authorizes vendor payment by accounts payable. Once the item has been processed in acquisitions, it is sent to cataloging for resource description and end processing, and is then added to the library's collection. The cycle is completed when the book is used by a patron for purposes of research and scholarship. It is ultimately consummated if the item is actually cited in the professional literature.

Every fall, the working relationship between acquisitions librarians and vendors can be observed at an annual acquisitions conference, a ritual known as the Annual Charleston Conference: Issues in Serials and Book Acquisitions in Charleston, South Carolina. Vendors showcase new products and services at the preconference, underwrite events, and generally network with acquisitions industry representatives. The acquisitions librarians communicate their concerns about the issues and trends in their industry. It has been suggested that this relationship between vendors and librarians at the conference is much too cozy.[12] For the most part, however, this conference has not just been a communication channel but has nurtured innovation within the acquisitions industry. It should be noted here that the scholarly publishing industry has been influenced by an increasing trend in mergers and acquisitions in which the information marketplace is moving from a traditional competitive marketplace to an arena of oligopolies. What this bodes for the library industry remains to be seen.

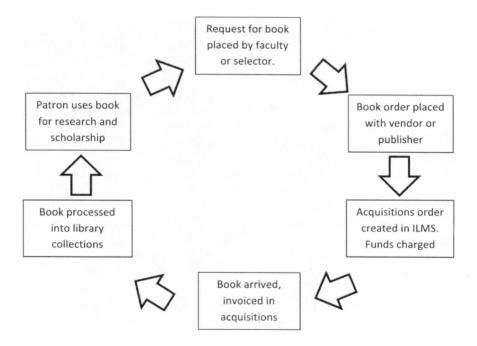

Figure 4.1.   The Acquisitions Cycle

In most academic libraries, acquisitions units are subsumed under the technical services infrastructure, where the core unit is usually, but not in all cases, cataloging. The function of technical services concerns processing acquired or donated library materials based on institutional practices and workflows. This process generates new library content for the academic community it serves. This raises a question: how does one measure organizational effectiveness regarding the processing of material in acquisitions? It has been argued that effectiveness can be evaluated using two measures.[13] The first measure is library materials purchased. The second measure is in terms of cost performance and budgeting. But what about the role of the traditional acquisitions staff in the process?

The traditional role of acquisitions staff in processing library materials is complex due to their intricate inter-institutional relationships with the network of librarians and staff within the library organization. These networks are described by what is referred to as informal communication ties, where the strength of the ties are predicated on the departmental relationships with the parent department.[14] For example, acquisitions staff have strong informal communication ties with technical services staff, such as catalogers, since they are typically located within the same departmental framework and share similar workflows or cultural similarities. Conversely, the acquisitions staff will likely have weaker informal communication network ties with public services staff, who are usually located outside of their division and who possess cultural differences regarding their respective workflows. It has been suggested that departmental organizational cultures, such as public and technical services, play a major role in academic libraries.[15] Yet the traditional role of academic libraries is changing to meet the demands of contemporary institutional environments. This requires a change in the scope of library acquisitions as cultural frameworks are shifting from print to digital.

The purpose of library acquisitions in traditional academic libraries, as previously noted, is to build collections to serve the needs of the institutional academic community. Traditionally, building collections meant the acquisition of print library materials. The emergence of the Internet, however, has spawned an expansive array of digital collections that has compelled academic libraries to restructure library resources and services. The traditional collection development model (also known as prospective collection building) is based on acquiring library materials under the assumption of "just in case" the content is needed by library users. This supply-side approach to accessing library content, which is library-centric, does not fit well in the digital environment.

CONTEMPORARY ACQUISITIONS IN ACADEMIC LIBRARIES: THE DEMAND-DRIVEN APPROACH

This section describes the emerging demand-driven digital innovations currently offered by the market that are used by library acquisitions units. Demand-driven methodologies used by the e-book vendor markets are examined in this section. This section addresses emerging economic models such as demand-driven acquisitions or Patron Driven Acquisitions (DDA/PDA), e-book subscription packages, and short-term loans. The second part of the section examines paraprofessional staffing trends described in terms of skill sets and demographics.

The traditional library-centric academy model, as previously discussed, focused on building collections through content ownership driven by supply-side economics based on a just-in-case approach. This model is predicated on the acquisition of print material through a framework of institutional structural library practices. With the establishment of the Internet as a standard tool for library practices came several digital innovations that have changed the library paradigm from a print-based to a largely digital culture. The future academic library, it has been suggested, will consist as an amalgam of networked print and electronic resources. [16] Transitioning to an electronic-based library follows three assumptions: most scholarly publications will shift their content to the online environment; scholarly publications will endure a paradigm shift that will render peer-review obsolete; acquisitions staff responsibilities, especially librarians, will change from a purchasing specialist perspective to a generalist approach, since they must have a broad background in nonlibrary areas such as IT and accounting, among others. [17]

Compounding the changes occurring within the library industry is a chronic global recession that is transforming the scope of how public service institutions do business with patrons. This recession has particularly impacted higher education institutions. Academic libraries, in serving their parent institutions, are caught in the crossfire. This has been exacerbated by the explosion of scholarly publishing over the last twenty years, which has not only logarithmically expanded the amount of information contributing to the disciplinary literature knowledge base, but has taxed the funding base needed to acquire library content. The upsurge in scholarly publishing has resulted in a shift of economic models in the information markets. Digital innovation is driving the changes in the traditional library organizational model. Acquisitions librarians are compelled to actively engage in creative thinking and become change agents to proactively meet the demands of their patrons, their library, and the future of acquisitions. [18] These transformations are shifting operations from a supply-side economic framework to a demand-side, market-driven, user-centric approach.

Facing new economic realities, contemporary academic institutions are tasked with new challenges to increase productivity in terms of products and services while using less fiscal resources. Key stakeholders in U.S. colleges and universities demand accountability from academic institutions.[19] A 2010 Association of College and Research Libraries (ACRL) report, *The Value of Academic Libraries*, identified a national concern among academic stake-holders regarding the value of higher education in the United States.[20] The underlying theme of the report is simple: accountability. The report noted these stakeholders demand that academic institutions provide evidence they were creating value regarding student educational needs and faculty research output. In turn, academic institutions were tasked with assessing the value and quality their respective higher education institutions were providing for their students and faculty. This report laid the foundation for a protracted discussion regarding the value of the academic library in higher education institutions. It mandated that the value of academic libraries should be measured in quantifiable terms. Two values were identified to directly measure the value of acquisitions: impact and return on investment (ROI). Impact, as an indicator of value, can be ascribed as a measure of organizational effectiveness.[21] For example, faculty research productivity, as an outcome, is measured by faculty publications cited in the literature and shows the impact of a faculty member's research in his respective field of expertise. ROI in academic libraries can be quantified by the relationship between faculty research productivity and the investment costs associated with building the library collections. For library acquisitions, these measures indicate how effective the acquisition of library resources is in serving the needs of and providing value for their library users.

Academic libraries are shackled with the challenge of chronically shrinking budgets while being held accountable for continuing to deliver high levels of resources and services. This compels academic libraries to efficiently allocate their finite resource base in serving their user communities. This requires contemporary academic libraries to continually seek institutional workflow improvements through innovative ideas and creative practices. One avenue that holds promise to meet this strategic vision for academic libraries is through demand-driven methodologies in the scholarly publishing marketplace.

New Economic Models: Demand-Driven Methodologies

The shift to a demand-driven, user-centric model coincides with a shift to a digital-based organizational culture predicated on acquiring electronic resources. This shift accompanies another movement from building collections based on content ownership to leasing collections based on content access. This change focuses on transforming the library organizational model from a supply-side economic framework to a demand-driven, market-based approach that is user-centric. This section explores demand-driven models pertaining to the acquisition of e-books.

The demands of the changing library culture coupled with shrinking budgets are forcing contemporary library acquisitions units to devise innovative solutions for acquiring affordable content. Digital innovations have made electronic access to content more attainable, but challenging cyberspace barriers such as licensing and copyright issues remain a consideration. Since e-books have entered the information marketplace, they have made a major impact due to technological innovations. For example, in a study of their DDA e-book program using the ebrary platform made available through YBP, researchers at the University of Iowa concluded that DDA programs were effective tools and held promise for both meeting user demand and building collections.[22] Since this study was made available, DDA models have steadily grown in use and popularity.

DDA came into existence in 1990 at Bucknell University when interlibrary loan (ILL) librarians started to acquire print books requested through ILL because they were unable to procure the material from other institutions.[23] They found it was more cost effective to acquire certain books than to borrow them. Eventually, academic vendors found the DDA model commercially viable. Over time, commercial DDA programs became particularly effective within e-book markets, and eventually the majority of DDA programs were implemented for the purchase of e-books.

DDA programs gained popularity from an acquisitions perspective because they streamlined acquisition workflows. Acquisitions staff did not initiate the ordering process since the acquisition of books was initiated when a trigger threshold was reached. Several academic vendors provide DDA programs, including YBP and Ingram, and programs vary by vendor. Implementing a DDA program requires attention to detail regarding variables such as the negotiation of program parameters similar to the implementation of approval plans. When a library establishes a DDA program, the assessment of the program should be guided by two principles: (1) whether the DDA serves the interests of the university community, and (2) whether the program increases the collection value (i.e., ROI).[24] The target market for DDA content is primarily students at both the undergraduate and graduate levels, although faculty are also involved in the DDA process. The DDA model allows patrons to access library content without being aware of the transaction. The input from the acquisitions staff is minimal since they become involved only after the library material is purchased through the vendor.

A multitude of DDA models have cropped up in the academic library marketplace, including several consortial DDA arrangements. These include the Colorado Alliance of Research Libraries (CARL), Five College Libraries, Orbis-Cascade Alliance (OCA), Triangle Research Libraries Network

(TRLN), and Washington Research Library Consortium (WRLC).[25] Consortial DDA programs are promising because they deliver content to the user by increasing economies of scale to a wider patron audience. This allows access to content that many smaller libraries could not afford on their own. They are proving to be effective demand-driven models that deliver savings to libraries in terms of funds and labor. Also, there are other advantages associated with DDA program models, such as (1) they compile usage statistics for the library acquisitions staff to use in assessing the value of the program for their users, (2) they provide robust tools for collection assessment purposes, and (3) they provide evidence to justify budget expenditures.[26]

A variation on the demand-driven methodology is the short-term leasing model. The short-term loan (STL) demand-driven model marketed by EBL, for example, is now affiliated with ProQuest. E-book STLs are similar to the traditional model of physically borrowing a book from a library. In this model, the user can access the e-book through a loan for a specified time period. The loan fees are negotiated between the vendor and the library. Each loan or short-term lease costs a fraction of the book's price, and savings are presumed under the assumption that few books that are loaned will be so heavily used that they will exceed purchasing costs.

Digital innovations, such as demand-driven technologies, have expanded the scope of academic libraries by providing access to content for its user-driven markets. Although certain issues need to be resolved, such as copyright restrictions and oligopoly entrenchment in the scholarly publishing industry, the trend toward user-centric library models is quickly moving academic libraries in new strategic directions. The shift from a content-ownership, just-in-case approach to building print collections to a leasing-content, e-resource, just-in-time approach to collection management is allowing libraries to efficiently use their scarce resources within a more flexible paradigm. Demand-driven acquisition technologies are providing innovative strategies for academic libraries to meet the needs of the changing demographics of their users in the academic environment. One important facet regarding library acquisitions still needs to be addressed: staffing trends.

Contemporary Staffing Issues in Acquisitions: Twenty-First-Century Skills

Staffing is another area of transformation in the acquisitions arena. In the traditional library acquisitions model, there are two basic acquisitions staffing lines: professional and paraprofessional. The career development of professional acquisitions librarians is not taught in library schools, although the Association for Library Collections and Technical Services (ACLTS) offers an online course, Fundamentals of Acquisitions, that provides a broad overview of library acquisitions processes.[27] Library schools that teach acquisitions include it as a component of either cataloging or collection development courses. Acquisitions librarians, for the most part, learn their skills through on-the-job training. This section focuses on paraprofessional staffing trends, since the majority of modern acquisitions work is performed by paraprofessionals. The author will examine two critical staffing issues: skill sets and demographics.

Traditionally, acquisitions paraprofessionals required few technical skills. Most tasks and activities associated with their positions were clerical in nature. Most acquisitions staff typically had a background in technical services or collection development. In the contemporary acquisitions landscape, however, the tasks and activities of the acquisitions paraprofessional are changing. There is a trend toward a reduction of clerical activities and an increase in advanced skill sets among acquisitions paraprofessionals.[28] In addition, there is a rise in outsourcing within technical services. This includes outsourcing of activities such as approval plans, cataloging, and invoicing, to cite a few examples. This has resulted in staff reductions that require contemporary staff to possess multiple skill sets to successfully work in library acquisitions. An examination of three skill sets for acquisitions paraprofessionals outside of the technical services arena (accounting, IT, and communication) is provided below.

Contemporary acquisitions paraprofessionals need a working knowledge of accounting fundamentals such as fund accounting. This is a methodology used by government and nonprofit entities that stresses budgeting or allocation of funds when accounting for expenditure of monies.[29] In traditional acquisitions organizations, there are two basic methods for purchasing library materials: payment by invoice and prepayment. When library materials are shipped with an invoice from the vendor, the acquisitions staff process the invoice for accounts payable to initiate vendor payment and to charge the appropriate fund account that was encumbered when the order was placed. When a library uses a prepaid account, they first deposit a set amount of funds as prepayment with a vendor; this establishes a deposit account. With this method, when material is acquired from that vendor, the account is charged and funds are deducted from the deposit account until depleted or replenished. These methodologies have served the library community well over the years. The implementation of e-commerce practices has opened up the use of credit card transactions. At the author's institution, for example, the use of credit card transactions has expanded acquisitions' ability to purchase library content and has facilitated access to new information markets. Although it has been noted that credit card use in the acquisition of library material results in savings for the unit and makes online purchases easier, it also creates bottlenecks to the workflow process by adding procedures and staff in the transaction mix.[30] The expansion of online purchasing and accounting technologies has made it a necessity for acquisitions paraprofessional staff to have basic accounting skills.

The second set of skills needed by acquisition paraprofessionals relates to information technology. IT skill acquisition has been documented as a critical skill for librarians.[31] The same case can be made for acquisitions paraprofessionals. As acquisitions organizations restructure to become more streamlined, the need for IT skills becomes critical. Downsizing and restructuring of acquisitions staffing, as well as outsourcing, in academic libraries has required the use of technological efficiencies to increase unit productivity while keeping pace with streamlined acquisition workflows. Contemporary integrated library management systems, which are complex databases with multiple interconnected modules, are becoming increasingly sophisticated, and that requires staff with a strong background in database management. The development of database management skills, beyond the need for a strong working background with bibliographic records, will become a critical skill set for acquisitions paraprofessionals. For example, batchloading skills will become a critical asset for the acquisitions paraprofessional since automated workflows have become increasingly prevalent in the e-resource environment. Looking ahead, other IT skills will be important for the contemporary acquisitions paraprofessional, such as Microsoft application skills for generating management reports.[32]

The final skill set needed by acquisitions staff is communication skills. Acquisitions staff interact with several key parties in the library arena, but especially with technical services staff such as cataloging. Library acquisitions staff, like other technical service positions, are grounded in highly routinized activities and rely on written and formal communication, particularly when dealing with policy issues. Since they usually do not engage in external and informal, interdepartmental communication processes, it is not surprising that acquisitions staff tend to effectively communicate intraorganizationally with other technical services staff rather than interorganizationally with public services staff.[33] However, they must effectively communicate with external stakeholders such as administrators and faculty, plus vendors and publishers. This requires good interpersonal communication skills and the ability to develop strong working relationships.

Another staffing consideration pertains to demographics. Over the last two decades, technical services demographics have changed. Traditionally, acquisitions paraprofessional staff were selected from the local job market, which usually supplied an ample pool of qualified applicants with a strong clerical skill base. Contemporary technical services staffing has experienced a major shift in library practices and demographics. It has been noted that there is a trend toward a reduction of professional technical services positions that has been attributed to retirement and reduced hiring.[34] This has resulted in workflow changes that necessitates, as noted above, hiring better-educated staff with multiple skill sets.

An important demographic issue related to staffing trends concerns work tenure. Recent observations of the current work force indicate that job hopping, or frequently changing jobs, is a common behavior among young people in the contemporary job market, which is a major market segment for the recruitment of library paraprofessionals. A study by CareerBuilder revealed that a quarter of workers surveyed under the age of thirty-five have held five or more jobs in their lifetime. The study also discovered that 45 percent of employers expect young new hires to stay only two years or less.[35] Whether this trend is due to higher mobility, the impact of the global recession, or job dissatisfaction remains unclear. Staffing issues, it can be certain, will bring challenges for the emerging contemporary acquisitions industry.

FINAL THOUGHTS: WHAT IS THE FUTURE OF LIBRARY ACQUISITIONS?

The intent of this chapter is to propose the argument that current library acquisition practices are in the midst of organizational transformations, which is accompanying the paradigm shift in the role that academic libraries play in higher education. The traditional library-centric, print-based culture, grounded in a bureaucratic organizational framework immersed in rigid library practices and institutional structures, is no longer efficient or relevant to serve the needs of the contemporary university environment nor its strategic institutional mission. The academic library organizational model is shifting to a user-centric, digital-based culture grounded in innovative institutional practices. The transformations are generating new demand-driven models and methodologies that are changing the acquisitions landscape. The contemporary academic library is immersed in a shift toward innovative, market-driven practices that are predicated on serving the needs of its users and community. Acquisitions is in the forefront of this transformation. This chapter provides evidence that supports this proposition that demand-driven methodologies are shaping the new acquisitions institutional environment.

This chapter gives a brief glimpse into what methodologies are making an impact in the library acquisitions arena from a demand-driven approach. Demand-driven methodologies, such as PDA and short-term leasing, deftly illustrate how user-driven models are starting to permeate the acquisitions environment to serve the needs of users not on a just-in-case, content-ownership basis but on a dynamic, just-in-time basis in which leasing content has become economical and affordable for academic libraries, which are engulfed in difficult economic times. Other demand-driven platforms, such as e-book subscriptions, print on demand, and evidence-based acquisitions are models that are penetrating the library content markets.

Staffing trends in academic libraries, as alluded to in this chapter, portend serious issues regarding the recruitment of qualified staff, especially at the paraprofessional level. Downsizing and the streamlining of workflows to create technological efficiencies in technical services processing will require the recruitment of paraprofessional staff with knowledge of more than the "library science" principles that was required from traditional technical services staff. The new acquisitions landscape will require savvy new staff with a strong grasp of accounting, IT, and communication skills above and beyond their knowledge of library practices, if they are to be successful in meeting the demands of the acquisitions industry in the twenty-first century. More importantly, however, is how the modern academic library organization can compete for the contemporary market of qualified candidates in the job pool. The contemporary pool of applicants are better educated, more likely to hold at least a bachelor's degree if not a master's degree (including those candidates with an MLS), and very tech savvy. If academic libraries are to compete in this market for the best recruits, they are going to have to offer competitive salaries, but how?

A more relevant question is what the future holds for acquisitions. We first need to consider the roles that are established in the current acquisitions environment. We noted that acquisitions librarians and vendors are establishing new relationships as new demand-driven methodologies emerge from the marketplace. It is essential that acquisitions librarians are proactive in their approach to the new marketplace. They must be proactive in establishing collaborative partnerships not only with the vendors but with their faculty responsible for institutional research productivity. The contemporary acquisitions organization is no longer responsible for building collections but for providing access to content no matter how the material is to be acquired. It means innovation, it means thinking outside the box. Sounds simple? Yes, it does, but then again, it is not an easy task.

NOTES

1. Wayne A. Wiegand, *Irrepressible Reformer: A Biography of Melvil Dewey* (Chicago: American Library Association, 1996).

2. Warren D. Huff, "Colleges and Universities: Survival in the Information Age," *Computers & Geosciences* 26, no. 6 (2000): 635–40.

3. John Leslie King et al., "Institutional Factors in Information Technology Innovation," *Information Systems Research* 5, no. 2 (1994): 139–69.

4. Joanne R. Euster, "The Academic Library: Its Place and Role in the Institution," in *Academic Libraries: Their Rationale and Role in American Higher Education*, no. 84, ed. Gerard B. McCabe and Ruth J. Person (Westport, CT: Greenwood, 1995), 1–14.

5. Megan Oakleaf, *Value of Academic Libraries: A Comprehensive Research Review and Report* (Chicago: Association of College and Research Libraries, 2010), http://www.ala.org/acrl/sites/ala.org.acrl/files/content/issues/value/val_report.pdf.

6. Stephen Ford, *The Acquisition of Library Materials* (Chicago: American Library Association, 1978).

7. Robert LaRose and Anne Hoag, "Organizational Adoptions of the Internet and the Clustering of Innovations," *Telematics & Informatics* 13, no. 1 (1997): 49–61.

8. Tony Becher, "Towards a Definition of Disciplinary Cultures," *Studies in Higher Education* 6, no. 2 (1981): 109–22.

9. John L. Campbell and Leon N. Lindberg, "Property Rights and the Organization of Economic Activity by the State," *American Sociological Review* 55, no. 5 (1990): 634–47.

10. Michael McPherson, "The Economics of University Investments in Information Resources," *Journal of Library Administration* 26, nos. 1–2 (1999): 73–77.

11. Liz Chapman, *Managing Acquisitions in Library and Information Services*, rev. ed. (London: Facet Publishing, 2004).

12. Donna M. Goehner, "Vendor-Library Relations: The Ethics of Working with Vendors," in *Understanding the Business of Library Acquisitions*, ed. Karen Schmidt (Chicago: American Library Association, 1990), 137–51.

13. Joseph A. McDonald and Lynda Basney Micikas, *Academic Libraries: The Dimensions of Their Effectiveness* (Westport, CT: Greenwood, 1994).

14. Mieneke W. H. Weenig, "Communication Networks in the Diffusion of an Innovation in an Organization," *Journal of Applied Social Psychology* 29, no. 5 (1999): 1072–92.

15. John M. Budd, "The Organizational Culture of the Research University: Implications for LIS Education," *Journal of Education for Library & Information Science* 37, no. 2 (1996): 154–62.

16. Ross Atkinson, "Reflection on 'The Acquisitions Librarian as Change Agent in the Transition to the Electronic Library,'" *Library Resources & Technical Services* 48, no. 3 (2004): 213–15.

17. Euster, "The Academic Library."

18. Carol Pitts Diedrichs, "Rethinking and Transforming Acquisitions: The Acquisitions Librarian's Perspective," *Library Resources & Technical Services* 42, no. 2 (1998): 113–25.

19. Oakleaf, *Value of Academic Libraries*.

20. Ibid.

21. McDonald and Micikas, *Academic Libraries*.

22. Karen S. Fischer et al., "Give 'Em What They Want: A One-Year Study of Unmediated Patron-Driven Acquisition of e-Books," *College & Research Libraries* 73, no. 5 (2012): 469–92.

23. Dracine Hodges, Cyndi Preston, and Marsha J. Hamilton, "Patron-Initiated Collection Development: Progress of a Paradigm Shift," *Collection Management* 35, nos. 3–4 (2010): 208–21.

24. William H. Walters, "Patron-Driven Acquisition and the Educational Mission of the Academic Library," *Library Resources & Technical Services* 56, no. 3 (2012): 199–213.

25. Christine N. Turner, "E-Resource Acquisitions in Academic Library Consortia," *Library Resources & Technical Services* 58, no. 1 (2014): 33–48.

26. Kay Downey et al., "KSUL: An Evaluation of Patron-Driven Acquisitions for Ebooks," *Computers in Libraries* 34, no. 1 (2014): 10–31.

27. See the course website at http://www.ala.org/alcts/confevents/upcoming/webcourse/foa/ol_templ.

28. Gillian S. Gremmels, "Staffing Trends in College and University Libraries," *Reference Services Review* 41, no. 2 (2013): 233–52.

29. Chapman, *Managing Acquisitions in Library and Information Services*.

30. Janet Flowers, "A Status Report on Credit Card Use by Acquisitions Departments," *Against the Grain*, 10, no. 5 (1998): 19, 27.

31. Debra A. Riley-Huff and Julia M. Rholes, "Librarians and Technology Skill Acquisition: Issues and Perspectives," *Information Technology & Libraries* 30, no. 3 (2011): 129–40.

32. Cynthia M. Coulter, "Technical Services Report," *Technical Services Quarterly* 22, no. 4 (2005): 77–82, dx.doi.org/10.1300/J124v22n04.

33. Hong Xu, "Type and Level of Position in Academic Libraries Related to Communication Behavior," *Journal of Academic Librarianship* 22, no. 4 (1996): 257–66.

34. Stanley J. Wilder, "Demographic Trends Affecting Professional Technical Services Staffing in ARL Libraries," *Cataloging & Classification Quarterly* 34, nos. 1–2 (2002): 51–55.

35. Jennifer Grasz, "Nearly One-Third of Employers Expect Workers to Job-Hop," Career-Builder, May 15, 2014, http://www.careerbuilder.com/share/aboutus/pressreleasesdetail.aspx?id=pr824&sd=5/15/2014&ed=05/15/2014.

Chapter Five

The Management of Electronic Resources

An Overview

Alice Crosetto

The advent of electronic resources created a ripple effect throughout librarianship. It is hard to think of one aspect of library services and support that was not impacted, including staff and position responsibilities, by the appearance of and dependence on electronic resources. One area that definitely felt the impact of electronic resources is the area traditionally named technical services, which typically includes acquisitions and cataloging.

Any discussion regarding the management of electronic resources should begin with the professional experience and knowledge of those individuals proposing to discuss this important topic, both current and perplexing. Unlike traditional print resources, librarians need to understand and accept one realization in acquiring electronic resources, and that is ownership, or more aptly, control. Print items are purchased and deposited in appropriate library locations. Electronic resources exist in the virtual environment, which often appears to have a life of its own and a unique set of considerations from print.

The veteran librarian tends to equate issues and concerns of electronic resources with their long-standing counterparts, print items. Decisions regarding electronic items may be rooted in established policies and procedures designed for print resources. A relatively new professional, beginning a career in librarianship with minimal to no experience in maintaining print resources, has little information on which to draw, hence drafting decisions for collection management is based solely on knowledge and interaction with the electronic. Considering the latitude of knowledge and experience of those in librarianship and the hallmark of the professional of being inclusive, our discussion should be broad enough to include both groups, including addressing the needs and responsibilities of individual libraries while providing well-founded and reasonable recommendations for the future.

As a veteran librarian, the author continues to struggle with knowing what policies and procedures designed for print items should readily transfer to electronic resources, if any. In attempting to identify best practices and standards for managing electronic resources, possibly the better route is to examine multiple factors, such as firsthand experience, recent literature, and current job descriptions posted to library employment websites or discussion lists. Firsthand experience provides real and substantial knowledge. This is the knowledge that is likely to find its way into publications and conferences, activities that contribute to one of our profession's most productive and beneficial characteristics, networking. Networking provides the impetus to create and maintain our faith in consortia or consortial endeavors and is often a layer that impacts our collections in both their development and management.

Literature containing research, case studies, theoretical essays, and the like is scripted by our peers. Sharing our library activities, successes, and even failures in publications and at conferences illustrates the camaraderie and collegiality of librarianship. Discussing and sharing at conferences enables librarians to interact and acquire immediate answers. Reading books, articles, blogs, and websites, to name a few resources, also provides a wealth of information. Our literature not only documents trends but also points to shifts in the library culture. By the 2000s, content in our literature saw a significant increase in the inclusion of information regarding electronic resources. One of the most noteworthy of acknowledgments and evidence of the importance of electronic resources is in the changing of the journal *Acquisitions Librarian* into the *Journal of Electronic Resources* in 2008.

Finally, but understandably not the last source of usable information, is perusing position descriptions posted to library employment websites, for example, the ALA JobLIST (http://joblist.ala.org/), or reviewing position descriptions posted to library discussion lists. Position descriptions list the detailed employment requirements of libraries and are based on long and painstaking evaluations and discussions of a library's specific needs. The increased number of library positions pertaining to electronic resources demonstrates the need for expertise in this area. Responsibilities detailing requirements pertaining to electronic resources are being included in current position announcements, and the position titles themselves reflect the need for individuals dedicated to the selection, acquisition, cataloging, and overall management of electronic resources. During the summer of 2014, the ALA JobLIST advertised the following positions: Acquisitions Coordinator of E-Resources and Serials, Electronic Resources Licensed Content Librarian,

Electronic Resources and Discovery Librarian, Electronic Resources Librarian, and Electronic Resources and Serials Specialist. The challenge of identifying the individual whose responsibility it is to oversee electronic resources is complex. For some individuals, additional responsibilities were added due to the natural progression and proximity of the requirements stemming from print resources.

Exploring not only this tripartite approach but also personal and sundry sources to understand how to manage electronic collections and databases, the author proposes that policies and procedures for print resources remain intact, but encourages library professionals to advance in the digital environment based on the needs dictated by the very nature of the resources' virtual existence. As we examine what would work best for our own libraries and what practices to employ, a brief look at the recent evolution of electronic resource management is beneficial.

BACKGROUND

As previously noted, it might be easier to transfer workflow policies and procedures established for print resources to electronic resources. What comes to mind is the old adage of trying to fit a square peg into a round hole. While this is not entirely accurate, it points to the need to address the unique features and characteristics of electronic resources. As illustrative as the change in journal titles can be to express the importance of updating existing practices regarding resources in the library, an even more substantial event occurred—the movement of creating modules within integrated library systems (ILSs) specifically designed to manage electronic resources. One example is Innovative Interfaces Inc. (III). By the early 2000s, III established the ERM—the Electronic Resources Management module. Understanding that electronic resources contained elements found in their print counterparts, for example, a title, the purchase cost, a vendor, III addressed the elements unique to the nonprint resource, such as renewal date, authentication details, and proxy data. [1]

The establishment of ERMs should be viewed as the exemplary result of the collaborative efforts between librarians and ILS providers. Once in place, the ERM and the substantial increase in the number of resources contained therein drove the need to revise responsibilities in library positions. In addition, the management of electronic resources themselves required a comprehensive strategy. It is against this backdrop that libraries redefined positions, including the updating of work responsibilities, and also established new positions dedicated to electronic resources. Within this new culture, several individuals identified the need to establish workflows that reflected the unique characteristics of electronic resources. One of the earliest was the chief strategist for EBSCO's e-resource access and management services, Oliver Pesch, who, during a 2005 conference held at Mississippi State University, presented a model depicting the life cycle of an e-journal.[2] Pesch's model consisted of five steps: acquire, provide access, administer, provide support, and evaluate and monitor. The model further revealed thirty processes associated with the main five steps, twenty-five of which were identified as unique to e-journals. Pesch noted that nineteen of the thirty processes were managed by an ERM. Expanding Pesch's model and using his firsthand knowledge of current ERM tools and current practices, Emery and Stone created TERMS (Techniques for Electronic Resource Management) in 2008. They employed their insight to identify what elements were missing when comparing current ERM systems with current practices.[3] The TERMS life cycle contains six steps: investigate, acquire, implement, evaluate, review, and cancel/replace. The additional step, investigate, was inserted at the beginning of the cycle, thus basically constituting a new action not shown in Pesch's life cycle.[4] The inclusion of this action may have been generated during the numerous discussions in which the authors engaged while developing their version of the electronic resource life cycle; Emery and Stone's own experience in library collection development and acquisitions may have suggested the importance of this activity, as equally valuable in acquiring electronic resources as it has always been for print purchases.

However, many libraries may lack the means to purchase an ERM. Adapting existing practices and software is necessary for libraries that lack an ERM. At a 2010 conference, Rick Kerns of the University of Northern Colorado Libraries shared how the technical services department reorganized personnel and evaluated position responsibilities and defined the e-resources workflow to address "the intangible, volatile, fast changing, and unpredictable nature of these materials."[5] Further discussions included how some position responsibilities were shifted and practices for print resources were moved into an electronic format.

Vendors have responded to the situation and provided the means to manage electronic resources. Ex Libris, a global leader in providing library automation solutions, created Verde, a stand-alone product that improves operational efficiency throughout the entire e-resource life cycle.[6] In addition to stand-alone products and ERM modules in ILSs, content providers also offer management services. EBSCO offers a subscription management service, which includes customizing options and analytics to evaluate usage. Analytics On Demand, Gale/Cengage Learning's new data solution, provides libraries with the essential support for "any library administrator looking to make smarter decisions, improve collections and better demonstrate the value of their library and its services."[7]

A further investigation of the literature will undoubtedly reveal numerous other examples of how libraries are adapting their current practices to meet the demands of electronic resources. Librarians will continue to publish their findings and share their experiences at conferences, from the local to the national level, to demonstrate how current positions are morphing and, in many libraries, new positions are being created to manage electronic resources.

THE THREE-PHASE CYCLE

Whether existing personnel need to embrace the management of electronic resources or newly hired individuals have to establish their work parameters, the author proposes using the following three phases when managing electronic resources:

- First, gather as much background information as necessary to make selections.
- Second, acquire the resource, which includes providing access and administrative support.
- Third, maintain ongoing evaluation, providing both internal and external assessment.

While this may seem like an oversimplification of the complex nature of electronic resources, these three key elements reflect the essential philosophy that provides the optimal resources that patrons expect from their libraries. Once these three basic rules are understood and followed, expanding your position's responsibilities into Pesch's model or TERMS should be a natural progression into successful management. One additional note regarding the phases: It is often challenging to determine when one phase ends and the next one begins. There is as much overlap between activities as there are stand-alone actions. It is easy to agree that workflows are typically fluid, which aptly explains why using the term *life cycle* to explain the management process is appropriate. Managing library resources is always an ongoing activity.

Gathering Information

Gathering background information is the initial consideration when identifying which resources should be purchased. Smaller libraries may have one or two individuals determine purchases, while larger libraries engage in collaborative efforts involving librarians and stakeholders outside the library. For example, libraries that support curriculum and research typically request input from instructors of specific subjects. Identifying relevant content for specific curricula and research is essential. Technical services librarians who gather information need to be aware of what reference, instruction, interlibrary loan, and other public services librarians, who are typically on the front lines, are being asked. Another important source of information is the vendor. Establishing relationships with vendors enables librarians to make purchase decisions based on negotiations with vendors regarding such specifics as available content, costs, trials, licensing issues, number of simultaneous users, and infrastructure compatibility. Knowing the particulars of high-priced electronic resource packages is paramount. One element of the gathering process involves comparing current print holdings against possible electronic coverage to detect unnecessary duplication. Print holdings are often withdrawn based on the extent of electronic coverage. However, knowing that you have the ability to provide access to content for the future provides an incentive to remove print copies from the collection.

Another consideration is being well versed in costs, both initial and ongoing. The more information you have during this phase, the better situated you will be throughout the whole management cycle. For libraries fortunate to belong to a consortium, this phase may not be as burdensome. The nature of the consortium means that libraries share not only the costs of resources but also the work involved in gathering information. This benefits the consortium as a whole as well as individual members. However, libraries need to be mindful that when purchasing electronic resources within a consortial environment, individual libraries have less control over the decisions and outcome.

Acquiring and Maintaining

The second stage is to acquire the resource. This section addresses access and administrative support. The in-depth knowledge obtained in the gathering information phase impacts this step. The more comprehensive the knowledge that is obtained while investigating possible purchases, the smoother the acquisition of and transition to electronic resources will be. Activities in this step (acquire resources, work with vendors, negotiate licensing, and manage platforms) are seen as primary requirements and responsibilities in many current job descriptions for electronic resources librarians. Additional responsibilities include establishing the workflow required to manage electronic resources, creating original or derived catalog records, working with appropriate individuals to establishing secure access for authorized patrons as well as resolving access problems, managing the display and promotion of electronic resources, and providing training sessions.

Evaluation

The last area of managing electronic resources is evaluation. Remembering that this is a circular process, this last action always pushes us along the life cycle right back to the first step, gathering information. As many libraries find themselves being driven by data and by the need to produce reliable statistics to justify funds allocated for services and personnel, this phase becomes the most critical in the process. Collecting and analyzing relevant data and applying metrics, the core of assessment, must be ongoing. Whether a library tasks a specific individual to conduct assessment, or individual units generate their own data, reliable and dependable data about the electronic resources remains crucial. Funding allocated for electronic resources continues to increase, and justifying the expense is routine as these resources are typically more expensive than their print counterparts and frequently contain ongoing associated costs for things such as licenses, access to back issues, vendor-supplied records, or refreshing the knowledge base. Not only does this data point backward to justifying recent acquisitions and possible renewal, but it also points forward and provides statistics that support collection analyses and further collection development decisions and purchases. Librarians may need several years of ongoing evaluation to be satisfied with purchases of some resources or the cancellation of others. As Emery and Stone state, "The best evaluation of a product or service happens within a three- to five-year time frame."[8]

Statistics have traditionally been generated by various library units. For example, access services produces usage numbers such as the number of patrons utilizing library space and circulation of resources, reference tracks the number and type of reference questions, and technical services identifies how many items have been purchased. While some of these traditional data-gathering venues can be used for electronic resources measurements, recent practice has seen libraries utilizing external sources for producing reliable and dependable usage data. As trustworthy as internally generated data should be, administrators often consider externally generated assessment to be more credible. Internally generated data is reliable and dependable; however, when generating data for electronic resources, individual libraries often lack the means to produce complex data due to internal software limitations as well as the multilayered facet of electronic files controlled by individual vendors and publishers. Lack of staffing is another challenge that hampers one's ability to generate this data.

Utilizing external sources for evaluation should not be viewed as questioning the credibility of internal sources. However, as librarians, we know the value of aligning ourselves and our libraries with larger entities. We realize the importance of standardizing our practices and relying on the profession's collective wisdom. Where would libraries be today without OCLC's pivotal role and guidance in bibliographic control via computerized cataloging, or Melvil Dewey's classification system? Numerous initiatives have been established to assist libraries in generating data. Project COUNTER (Counting Online Use of Networked Electronic Resources), launched in

March 2002, sets the standards that facilitate the recording and reporting of online use statistics in a consistent, credible, and compatible way.[9] Another noteworthy initiative, which was commenced in 2007 by the National Information Standards Organization (NISO), is the Standardized Use Statistic Harvesting Initiative (SUSHI). According to online documentation that details its basic functions, "SUSHI protocol provides instructions to automate the collection of usage statistics reports from compliant vendors, which you'd otherwise manually download from a vendor website or receive via email."[10]

The importance and value placed on gathering data from electronic resources is demonstrated, first, in the establishments of these initiatives, and second, in their compatibility with other entities. SUSHI 1.6 supports COUNTER reports and non-COUNTER reports and produces reports designed specifically to address consortial needs. Among its features, SUSHI can be configured with a library's ERM, and online instructions are provided for a locally developed data-reporting system. Smaller libraries as well as larger and multilocation libraries will benefit from initiatives such as COUNTER and SUSHI.

CHALLENGES

Challenges always exist in librarianship. In managing electronic resources, individuals need to be aware that some challenges are inevitable and others that may arise can be addressed, both quickly and appropriately. The following challenges fall under the former category and by no means represent a comprehensive list. One of the first challenges, a long-standing concern throughout all facets of librarianship, is funding. The costs that typically apply to electronic resources are an initial charge that might be hefty due to content coverage and ongoing costs. Regardless of how much information about costs is gathered from vendors as suggested in the first step, sometimes ongoing charges increase at such substantial rates that libraries are not able to support continued accessibility. While this represents the external challenge of costs, the internal challenge may be that assurance of funding is provided at the moment that electronic resources are acquired; however, few if any library administrations can guarantee continued funding in perpetuity. Another aspect to be monitored is possible change in content coverage. The likelihood of publishers changing available content does occur. Embargoes and changes in ownership may decrease coverage. As mentioned earlier, this becomes troublesome and disheartening when decisions to withdraw print resources were based on the availability of the electronic counterpart. Another management challenge is that purchasing electronic resources in reality means paying for access, that is, the library is buying a connection. The ease of accessibility needs to be balanced with factors often beyond our control. A disruption in service can be created by power outages, or inaccessibility and downtime can occur due to vendor or internal system maintenance. Connectivity issues include any user authorization problems that need to be addressed by the appropriate individuals as quickly as possible. One final challenge is securing viability and usage for electronic resources. Several recent job descriptions list promoting electronic resources within the library as well as to external stakeholders as one of the primary responsibilities of the electronic resources librarians. During these data-driven times, analytical statistics, including usage data, which is often generated by visibility via marketing techniques, is as important for electronic resources as it is for print items.

E-Resource Collection Development

E-resource collection development has been a challenge for library professionals. Collection policies for print resources can be extended to electronic resources, but with some limitations. E-resources provide challenges not associated with print, such as licensing and access considerations, pricing, ownership, and archiving. IFLA has produced an excellent guide for libraries to e-resource collection development that is freely available online.[11] Some of the considerations for collecting e-resources as outlined in this guide include technical feasibility, functionality and reliability, vendor support, supply, and licensing.[12]

Selecting and acquiring resources is a complex process that involves a larger number of individuals than typically required when selecting their print counterparts. An institution may have a team or group who are charged with investigating and acquiring electronic resources. Rutgers University Libraries uses their Electronic Resources Team to fill this function for databases and e-journals. This group also works cooperatively with Central Technical Services to purchase e-books and packages. The responsibilities of the Electronic Resources Team include:

- Investigating requests for new e-resources
- Overseeing the entire e-resources acquisitions process
- Monitoring and maintaining access to ensure continuous access to resources is provided
- Compiling and maintaining database and e-journal usage statistics
- Providing ERMS management.[13]

Vendor Support

Vendor support is a critical consideration for e-resource acquisition and collection development. In addition to securing the optimal pricing and access, the type of ongoing support the vendor provides is paramount. E-resources are pricey and not all requests for a resource can be realistically honored, particularly if a resource duplicates content provided by another resource or will appeal to a select small audience. This is a good case for requesting a trial so that the product can be tested and evaluated. [14] Making trials available to users is a good way to get feedback from experts that can be used to guide decisions on whether to purchase a resource. Vendors who want to secure the sale of a resource should provide a demonstration of their product and also provide user training and support. [15] Additional considerations include the ability to customize products for a library's specific needs, data archiving and back up if the vendor declares bankruptcy, and the ability to provide quality statistical reporting. [16]

Weeding E-Resources

As with other types of library resources, there is a need for applicable weeding policies and procedures for e-resources. These resources may become outdated or obsolete, or new editions may become available, and it is in the library's best interest to provide the most current resources to their users, particularly in the case of research libraries. Some selectors prefer to pay for an e-book that can be withdrawn or swapped out when that content is obsolete, rather than deciding whether to withdraw a print copy or if there is sufficient shelf space to accommodate various editions of the print. Many patron-driven acquisitions plans (PDAs) and e-book lease programs include provisions for swapping out older or little-used titles, yet libraries seem to have not considered the applicability of weeding for e-books. This may be due to the fact that libraries are just starting to embrace e-books and their potential to serve a large number of users simultaneously. However, these resources are costly and frequently more expensive than their print counterparts, and careful attention must be paid when acquiring them and also providing oversight of them.

Selectors and collection development librarians may work with technical services librarians to identify e-resources that should be withdrawn from the library catalog, as is done for print titles. [17] E-resources purchased for a consortial program may be eligible for weeding projects, but not for individual participating libraries. After titles to be withdrawn have been identified, care must be taken not to withdraw the wrong record (this could happen if there are similar titles in the catalog). If a library uses merged format records, withdrawing the e-book may be achieved through tweaking the record. Libraries that participate in union catalogs such as OCLC will also need to arrange to delete their holdings from the database.

The author has developed a short list of considerations to address when planning to weed e-resources:

- Print materials are weeded due to low use or lack of currency. The same consideration may be given to e-books.
- Revised and newer editions of e-books should be regularly weeded.
- Data should be collected and analyzed before any decisions are made to weed a title. Factors to be evaluated include the number of times an e-book was accessed or downloaded or whether a title from a PDA project was purchased.[18]

Providing access to obsolete or unused e-books benefits no one. Academic libraries typically pay maintenance fees to ILS vendors that may be based on the number of records in their catalogs, which can cause greater fees. Unused or underused titles occupy space that could be better used for more current titles, and can also generate undesired search results for users. "We must understand that virtual shelf clutter can obscure good content from bad."[19]

CONCLUSION

How are libraries and their librarians expected to manage the complexity of electronic resources? What are the best practices for managing collections, databases, and all electronic resources? Librarians have utilized their knowledge and firsthand experience to know what their libraries and users want and expect. Vendors always seem to be willing and prepared to assist libraries by providing the support and collaborative strategies that strengthen their relationships with libraries. This synergy results in better library services and, more importantly, satisfied patrons. The management of electronic resources, as with all library resources, is undoubtedly library specific, that is, what works for one library may not work for another.

Librarians in all types of libraries will continue to operate as they have since the beginning of the library's existence: use firsthand knowledge acquired along the way, discuss your concerns and needs, ask the necessary questions, share your findings, see what others are doing, address the needs of the situation, identify the appropriate individuals, and continue to evaluate resources and services. We need to keep moving forward and provide the best library services and support.

NOTES

1. "Our Story," III, http://www.iii.com/about/story.

2. Robert E. Wolverton Jr. and Oliver Pesch, "Conference Report: E-Journal Services, Tools, and Standards: An Agent's Perspective," *Serials Librarian* 51, nos. 3–4 (2007): 209–13.

3. Jill Emery and Graham Stone, "Chapter 1: Introduction and Literature Review," *Library Technology Reports* 49, no. 2 (2013): 5–9.

4. Nathan Horsburgh, "Managing the Electronic Resources Lifecycle: Creating a Comprehensive Checklist Using Techniques for Electronic Resource Management (TERMS)," *Serials Librarian* 66, nos. 1–4 (2014): 212–19, dx.doi.org/10.1080/0361526X.2014.880028.

5. Ning Han and Rick Kerns, "Rethinking Electronic Resources Workflows," *Serials Librarian* 61, no. 2 (2011): 207–14, dx.doi.org/10.1080/0361526X.2011.591042.

6. See Ex Libris, "Verde," http://www.exlibrisgroup.com/category/VerdeOverview, for more.

7. See http://learn.cengage.com/analytics for more.

8. Jill Emery and Graham Stone, "Chapter 5: Ongoing Evaluation and Access," *Library Technology Reports* 49, no. 2 (2013): 26–29.

9. Alice Crosetto, "The Use and Preservation of E-books," in *No-Shelf Required: E-books in Libraries*, ed. Sue Polanka, 125–34 (Chicago: American Library Association, 2011).

10. National Information Standards Organization (NISO), "SUSHI for Libarians," http://www.niso.org/workrooms/sushi/librarians/.

11. Sharon Johnson et al., *Key Issues for E-Resource Collection Development: A Guide for Libraries* (The Hague: IFLA, 2012), http://www.ifla.org/files/assets/acquisition-collection-development/publications/electronic-resource-guide-en.pdf.

12. Ibid.

13. Rutgers University Libraries, "Electronic Resources," http://www.libraries.rutgers.edu/rul/staff/dts/electronic_resources/electronic_resources.shtml.

14. Johnson et al., *Key Issues for E-Resource Collection Development*.

15. Ibid.

16. Ibid.

17. Barbara E. Hightower and John T. Gantt, "Weeding Nursing E-books in an Academic Library," *Library Collections, Acquisitions & Technical Services* 36, nos. 1–2 (2012): 57.

18. Alice Crosetto, "Weeding E-Books," *Booklist Online*, October 18, 2011, http://www.booklistonline.com/Weeding-E-books-Alice-Crosetto/pid=5152179.

19. Roselle Public Library District, "RPLD Ebook Collection Management: eSelection & Weeding," http://rpldebookcollmgt.wordpress.com/weeding/.

Chapter Six

Research Data and Linked Data

A New Future for Technical Services?

Sherry Vellucci

Data curation challenges are increasing as standards for all types of data continue to evolve; more repositories, many of them cloud-based, will emerge; librarians and other information workers will collaborate with their research communities to facilitate this process.— Association of College and Research Libraries (ACRL) Research Planning and Review Committee [1]

[Linked Open Data] is moving to a global scale. . . . Openness, collaboration, and cooperation will bring progress and carry us forward into the world of linked open data.—Yoose and Perkins [2]

The library literature is awash with articles that discuss the future of academic libraries in terms of data. [3] Many versions of the term appear in the context of research, including research data, big data, data management, data profile, data life cycle, data curation, data services, data citation, and data literacy. What changes in research practices and emerging research needs offered librarians opportunities to engage with the research data process when their traditional support role is to build collections, provide access to the published research record, and offer assistance finding and acquiring data sets? The evolving research and publication landscape may present new and exciting opportunities for outreach and collaboration, but what does this new research data vision mean for technical services librarians?

In the context of the Semantic Web, the term *data* appears as linked data, open data, linked open data (LOD), and Web of data. For many years catalogers and metadata specialists have witnessed constant change in almost every aspect of their work—from cataloging codes, metadata standards, and record formats to digital libraries, markup languages, and the transformation of library catalogs into discovery systems. As technology and user expectations change, information organization resides in a world of perpetual beta! Just when catalog and metadata librarians are adapting to these many changes, linked data appears on the horizon with the potential to turn things upside down once again. Where did the idea of linked data come from, and will it persist as a new direction for cataloging and metadata?

A literature review confirms the importance of data in the future of academic libraries. Library participation in data curation is included in several recent "Top Trends" lists. In the June 2014 issue of the *Association of College and Research Libraries News*, the theme of the biennial article "Top Trends in Academic Libraries" is "deeper collaboration."[4] Data is cited as the top trend and includes three subcategories: (1) new initiatives and collaborative opportunities; (2) cooperative roles for researchers, repositories, and journal publishers; and (3) partnerships related to discovery and reuse of data.[5] Deeper collaboration perfectly describes the trend for librarians and researchers working more closely together. Also in 2014, the Library and Information Technology Association's (LITA) "Top Tech Trends" similarly includes research data management, big data, open data, and the Semantic Web of linked data.[6]

In their report on data curation as an emerging role for academic librarians, Walters and Skinner see the organizational structure of libraries "focusing less on the public and technical services paradigm of old (front of the house and back of the house . . .) and more on building the trio of strong infrastructures, content, and services."[7] This new type of organizational structure supports a broad view of resources and services intended to facilitate extensive collaboration for data curation and preservation services.

Research data and linked data may seem to be associated with different spheres of library activities, but both are concerned with data organization, discovery, access, and support of shared data beyond the library, and both are addressed here. This chapter examines many aspects of research data from the perspectives of researchers and librarians. It briefly examines events prior to the library's greater involvement with research data, looks at how librarians gained some fundamental knowledge and skills to assist with the tasks involved with research data curation, and discusses why researchers began to place more emphasis on data management. It then examines the stages of the data life cycle, the components of a data management plan, the purpose of application profiles, and the usefulness of standardized vocabularies and ontologies. The chapter then discusses the connection between the Semantic Web and linked data and how this integrates with research data, standards, and its future for the shared library. Metadata is a common factor among these topics. The chapter concludes with a discussion of options for librarians to expand their data expertise or retool for a new future.

WHY DATA, WHY NOW? A PERFECT STORM OR A PERFECT PARTNERSHIP?

Over the last decade, changes in many sectors of higher education converged to force academic libraries to reassess their roles and functions. The reasons behind these changes are many and complex, but the end result was an emerging focus on open access (OA) to information and sharing, repurposing, and curating research data. Rapidly advancing technology, such as expanding bandwidth for faster data transfer and lowering costs for data storage, provided the necessary infrastructure enhancements that enabled new methods for collecting and working with large research data sets. Technology was a major catalyst, but not the sole catalyst, for change. The confluence of many factors appeared to create a perfect storm, generating a data surge that challenged the ability of librarians and researchers alike to make data meaningful and useful beyond the immediate research project. We can trace the beginnings of a data paradigm shift for libraries and researchers back to several critical incidents; these include the emerging OA movement, new approaches to scholarly communication and publishing, new mandates from funding agencies requiring data management plans, and the development of institutional repositories.

Open Access and the Changing Scholarly Communication Landscape

The critical incident that drew researchers' attention to the need to manage their data more effectively came from government funding agencies and the OA movement. The combination of escalating research journal costs and shrinking library budgets meant less available access to research articles—a key driver leading to library support for OA.

The lengthy lag time between completion of research projects and publication of results posed another serious problem for both researchers and government funding agencies. The fundamental principle of scientific research is the ability to replicate the research, since scientific research is cumulative, often incorporating the findings of earlier work. It is not surprising, then, that many scientists and funding agencies found the expensive and relatively slow publishing models a hindrance to the rapid advancement of science. Unhappy with current publication practices, the National Institute of Health (NIH) proposed that papers describing research funded by their agency be deposited in an open-access database (i.e., PubMed Central).[8]

Emerging digital publishing models and ever-increasing technological capacity make it possible for published research articles to link to the supplemental data on which the study was based, thus making it available to the wider public.[9] Openly accessible research *data* makes it easier to replicate studies and repurpose data for other research projects, thus circumventing the time-consuming process of collecting data anew. But in order for data to be reused, it is necessary to provide documentation that sufficiently describes the data, ensures its quality, and makes it viable for reuse. The National Science Foundation (NSF) mandate that requires all funding proposals to provide an explicit data management plan has had a major impact on the scientific community, and it seems likely that government mandates will increase. Under the Obama administration, the government is rapidly moving forward to support OA to data. In May 2013, the President issued an Executive Order that outlined an Open Data Policy as the default model for government publishing; [10] in June 2013 the G8 leaders endorsed the five strategic principles of the Open Data Charter; [11] and in May 2014 the government followed up with the U.S. Open Data Action Plan, "which outlines new commitments as well as plans for enhancements and releases of certain data assets across the categories set forth by the [Open Data] Charter." [12] The new national and international policies underscore the importance placed on data in a global context. Some researchers see these mandates as an additional burden and have neither the time nor the expertise to manage such data plans. Librarians saw this as an opportunity to offer assistance in innovative ways that were not usually associated with librarians.

Institutional Repositories

The critical incident that prepared librarians to engage more collaboratively with researchers in managing their data was libraries' campuswide leadership role in creating institutional repositories at the beginning of the new millennium. [13] The process of designing, building, and populating an institutional repository offered countless opportunities for innovation. Professionally, technical service librarians gained or enhanced their knowledge, skills, and experience in areas such as project management and systems analysis; determining functional requirements for hardware, software, and metadata needed to support a repository; conducting research that honed survey, interview, and observation skills to discover the needs and information-seeking behaviors of different users; developing a workflow process for preparing digital objects for archival-quality preservation; working with many new metadata schemes; learning new data encoding methods such as XML, XSLT, and RDF; gaining knowledge of open-access issues; understanding intellectual property rights and copyright laws for digital objects; refining problem-solving skills; and costing out the expenses of staffing this new service and providing data storage.

Library culture began to shift as scholarly communication and technical services librarians increased their collaboration skills and raised their visibility by working more closely with faculty, information technology (IT) staff, and colleagues in other library departments. Collaboration with faculty often involved explaining open access, author rights, and the purpose of institutional repositories, as well as helping them deposit their publications. These interactions frequently enhanced librarians' knowledge of a faculty member's research and the terminology of different disciplines, while fostering trust between faculty and librarians. Collaboration with other academic units in the institution, such as the Graduate School and Honors Program, was also necessary to develop policies for depositing students' electronic theses and dissertations in the repository. Collaboration with IT staff was necessary to build the information architecture for a repository that meets the functional requirements laid out for hardware, software, and metadata. The collaborative process provided a common ground where librarians and IT technicians could learn each other's terminology, priorities, technical needs and limitations, and cultural differences. Within the library, the cross-functional nature of the work required to build, maintain, and provide a full-service institutional repository pushed the boundaries of the traditional organizational structure, and involved cataloging and metadata services, scholarly communication, and library liaisons to academic units, special collections, and archives. As frequently noted, collaboration is a critical part of research data services, and for some librarians it represents a new working model that centers on a project and team work rather than an individual narrowly focused on a single item or service.

The knowledge and skills enhanced or gained through the process of building an institutional repository laid a strong foundation for librarians to assume many of the tasks required to make data accessible for the long term. The government funding agencies' policy mandates that submission of data management plans with grant proposals compelled many researchers to seek expert assistance that allowed them to focus on their research, rather than spend valuable time learning systems for data curation. These factors make possible a synergy between librarians and researchers leading to greater collaboration on research data curation.

RESEARCH DATA

The conduct of research in all areas of study is changing and producing increasing amounts of data in digital form. In her introduction to cyberinfrastructure and data for librarians, Gold notes that "data is the currency of science, even if publications are still the currency of tenure. To be able to exchange data, communicate it, mine it, reuse it, and review it is essential to scientific productivity, collaboration, and to discovery itself."[14] Gold's statement focuses on science, but it is just as applicable to research in most other subject domains. The term *data* itself is somewhat vague in that it can apply to almost any type of evidence collected for the purpose of informing research questions. The term also applies to both types and formats of data. Types are a higher-level category including observational, experimental, derived, compiled, simulated, quantitative, and qualitative data. Formats are more specific than types and may include numeric, coded, textual, images, maps, audio files, lab notes, sensor data, survey data, field notes, samples, climate models, economic models—the list goes on. Pryor calls data "the primary building block of all information, the lowest level of abstraction in any field of knowledge, where it is identifiable as collections of numbers, characters, images or other symbols that when contextualized in a certain way, represent facts, figures or ideas as communicable information."[15] This lowest level of abstraction is often referred to as raw data. Data in this raw form frequently must be processed in some way before analysis. For example, the notes taken or recorded during a focus group interview must be transcribed and coded or categorized before they can be manipulated during analysis; or data collected by instruments in the field may need to be converted to a different file structure for analysis. Deumens et al. identified three phases, or categories, of data: *raw data* from initial observations, *intermediate data* that has been processed for analysis, and *final data* showing results of the research project.[16] Some data sets are continuously added to, or added to at intervals over time. In such cases, the data provides a "snapshot" at a specific point in time but may not be permanently fixed for years.

Today's scientific research can generate massive amounts of digital data using technologically advanced instruments that gather data at an unprecedented rate. Bartolo and Hurst-Wahl differentiate big data by the "3 Vs: Volume (how much); Velocity (how fast); and Variety (how complex)."[17] No matter the forms, types, or quantity of research data, research benefits greatly if the data is structured, described, and preserved in an accurate and systematic way that facilitates discovery, access, use, and sharing with other researchers.

Library Research Data Services

Before beginning to develop research data services, librarians should identify which services are needed by researchers on their campus and what services are already available. This will help to identify any service gaps and overlaps, avoid expensive duplication of effort, ensure that different services are based in the unit that is best equipped to offer it, and save time and money for all stakeholders.

Researchers differ in their approach to managing their research data, and their need for assistance will vary. Styles range from researchers who want the responsibility and control of the data to remain completely within the research team with no outside assistance from the library, to those who are receptive to librarians helping with the full spectrum of data services. Lage, Losoff, and Maness conducted an ethnographic study that resulted in the creation of researcher personas designed by aggregating data gathered during interviews with researchers regarding their data curation needs.[18] The various personas "represent the range of attitudes and needs regarding the type of datasets created, existing data storage and maintenance support, disciplinary culture or personal feelings on data sharing, and receptivity to the library's role in data curation."[19] An interesting finding from this study showed that a researcher's receptivity to librarians having a role in data curation did not necessarily correlate with their need for assistance due to a lack of support from other units on campus. Instead, a greater impact on receptivity was the culture or philosophy of the researcher's particular discipline vis-à-vis sharing data and collaborative research projects.[20] These personas provide a different and creative approach to developing researcher profiles and offer useful disciplinary insight into a researcher's potential data management style that will help when deciding on and marketing new data curation services. Another approach to determining a researcher's need for assistance with a data management plan that also provided information on receptivity of librarians was undertaken by Steinhart et al., who surveyed researchers to ascertain how well prepared they were to meet the new data management plan requirements mandated by the National Science Foundation.[21] Their findings revealed that (1) researchers were unclear about the meaning of the requirements and how to implement them; (2) they were uncertain whether their data met standards in their discipline; (3) most assigned no metadata and did not know if a metadata standard existed for their discipline; (4) most were willing to share their data, although many indicated that there were circumstances under which they would not; and (5) researchers welcomed "offers of assistance—both with data management planning, and with specific components of data management NSF asks them to address in their plans."[22] Steinhart's findings are supported by a 2012 study by the Council on Library and Information Resources (CLIR), which reported that researchers queried in their study "repeatedly cited a lack of time to conduct basic organizational tasks, let alone time to research best practices or participate in training sessions."[23] These studies demonstrate a need for data management plan services, even though some researchers might be reluctant to seek assistance. Librarians should understand and respect researchers' data management styles, but they should also make sure that researchers are aware of the research data services offered by the library.

Research data services include activities that cover the entire spectrum of data curation and involve librarians across most library units. Tenopir, Birch, and Allard offer the following definition of research data services:

Research data services are services that a library offers to researchers in relation to managing data and can include informational services (e.g., consulting
with faculty, staff, or students on data management plans or metadata standards; providing reference support for finding and citing data sets; or providing web guides and finding aids for data or data sets), as well as technical
services (e.g., providing technical support for data repositories, preparing data
sets for a repository, deaccessioning or deselecting data sets from a repository,
or creating metadata for data sets).[24]

This definition indicates the wide range of services that can be offered by
the library and engages librarians who work in many library units, including
collection management, acquisitions, cataloging and metadata services, library systems/IT, scholarly communications, reference, and instruction. It is
clear that a majority of services listed here fall within technical services and
amount to a broader role for technical service librarians than is commonly
believed.

Taking a broad, institution-wide approach, Wakimoto found four key
factors essential for developing research data services.[25] These included (1)
collaboration, which is critical to address the full spectrum of digital curation
services; (2) partnership among the three key campuswide units: the University Libraries, Research Computing, and the Office of Research; (3) sustain-
ability of the socio-technical infrastructure for successful implementation;
and (4) institutional culture as a significant factor when determining what
research data services are needed and how those services might evolve in the
future.[26] These key factors are echoed throughout the literature and will be
the top-level metrics of success for library data curation services.

Tenopir, Birch, and Allard conducted a survey in 2012 to discover what
services were being offered by academic libraries. The study found that a
minority of academic libraries offered research data services, but "a quarter
to a third of all academic libraries [surveyed] are planning to offer some
services within the next two years."[27] This growth prediction is supported in
an ACRL environmental scan[28] and by a growing body of literature[29] that
indicates rapidly mounting interest and a strong future for these emerging
library services.

Responses from a 2013 Association of Research Libraries (ARL) survey
identified two categories of research data services: broad, long-standing library services, and services that are more specific to data management.[30]
Many of the services listed in the first category are presently offered by many
libraries as part of their wider service mission. Services in this broad category include the following:

• Helping researchers locate and use data sources
• Data set acquisition
• Copyright and patent advising

- Support for geospatial analysis
- Institutional repositories

Among the libraries that have implemented some form of research data services, the ARL study found the following services that were specific to data management:

- Online data management plan resources
- Data management plan training and consulting
- Digital data repository services
- Long-term data management and preservation advice
- Training/support for the software application DMPTool[31]
- Consultation on data management plan services for grant proposals
- Consultation on data management best practices (online and workshops)
- Help in identifying and applying appropriate metadata standards
- Advice on data citation, data sharing, and access
- Assistance with file organization and naming (also may be offered elsewhere on campus)
- Data storage and backup (also may be offered elsewhere on campus)
- Data archiving assistance (IR with data sets, digital repository with data sets, and data-specific repositories)[32]

In addition to these more common services, some survey participants also supported data publication, data rights management, and digital image data conversion. Not every academic library offers, or should offer, every service. The services offered by the library should fit the needs of their particular user population and the ability of the library to offer the research data services with the staff, expertise, and budget available to the library for this purpose.

User-Centered Focus for Services

Currently, large university research libraries are the most obvious institutions to offer research data services. This is supported by the survey conducted by Tenopir, Birch, and Allard, whose findings indicated that libraries in larger universities, at doctoral granting institutions, and on campuses that receive NSF funding are more likely to offer or plan to offer research data services.[33] It is understandable, then, if libraries in smaller institutions find the many articles on big data curation off-putting or not applicable to their everyday work environment. Data curation, however, is also important to research endeavors in smaller universities and liberal arts colleges across all disciplines.[34] Of course, not all data sets are "big," but that does not mean they are not important for research.[35] Carlson notes that the majority of research conducted in the science, technology, engineering, and medicine (STEM) areas is smaller research projects, with data dispersed around campus, residing on the PCs and laptops of small research groups or individual researchers.[36] Smaller, dispersed research data sets may actually present more difficulties for data curation. According to Akers, "Data from smaller studies may be captured in a variety of file formats with no standard approach to documentation, metadata or preparation for archiving or reuse, making its curation even more challenging than for big data."[37] Dispersed research data also requires librarians to make greater outreach efforts to discover and work with these researchers. Toups and Hughes stress the importance of interpersonal engagement with researchers to ascertain their data curation needs and the benefits of the smaller academic setting for face-to-face discussions.[38] On a broader scale, an environmental scan is a useful tool to identify the extent and types of research data services needed on campus and provides an opportunity for librarians to interact with researchers. A focus on user needs is the best path to a successful research data services program.

We also tend to think of data as the purview of faculty, but in fact, all types of data are increasingly collected, transformed, and used by other researchers in the academy, including students and librarians. Although graduate students are required to take courses in research methods, often there is little or no instruction focused on the process of data curation. This lack of education leaves graduate students unprepared to deal with the full life cycle of research data, which, at best, results in senior researchers using valuable time to train graduate assistants; at worst, the data may not be able to provide the necessary information to answer the research question, support the hypothesis, or be easily usable.[39] At the undergraduate level, inquiry courses are being integrated into core curricula,[40] and the growth of undergraduate research conferences demonstrates a need to grasp the importance of data management earlier in a student's academic career.[41] In this regard, data literacy is a new area for instruction—a service that should be proactively marketed and offered by librarians as part of a comprehensive plan that targets methods of instruction for specific user groups, depending on the users' existing levels of expertise.[42]

Research Data Curation

Data curation involves a set of activities that parallels the research process and ensures the current and future reliability of the research data. In its Charter and Statement of Principles, the Data Curation Centre (DCC) defines data curation as "maintaining and adding value to a trusted body of digital research data for current and future use; it encompasses the active management of data throughout the research lifecycle."[43] One of the operative terms in this definition is *trusted*, which refers to quality assurance and quality control. Procedures to safeguard quality include use of appropriate standards and best practices for data structure, organization, description, processing, and interoperability; careful and ongoing data inspection; and documenting these decisions to create trustworthy data sets that enable other researchers to replicate the study and reuse the data with confidence.

Shreeves and Cragin offer another definition of data curation as "the active and ongoing management of data through its lifecycle of interest and usefulness to scholarship, science, and education, which includes appraisal and selection, representation and organization of these data for access and use over time."[44] This definition identifies some tasks in the data curation lifecycle and circumscribes the length of curation to the period when the data is of interest and useful. Implicit in this statement is the notion that not all data needs to be retained indefinitely. This decision may be determined by the funding agency, the researchers' institution, or the researchers themselves, and should be reviewed periodically throughout the project.

Data curation is the area that typically engages technical services librarians. As mentioned earlier, to some extent librarians possess the fundamental knowledge and expertise to help researchers manage their data in meaningful and useful ways, especially with their metadata needs, and of course some librarians are specialists in this area. Still, a steep learning curve exists in other areas of research data curation. Data sets differ in several ways from the typical research products with which librarians commonly work. In 2007 Gold stated that "librarians are much less familiar with the data-generating research phases of the scientific research cycle than with post-research phases of reporting, communication and publication."[45] She went on to cite several challenges, including a lack of general understanding of the various methods used by e-science to collect, process, analyze, and curate research data, as well as differences of understanding between researchers and librarians of seemingly common vocabularies. Even so, recognizing several areas where they could assist in the data curation process, librarians remained keen to tackle the challenges and began to update and enhance their knowledge and skills. Three years later, Gold acknowledged that "The library profession has demonstrated significant conceptual progress in characterizing and understanding data curation both in theory and in practice."[46] One need only look at the number of webinars and workshops offered in data management, curation, and preservation to understand librarians' desire to enhance their knowledge and learn new skills to support this emerging area of their field.

The Research Data Lifecycle

The purpose of a data lifecycle model is to guide the data planning process and provide the general framework for data management and curation. To provide the needed support services for data curation, librarians must first understand the components of the research process and the phases of the research data life cycle. The best practice is to develop the data lifecycle model in conjunction with each stage of the research plan (often called the *research* lifecycle model). A research data life cycle groups related activities together into stages that are often sequential and dependent on the previous stage. For example, the planning stage involves deciding on the type of data that is needed to answer the research questions and determines how the data will be gathered and stored. The next stage involves collecting the data, but this is dependent on the data specifications determined in the planning stage. Some stages in the data life cycle may be iterative—for example, after data is collected and examined, new or additional data might be required, and the collection stage begins again. The groups of activities continue throughout the data life cycle and on into the archiving and preservation stages after the research is completed.

The research data life cycle is represented as a graphic conceptual model at a high level of granularity. Each subject domain and research project tends to develop its own data life-cycle model that fits its particular needs. For this reason, no model is one-size-fits-all, but there are life-cycle stages that are common to most research and can be adapted to a particular research project. The Committee on Earth Observational Satellites maintains an ongoing compilation of data life-cycle models that currently consists of fifty-five models across various disciplines.[47] Some of the models included are quite simple, while others are much more complex.

Figure 6.1 is an example of a simple life-cycle model. Adapted from a model developed by the United State Geologic Survey (USGS),[48] it uses a linear matrix structure expanded to eight sequential primary life-cycle stages. The matrix below the primary-stage arrows indicates processes that are non-sequential and ongoing throughout all phases of the research project.

The *research* lifecycle outlines all stages of activity for the entire research project, while the *data* lifecycle covers the stages where some type of activity involving data occurs. In reality, the data lifecycle is embedded in the research lifecycle. For this reason, many models combine the research and data

Figure 6.1.   Linear Matrix Life Cycle Model. *Adapted from the USGS Linear Data Lifecycle Model*

lifecycles into one, which contextualizes the data within the overall research project. Figure 6.2 shows the research lifecycle model from the University of Virginia and is an excellent example of a contextual model that includes both the research life cycle and the data management lifecycle.[49]

The Virginia design expands on a linear model, beginning with the first stage in the *research* lifecycle—planning and writing the research proposal—and continues through the end of the research project and the data archiving process. The Virginia model also incorporates features of a nonlinear or cyclical model that includes recursive stages for additional data discovery, collection, analysis, repurposing, and reuse. This contextual model includes data preplanning as part of the research proposal writing phase. During proposal writing, librarians can assist researchers with discovery of existing data sets and begin to gather information that identifies the types of data and data events that will occur during the research project. This stage also provides an opportunity for librarians to gain knowledge of the nature of the data being collected and to help structure the data model for optimum access, use, archiving, and sharing. In the Virginia model, the detailed data management plan is developed in the "Project Start Up" stage, which begins after the project is funded. These first two stages are sometimes considered conceptual or administrative in nature because much of the activity entails planning and testing research tools and processes.

The more dynamic data lifecycle phases begin with data collection and run through data analysis and data sharing; recursive activities with data can occur anywhere during these stages. The analysis phase involves processing data to enable analysis and interpretation that facilitates sense making for researchers to grasp the implications of the data as they relate to the research

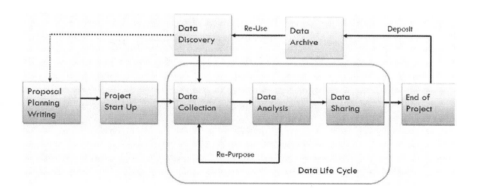

Figure 6.2.   The Research Life Cycle. *Figure reproduced with permission from the University of Virginia Library, Research Data Services. © 2014 by the Rector and Visitors of the University of Virginia*

questions. There is always the possibility that data-gathering instruments may need recalibration, or the data may need to be reprocessed, updated, and cleaned (i.e., duplicates removed, checked for missing data or other errors). Data sets might also be merged at some point to integrate new data or conduct a meta-analysis. Data manipulation makes identification of different versions of the data a critical part of ongoing data maintenance throughout the project. The data is then prepared for sharing. This could involve structural or format conversion to a required file format standard or, if not already completed, stripping the data of any information that could identify participants, if the research involved human subjects, or other sensitive data. When the data is configured for sharing and the research results written up for publication or other forms of dissemination, the data set should be fixed at that point in time to represent a snapshot of the data used to support the results of the published article.[50] The data snapshot is then archived, but that does not necessarily mean that data collection is completed. Many longitudinal studies will continue to generate data and produce project reports over time. A new fixed data snapshot should document the data used in each report or published article.

The end of the research data lifecycle deals with postresearch data activities that include data archiving, discovery, and preservation. Open access databases and some subscription journals link the published research article directly to the supporting data, rather than making the reader search elsewhere to locate and reuse the data from the study. At this point, the data can either be discarded from short-term storage or archived and preserved in long-term storage for the length of time determined in the data management planning document.

It should be noted that not all researchers are eager or able to share their data. In addition to issues of confidentiality and privacy, other reasons for withholding data publication include research that results in proprietary products, time embargoes imposed by funding sources or industries, or a desire to publish the research findings in articles prior to releasing the data.[51] Cragin et al. conducted in-depth interviews with researchers to examine data sharing in more detail and found that research discipline was not the predominant factor in willingness to share research data.[52] Researchers were most willing to share their data with other colleagues in the same field. Also, "willingness to make data available increased as data were cleaned, processed, refined and analyzed in the course of research."[53] Several researchers were concerned due to personal experience, where their data had been misused, misinterpreted, and cherry-picked by industry to support efficacy claims about their products.

Another problem of concern to researchers is the lack of attribution or inaccurate data citation by other researchers who used their data.[54] International groups are working to make data identification and citation easier.

DataCite is dedicated to helping researchers discover, access, and reuse data.[55] The DataCite membership took the lead in developing the "Joint Declaration of Data Citation Principles"[56] and currently focuses on working with the publishing community to assign digital object identifiers (DOIs) to data sets to provide unique identifiers. While this cannot negate ethical problems, it certainly is a step in the right direction for proper citation. DataCite has also created a metadata scheme and best practices to facilitate consistent and accurate citation of data sets.[57]

When first implementing new research data services, a researcher's lack of awareness of the data services offered by the library may be a barrier to collaboration at the outset of the research planning stage. Librarians are often called upon for help in the middle of a project lifecycle, after data is collected, or in other cases when the project is finished and the researchers are seeking a place to archive their data. Librarians can enter the data lifecycle at any point to help with data curation, but the further into the research lifecycle, the more difficult it may become to apply best practices to the data curation process. The activities for each stage of the research lifecycle model provide context for the stages of the data lifecycle model, which in turn provides a framework for the data management plan.

Data Management Planning

A data management plan provides the written documentation that describes the data and the data events needed to support each stage of a research project's life-cycle model and identifies the persons responsible for each activity. Just as development of the data life-cycle model overlaps with development of the research life-cycle model, an outline of the data management plan will begin to take shape as decisions are made regarding the data life-cycle model.

It may seem counterintuitive to say that priorities for crafting the data management plan should focus on the researcher, not the data, but adopting a user focus will ensure that the data is fit for purpose. When the focus is solely on the data, the end result may be an elegant data management system that cannot be used by others or is not interoperable with other systems used by the particular discipline for discovery, access, storage, retrieval, and archiving. The best way to ensure that the user remains central to the plan is to work as a data management team, with members from the research project, library, research computing center, and other campus units with the required expertise.

Within a broad context, a data management plan can be viewed as consisting of three primary stages: the active research data phase (data planning prior to and during the research project), the end-of-project phase (review data documentation and data sharing plans, check adherence to ethical and legal policies), and the final postresearch archiving phase (review retention specifications, data growth, access, security plans, and preservation plan). Thinking in this broad context at the inception of the plan will enable decisions made for each component of the data management plan to result in the most effective use, reuse, and storage of the data.

Data management plans may take many forms and include different component parts. Data management plan checklists, which outline details of the content to include in the plan, are readily available. [58] While these checklists vary, some common components include an introduction, data description, documentation, metadata, intellectual property rights, backup and storage, security, dissemination and sharing, maintenance, archiving and preservation, data attribution, and plan administration. Figure 6.3 offers basic questions to consider for each category when developing a data management plan.

Most data management plans found in the literature are written for researchers, not librarians, and it may be unclear exactly what role the librarian has or where a librarian fits into the overall process of developing a data management plan. Ultimately, the researchers will make this decision— hopefully, with knowledge of the data services available to them. Generally, librarians serve as consultants in their areas of expertise, extending their knowledge to the research process and data collected in a given discipline to perform successfully as a data management plan consultant.

A good way to start a collaborative data management plan partnership is for librarians to reach out to researchers to create data curation profiles. [59] Developed by Purdue University and the University of Illinois, the data curation profile is an instrument that provides a structured method to outline and document information about a researcher's data needs throughout the multiple stages of the research process in a particular subject area. [60] The process for developing a data curation profile starts with the librarian conducting an in-depth interview with the researcher to identify requirements related to data curation in their particular area of research. That information is then used to create a profile in a concise, structured document that is suitable for sharing. [61] The profile information can then be incorporated into a data management plan. Because data curation profiles register the details of the research process in a specific subject field, they can be adapted to serve as a basis for developing future data curation plans for other research conducted in that subject domain. Purdue maintains a data curation profiles directory containing completed subject profiles that have been reviewed and deposited for sharing, reuse, and preservation. [62] Not only do data curation profiles provide in-depth details of a particular research process, they help break down cultural barriers by demonstrating the librarian's desire and ability to understand the researcher's work and data needs, which helps to develop a more trusting, collaborative relationship.

Data Management Planning Questions

Introduction: What is the context for the research and the data management plan? Who is the funder and what is the project ID? What internal and external policies apply to the data (funder, institution, researcher, journal)? Who is the contact person for the project? The data?

Data description: What type and format of data are needed to inform the research questions? Is there existing data? How will the data be collected (methods, equipment, software)? What will be the growth rate and will it change frequently? What conventions will be used for file organization and directory and file naming? Are tools or software needed to create/process/visualize the data?

Documentation: What documentation is needed to replicate the project and reuse the data (data collection procedures, codebooks, data dictionaries, data definitions, data processing and analysis methods, reports, publications, website)?

Metadata: What metadata standard, controlled vocabularies or ontologies will be used to describe the data? Do discipline specific standards exist? How will the metadata be created or captured? How will the different versions of data be tracked? Will technical, administrative and rights management metadata be used to facilitate discovery, retrieval, interoperability and sharing of the data?

Intellectual property rights: Who will hold the intellectual property rights to the data, and how will IP be protected if necessary. Will a Creative Commons license be used? Are there any copyright constraints (e.g., copyrighted data collection instruments) should be noted.

Backup and Storage: How will the data be backed-up and how often? What volume of storage is needed? What media/formats will be used? Where will the data be stored during the project? How will the data be stored, maintained, archived and preserved for the long term? What version(s) of the data will be retained and for how long, or will the data be discarded at the end of the project? What repositories are available for data storage and deposit? Are there subject specific repositories?

Security: What type of security is there to safeguard the data? Are there confidentiality, privacy, commercialization, high-security or ethical restrictions? How will data access be managed during the project?

Dissemination and sharing: Who is the audience? How will potential users discover and retrieve the data? Where and when will a report/article be publish? Will the data be shared? Will it be linked to the article? Is there an embargo period on access to the data and if so, how long? What tools/software are needed to access, visualize and retrieve the data? Will data access be mediated?

Maintenance, archiving and preservation: What data should be retained, shared and/or preserved? What are the foreseeable research uses for the data? Will the final format of the data files be in a sustainable format for long term access? Will supporting documentation be archived with the data? Who maintains the data after the project is completed? Are there subject archives suitable for the data? Are there costs for long-term storage?

Data attribution: How should the data be cited? Will the publisher assign a DOI? Where will the desired citation form be published?

Plan administration: Who is responsible for each activity or event in the data process; and how much will each activity or event cost? Who will assure that the Data Management Plan is followed? When will the plan be reviewed or revised?

Figure 6.3.   Data Management Planning Questions

Metadata for Research Data

"Metadata is structured data that describes a resource [i.e., research data], identifies its relationships to other resources and facilitates the discovery, management and use of a resource."[63] It provides the contextual basis to identify, authenticate, describe, locate, and manage research data and related resources in a precise and consistent way. Metadata can help researchers find their own data more efficiently by bringing consistency to all documents and data in a research project. When subject-specific metadata are applied, they extend consistency to other research projects in that same discipline. Using a standard metadata scheme to describe a data set facilitates interoperability and makes integration of data sets much easier. With the new cultural shift toward research transparency and data sharing, many journal publishers and subject repositories now designate specific metadata requirements for data deposit.

In the context of a data management plan, a strong case can be made for assigning metadata to research data, but many researchers are confused by the term *metadata* and do not understand the important functions that metadata serve. Based on a study conducted at Purdue University, Carlson notes that researchers "often do not have a sense of what metadata should be applied to their data set to enable it to be discovered, understood, administered or used by others."[64] Discipline-specific metadata schemes can be extremely complex, making them difficult and time consuming to apply. In response to this problem, many schemes have identified a *core set* of elements that create a basic level of description; examples include Dublin Core, Darwin Core, and TEI Lite. Researchers can also select essential elements from a specific scheme to create their own core metadata, but this should always be documented for future understanding and use. Metadata librarians can provide a wealth of knowledge and expertise to assist with these activities, but it is important when developing library data services that outreach efforts to researchers are clear, precise, and jargon free.

Types and Functions of Metadata

Many metadata standards are developed and maintained by discipline communities to support the specific needs of that group. Each community tends to define different types of metadata grouped by the functions they perform. Greenberg defines the general functions of research metadata as discover, manage, control rights, identify versions, certify authenticity, indicate status, situate geospatially and temporally, and describe processes and architectural structure.[65] Librarians typically think in terms of the more generic FRBR (Functional Requirements for Bibliographic Records) user tasks—find, identify, select, and obtain—and categorize metadata functions as descriptive, administrative, and technical, containing subcategories such as intellectual property rights and usage, events, preservation, and structure. There is not universal agreement on the definitions for these categories, and subcategories are often considered primary categories in their own right. These three broad categories are not mutually exclusive. Metadata elements can overlap boundaries, complicating any categorization of elements. For example, is the time period of data collection a descriptive element, an event, or both? Regardless of how they are grouped, the important consideration is that the functional requirements are appropriate to the specific research project and data sets.

Descriptive research metadata performs functions similar to metadata used in library catalogs but uses many different elements and standards. In the broad view, research metadata is used to enable researchers to *find* the data sets based on their search terms, *identify* which data sets are appropriate for their research needs, *select* the best data set for their purposes, and *obtain* the selected data set. Descriptive metadata for research data sets, however, will vary depending on the subject domain and type of data and will contain data-specific elements such as data identifiers; methods of data collection and source of data; variable names, labels, and groups; sampling procedures; greater specificity/technical subjects; geospatial and temporal information; and data citation form. Descriptive metadata equates to Greenberg's functions of discover, identify versions, situate geospatially and temporally, and indicate status.

Administrative metadata provides information that is needed to manage and maintain data sets. This is where much of the data life-cycle information is recorded. These metadata elements might provide information about the data management plan, including names and contact information of persons responsible for various data-related tasks; file sizes and naming conventions; data processing methods; equipment and software used to process and analyze data; maintenance and update frequency; status of the data (raw, processed, final); tools necessary to view the data; and data storage information. Administrative metadata also includes rights information about ownership, intellectual property, usage data (including restrictions on use, reuse, and sharing); and event data (including information about data capture, integration with other data, observational occurrences, information about data processing and analysis, and data retention or disposal information). Administrative metadata equates to Greenberg's functions of manage, control rights, certify authenticity, and describe processes.

Technical metadata includes information on the metadata scheme structure used; the technical specifications for format types, encoding, viewing, processing, storing, and exchanging data sets; data validation methods; and information needed to migrate and curate the data for long-term preservation as software and hardware change over time. Technical metadata may also include structures used to link the data set to related objects such as journal articles, different versions of the data, and additional forms of documentation related to the data set.[66] Technical metadata equates to Greenberg's functions to manage, certify authenticity, and architectural structure. Consistent data values (i.e., standards) are critical to all categories of metadata to ensure the most useful data organization and description, provide relevant data retrieval and integration, and facilitate preservation, sharing, and reuse.

Standards

The Environmental Protection Agency offers this definition for data standards: "Data standards are agreed-upon definitions, formats, and procedural rules for commonly used data sets that are needed to reduce the complexity of data manipulation and to make the exchange and integration of data more efficient."[67] Standards are an essential part of creating high-quality, trustworthy metadata, for without standards automatic metadata creation, discovery, interoperability, data sharing, and long-term preservation would be a considerable challenge. Key to the success of data curation, standards provide tested and trusted models that define best practices. In the metadata environment, several types of standards are used, including those for structured metadata schemes, content, vocabularies, and syntax. Some standards (i.e., standard metadata schemes) may incorporate other standards, such as directions for how to enter data content and specifications for what vocabularies to use for data values and what syntax scheme to use.

Structured Metadata Schemes

Standardized metadata schemes define the number and types of elements in the metadata structure and range from a simple general scheme such as the Dublin Core Metadata Element Set (DCMES), with only fifteen elements designed to describe all types of resources at a high level of granularity, to subject-specific metadata schemes with dozens of elements that provide great depth of detail, such as the ISO 19115-1:2014 Geographic Metadata scheme.[68] The DCMES is the most commonly used international metadata standard, largely due to its high level of description and simplicity, which enable it to function as a switching language to facilitate interoperability and easy metadata harvesting. When metadata schemes other than DCMES are used to describe a data set and are then mapped to the DCMES elements, it expands the ability to share research data exponentially.

Subject-specific metadata schemes proliferate across the wide spectrum of research disciplines and it would be impossible to cite them all here. Determining which metadata standard is most appropriate for a given data set is a complex and, as noted, confusing decision. The Data Documentation Initiative (DDI) metadata scheme is used widely for social science data sets, for it uses a hierarchical structure that describes the research project, the data sets used in the project, and the variables used in the data sets.[69] The ISO 19115-1:2014 Geographic Metadata scheme is used by many disciplines, but a majority of subject-specific communities have devised their own metadata. To alleviate the problem of finding the right metadata, the Data Curation Centre (DCC) maintains a discipline-based list that includes not only information about a metadata standard but also application profiles, tools to im-

plement the standards, and use cases of data repositories that currently implement them.[70] The five broad DCC disciplines include:

1. Biology (10 schemes, 13 extensions, 12 tools, and 30 use cases)
2. Earth Science (9 schemes, 16 extensions, 14 tools, and 27 use cases)
3. Physical Science (7 schemes, 6 extensions, 13 tools, and 19 uses cases)
4. Social Science and Humanities (5 schemes, 3 extensions, 6 tools, and 12 use cases)
5. General Research Data (8 schemes, 4 extensions, 5 tools, and 8 use cases)

The DCC listing has a strong European focus and is by no means comprehensive. Other subject-specific metadata lists include the JISC Digital Media Guide[71] and the Society of American Archivists Metadata Directory.[72] The most comprehensive inventory of metadata standards for the cultural heritage domain is Riley's visual mapping of the metadata landscape, which includes over one hundred standards for metadata schemes, content standards, controlled vocabularies, and syntax, structural, and markup standards.[73] Large government agencies such as the National Aeronautics and Space Administration (NASA),[74] National Oceanic and Atmospheric Association (NOAA),[75] and the EPA[76] have research data and metadata standards for their agencies' projects to provide consistent data description for data sharing and integrating with other data sets. Finally, many research university libraries regularly include lists of metadata in their guidelines for data management plans. Guidelines that were created using the Springshare LibGuides tool are open access and can be searched on the LibGuides Community website.[77]

Content Standards

Content standards are the formal rules that provide general guidelines or detailed requirements for each metadata element. This type of standard acts as an input guide for content for metadata elements that are not automatically populated or when no controlled vocabulary or syntax applies.[78] A content standard might explain how to enter a person's name, when to use capitalization, or how to format a date. Content standards are not new to librarians, as all cataloging rules up to Resource Description and Access control metadata content. Examples of other formal content standards include Cataloging Cultural Standards (CCO), Describing Archives: A Content Standard (DACS), the Federal Geographic Data Committee's Content Standard for Digital Geospatial Metadata (FGDC CSDGM), and Access to Biological Collections Data (ABCD). Informal content standards are the best practices defined when a new subject-specific metadata is created and should be recorded in an application profile.

Content standards also specify what information to use for the values of specific fields. For example, a content standard might stipulate what label is assigned to a particular metadata element; indicate whether a specific element is mandatory, recommended, or optional; or identify a specific thesaurus to be used for the subject or spatial elements.

Vocabularies, Taxonomies, Ontologies

Controlled vocabularies are another type of standard that is used to bring accuracy, clarity, and consistency to metadata. In its broadest sense, a controlled vocabulary is any standardized list of terms, or set of words, selected by a community to describe and bring meaning to a data set or a group of data sets. Some vocabularies control for synonyms, disambiguate similar objects, or are used for indexing and provide a semantic relationship structure. Vocabulary control greatly improves precision and relevance in retrieval by identifying and collocating equivalent and related objects. Research data semantic vocabularies are frequently designed to be specific to the terminology used by the subject community.

The continuum of vocabulary control moves from the simple list, subject heading lists, and authority files to the more complex thesaurus, taxonomy, and ontology structures. A list is a simple group of terms for a category of things. The terms may be coded data to use as surrogates for such things as countries, languages, variables, and roles. They are widely used in dropdown menus to limit choice as a feature of a metadata input template and are especially useful in the research metadata context to assist data entry and ensure consistency.

Both authority files and subject heading lists are an integral part of technical services workflow, needing no further explanation here. Many general and subject-specific authority files are used to describe research data, and domain-specific metadata best practices will identify these.

Over the years, the Library of Congress Subject Headings (LCSH) have moved in the direction of a thesaurus by using standard relationship indicators, but LCSH is excluded from the thesaurus category because it does not maintain a hierarchical structure. Subject heading lists describe a wide range of topics and do not contain the level of subject depth that is needed for a very specific subject discipline, but depending on the type of research, the LCSH may be adequate for some data sets.

Increasing in complexity, taxonomies, also called classification schemes, are collections of controlled vocabulary terms, or a classification code, organized into a hierarchical structure primarily in an online environment. Each tier of the hierarchy inherits the attributes of the tier immediately above and becomes more specific as you move down the hierarchy. Taxonomies are limited to broader/narrower relationships with no particular entry term, since any term may be part of multiple hierarchies.[79] This allows the context of the vocabulary to change depending on the preferred term at the top of the taxonomy and makes them useful for searching in the online research data environment. The term *taxonomy* has become a catchall used by many in the online environment to refer to any type of vocabulary, causing confusion by ignoring distinctions among the different types of subject standards.

A thesaurus represents the vocabulary of a specific subject; it adds layers of complexity to a taxonomy and differs in a number of ways. A thesaurus is arranged in a known order and strict hierarchical structure so that the various relationships among terms are displayed clearly and identified by standardized relationship indicators (BT, NT, RT, etc.).[80] Not all terms in thesauri are preferred terms, so in addition to the broader/narrower relationships used in taxonomies, a thesaurus includes *Use For* (UF) and *Use* to identify the preferred term and refer from the nonpreferred term, thus controlling for synonyms. Thesauri also include relationship terms (RT) for subjects that are related to the preferred term but not included in same hierarchy. Context is provided in thesauri in the form of scope notes (SN). Thesauri are among the most heavily used controlled vocabularies for data and are available for most subjects ranging from the *NASA Thesaurus*[81] to the *Art and Architecture Thesaurus*.[82]

The final type of controlled vocabulary on the continuum is the ontology. Ontologies define the concepts and semantic relationships in a specific knowledge domain and are presented as a formal model. Ontologies represent the most advanced point on the continuum, in the sense that taxonomies and thesauri are fixed vocabulary languages for subject description, while ontologies have open vocabularies.[83] In a closed vocabulary language, the number of concepts is open, but the language used to describe them is considered closed if the allowable relationships are fixed and limited. Since taxonomies allow only one relationship in the hierarchy (BT/NT) and thesauri use a limited number of relationship types (BT, NT, RT, UF/Use, and SN), both are closed vocabularies. Ontologies, on the other hand, allow the creator of the subject description language to define many more semantic relationships—for example, hasColor, isSister, hasDisease—making it more flexible and robust.[84]

As with taxonomies, people use the word *ontology* to mean any type of controlled vocabulary, adding to existing terminological confusion. Ontologies, like taxonomies and thesauri, are developed for a specific domain, making them an important vocabulary resource for research data sets. The original Greek term meant "the science of being" and was used by a branch of metaphysics that attempted "to organize the universe and its components into a scheme with explicit formulation of their possible relations."[85] With the advancement of technology in the late twentieth century, the term was co-opted by the information architecture and science domain and repurposed for use in information retrieval.[86] As an open vocabulary with many allowable semantic relationships, ontologies retain hierarchies but are increasingly structured as a Web network and are largely developed outside the immediate library community. Because of this, the language used in defining the components and structure of ontologies may sometimes be a bit unfamiliar to librarians, but most of the concepts are not. Gruber offered the most well-known and succinct definition of ontology: "an explicit formal specification of a shared conceptualization."[87] Vanopstal et al. offer an excellent explanation of Gruber's definition by parsing the component parts:

> Firstly, "explicit" means that the concepts included in the ontology are clearly defined, as are the constraints on their use. "Formal" refers to the language of the ontology. A formal language is computer-readable: the computer "understands" the relationships—also called "formal semantics"—within the ontology. This way, they can be used to support computer applications. . . . The last components of the definition, *shared* and *conceptualization*, imply that this abstract model of phenomena in the world has been agreed upon by a group of users or experts.[88]

Thus an ontology has clearly defined terms, which are vetted by experts in the subject domain, and tells how they can be used; however, the term *formal specification*, or *formal language*, might prove confusing. In this context, it does not refer to the language of subject terms; it means a type of structural language, such as the Resource Description Framework (RDF).

Ontologies consist of concepts, properties and instances. Concepts are the primary element and are grouped into classes. An instance (also called an individual) is a specific member of a class, that is, the real-world object referred to by the concept. Properties, or attributes, define the relationships between classes and instances. Both classes and properties may have subclasses and subproperties (a parent-child relationship), both of which inherit the characteristics of the parent class or property.

When the terms and relationships are clearly defined and a formal structural framework such as RDF is implemented, computers can use the hierarchical class/subclass structure to make inferences about like things. For example, if the subclass *cuckoo clock* is a type of class *clock*, and class *clock* is a type of *timepiece*, then a *cuckoo clock* must be a type of *timepiece*. When encoded in RDF-based ontology language, such as the Resource Description Framework Schema (RDFS) or the Web Ontology Language (OWL), the ontology becomes a computer-actionable model that enables logical inferencing.[89] Tools exist to help create ontologies. *Protégé* (http://protege.stanford.edu/) is one of the more popular applications for this purpose.

Syntax Standards

Syntax standards are the final type of standards discussed for metadata in this chapter. They provide the encoding/packaging to make the metadata machine readable and enable data to be integrated and exchanged with different systems. Librarians have worked with electronic syntax standards for many decades in the form of the MARC record format. In recent years, with the advent of the web, new markup languages are used.

The mother tongue of markup is the Standard Generalized Markup Language (SGML), from which other markup languages are derived. The most commonly used encoding standard today is the eXtensible Markup language (XML), which is designed to *describe* data and focuses on what the data is, as opposed to HTML, which was designed to *format and display* data on a web page. By removing the display function, XML becomes a more flexible and powerful syntax for exchanging data—the primary function needed for linking and transferring data on the web. Since no tags are predefined, an XML schema can be created for a general or specific subject domain, making it adaptable for metadata and research data sets. XML is used widely by metadata schemes to provide the encoding structure. Other types of XML applications extend the functionality to enable searching. One important feature of XML is the ability to use namespaces, a type of uniform resource identifier (URI) that links directly to the vocabulary term. Rather than entering the literal name for a concept like *Brooklyn Bridge*, a URI can be entered that links to the specific term in the Library of Congress Subject Authority File (http://id.loc.gov/authorities/subjects/sh85017204).

The different types of standards used for metadata are the critical underpinnings for systems that describe, maintain, process, discover, integrate, exchange, share, reuse, and preserve research data. A vital accompaniment to a metadata scheme is documentation of the standards employed and the best practices for using the scheme. This type of documentation is especially important when project personnel change, or when altering an existing metadata scheme.

Application Profiles

Sometimes no metadata scheme exists that can meet all the needs of a particular research project. To avoid a proliferation of schemes and duplication of work, one should check that no subject scheme already exists that could be adequate for the specific community or local project needs. Modifying an existing scheme could be a useful option, but the modified scheme should follow accepted standards to allow metadata and data sets to be interoperable with data in other repositories. The modified scheme should be fully documented so others will be able to find the data and reuse the newly modified metadata scheme for similar projects.

If only a minimum number of elements from one metadata scheme are used, this is referred to as a *core* scheme. For example, if only ten elements of the ISO 19115-1:2014 metadata standard are used, the modified scheme might be called a Geographic Core Element Set. A modified scheme is a new *application* of the existing scheme that should document, or *profile*, the way it will be used or extended. The final result is creation of an application profile (AP). APs consist of data elements drawn from one or more metadata schemes and customized for a particular local application.

Many application profiles exist, as well as AP data models for creating new ones. The Dublin Core Metadata Initiative (DCMI) group created the Dublin Core Application Profile (DCAP) model to assist the AP development process.[90] "The DCAP defines metadata records which meet specific application needs while providing semantic interoperability with other applications on the basis of globally defined vocabularies and models."[91]

The first step in the AP development process is to determine the functional requirements, or what you want the metadata to accomplish—for example, interoperate with other schemes, assist in identifying intellectual property rights, provide information for preservation migration, and so on. The next step is to create a domain model that characterizes the things that exist in the subject community's universe that the metadata will describe, such as the concepts, people, events, and relationships that exist between them—for example, temperature data recorded by person X using instrument Y. Following the domain model, identify the list of metadata elements needed for the metadata scheme (for the data concept alone, this domain needs elements for data set identifier, name, type, date, version—the list goes on for each element needed for persons and instrument type). The next step is to define the specific elements and provide guidelines for how they are used. This data set description is usually formatted as a table and provides, at the minimum, the element name, label, status (mandatory, recommended, optional, etc.), repeatability, type, and source of data value, standards used for vocabularies and syntax for each element. Figure 6.4 shows the more complex Singapore Framework, which provides a three-tiered contextual model of the DCAP. The top tier diagrams the *application profile* layer; the middle tier diagrams the *domain standards* used; and the bottom tier shows the *foundation standards*, including the metadata syntax and structural standards. The things documented will vary depending on the environment in which the metadata will operate. If the environment is the Semantic Web and linked data, the content categories will include *namespace* information as the source for a particular element.

The Semantic Web and Linked Data for Libraries and Research

Interest in ontology development has surged due to the convergence of three factors: (1) research data migration to the digital environment, (2) the web providing the platform for linking data, and (3) the Semantic Web gaining a foothold among researchers and librarians. As noted above, ontologies are constructed to function in the web environment and rely on sophisticated linking architecture for their structure and use. To understand better the functional application of ontologies, therefore, we must be familiar with the Semantic Web and linked data.

Miller describes the current web environment as a web of linked *documents* with unstructured data that relies on manually created hyperlinks that do not specify the nature of relationships among records; searches that match keywords in documents; and relevance-ranking algorithms. This creates a system suitable for humans but not terribly precise and of little use to machines.[92] In contrast, he describes the Semantic Web as a distributed web of *linked data* that connects structured, semantically meaningful metadata using semantically meaningful links, making parts of the web similar to a database with database functionality. The use of standardized vocabularies along with this linking data architecture makes the Semantic Web system suitable for

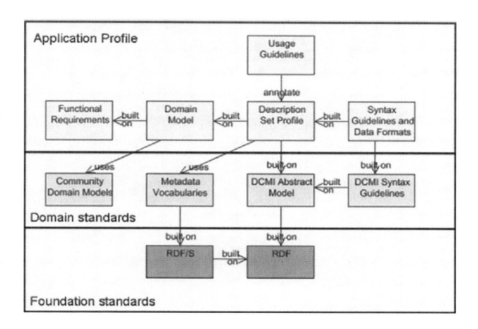

Figure 6.4.   The Singapore Framework. *Reproduction of the DCMI Singapore Framework. http://dublincore.org/documents/singapore-framework*

machine queries that will result in greater retrieval of more relevant search results and the ability to integrate data sets more easily, improving access for humans.[93] Openness is the bedrock for both the Semantic Web and linked data, for if data remains encapsulated in closed databases or library catalogs, where it is accessible only by searching each database separately, the Semantic Web and the linked data structure will be limited in its retrieval capacity. The cultural shift to open research data reinforces the importance of both the Semantic Web and linked open data capabilities.

What Miller describes as the Semantic Web is the architecture for *linked data*. In essence, linked data represents metadata *records* deconstructed into individual components of *data* (i.e., elements), rendering the data within the record structure independently retrievable. To accomplish this and maintain the context provided by the full metadata record, it is critical to use controlled vocabularies for consistency and a structure that provides for inclusiveness of a metadata record, while separately linking to the individual elements. The Resource Description Framework (RDF) data model meets this need.

The extensive literature on the RDF data model is coupled with literature on linked data. As the MARC communication format provides the structure for library catalog records, RDF is the communication architecture for linked data, and as MARC tags are the syntax for catalog records, XML is the normative syntax for the RDF, although other markup languages can also be used. The basic RDF model is expressed as a graphic using a three-part RDF statement (RDF triples) about a particular resource and its relationships. RDF statements are expressed as a Subject—Predicate—Object (e.g., <This chapter><has creator><Sherry Vellucci>). Each element in an RDF statement should have a unique identifier expressed by a URI that links to the specific term in a standard source, elevating authority files and controlled vocabularies to the gateway of linked data. In the Semantic Web linked data environment, each metadata element may have one or more RDF statements, and each metadata record can contain numerous RDF triples. The example above would be expressed in RDF as:

```
<dc:title xml:lang="en" rdf:>This Book</dc:title>
<dc:creator rdf:resource=http://viaf.org/viaf/106125310"/>
```

For the computer to understand what the syntax is saying, the beginning of the record declares that this record uses the namespaces for RDF, XML, Dublin Core, and the Virtual International Authority File. If we had a namespace for "This Book," that URI would also be declared.

While research data curation is becoming an established service, libraries have been slower to transform catalog records into linked data. Although linked data may be easier for catalogers to grasp because it deals with the elements of the familiar bibliographic record, conversion to linked data would involve enormous numbers of catalog records and a better understanding of RDF and XML. Recently, however, linked data appears to be gaining support from the library community with growing evidence that OCLC and the Library of Congress (LC) are exploring the possibilities for making linked library data accessible to a global user population.

LC has implemented a Linked Data Service,[94] which offers an impressive array of authority file, general and specific controlled vocabularies, classification, MARC languages, code lists, type lists, and so on converted into URIs and many different formats, including RDF and XML. This extensive project provides preformatted values for many components of linked data triples that will be useful for research data sets and lowering the bar for libraries to enter the Semantic Web community. For examples of linked data in context, Southwick and Lampert's presentation on RDF and linked data offers an excellent overview of its use for a library digital collection, accompanied by many useful examples.[95]

As of this writing, OCLC Research is exploring several different aspects of linked data, including an extensive survey to discover who is currently using linked data; which institutions are consuming or publishing linked data and why; and descriptions of technical details, production examples, and implementer advice. The results show a small group of respondents have actually implemented linked data projects. Of the 122 respondents, ninety-six have implemented a linked data project and seventy-six projects were described. "Of the 76 projects: 27 are not yet in production; 13 have been in production for less than one year; 12 have been in production for more than one year but less than two years; 24 have been in production for more than two years."[96] It will be interesting to follow up to see how quickly the implementation trend moves forward, particularly after OCLC fully implements a linked data WorldCat.

PROFESSIONAL DEVELOPMENT

Cultural Barriers

Data management is the area in which technical services librarians' knowledge and expertise can shine, but there may be cultural barriers to address before some researchers are willing to change their current data management practices to enable librarians to provide this service. Pryor identified two challenges that librarians must overcome: the lack of "parity of esteem with the research community," which leads to a lack of credibility; and a need to "persuade and demonstrate that they have a material contribution to make, one that is likely to be of tangible benefit to researchers and the research programme."[97] To collaborate effectively, it is incumbent upon librarians to understand the nature of the research process, the types of data, and data collection methods in a researcher's subject field to establish credibility and trust. Liaison librarians have a depth of knowledge in specific disciplines and subjects and could serve as internal consultants to help librarian colleagues expand their knowledge base. Preparing for and conducting an interview with a researcher to develop a data curation profile is one of the best ways to learn about the research process in a specific subject domain.

Resources for Professional Development

Prior to focusing on the details of data management planning and curation, librarians should begin by familiarizing themselves with the policies and procedures of the local institution; this information is usually maintained by the Office of Research. Websites of government funding agencies provide guidelines to meet their data management plan requirements, and these should always be followed when submitting a grant proposal. Page length limitations are often set for the data management plan portion of a funding proposal, which can restrict the amount of detail included, but that does not preclude adding greater depth of detail to the project's operational data management plan. Librarians should be aware that different directorates within the same large agency, such as the NSF, will have different requirements. Many librarians create data management and curation LibGuides to make this information accessible to researchers at their institution. The majority of LibGuides can be shared freely and reused by other librarians. As of this writing, over seventy data management LibGuides are available from the LibGuides Community website.[98]

Fortunately, a great deal of information is available online. The Digital Curation Centre in the United Kingdom provides a wealth of information on their website under the *Resources* and *Training* tabs, including tutorials, checklists, and briefing papers.[99] The DataOne website (Data Online Network for Earth) has a page for librarians called the Librarian Outreach Toolkit with a "Primer on Data Management," marketing materials, and talking points for discussions with researchers.[100] The *Education* tab contains ten downloadable lesson modules that cover most areas of the planning process and a database with information, and links to a variety of software applications useful at different stages of the data life cycle. DataOne also links to the Data Management Planning Tool (DMPTool), which "is a means for researchers to develop practical data management plans consistent with agency requirements and available resources."[101] In addition to being a repository for social science research data, the Inter-university Consortium for Political and Social Research (ICPSR) website has a section titled *Resources for Instructors*, including learning guides with exercises for teaching students about data, a section on data management and curation that includes suggested metadata elements for DDI metadata and information on data to exclude for confidentiality purposes, and a selection of curation tools and services.[102] Librarians should be aware that most resources provided by these organizations are targeted at researchers, but they all provide excellent education materials for librarians as well.

The Data Curation Profile website at Purdue University contains a toolkit composed of a user's guide, an interviewer's manual, an interview worksheet, and a template for creating the data curation profile.[103] The project also maintains an open-access repository of profiles for a variety of subject areas and encourages librarians to deposit and share their locally created profiles. The depth of information provided by the Data Curation Profile website is an invaluable resource for librarians just beginning to develop research data services, or a timesaver for librarians more experienced with this type of data service.

MANTRA is a free online course for research data management training offered by EDINA, the designated National Data Centre at the University of Edinburgh.[104] The self-paced curriculum consists of eight modules covering the important components of data management planning and data handling tutorials, using SPSS, R, ArcGIS, and NVivo software. Each module consists of twenty-five slides that include videos, links to resources, templates, and brief quizzes. MANTRA also includes a "Do-It-Yourself Research Data Management Training Kit for Libraries."

LC provides an online curriculum, Digital Preservation Outreach and Education. Although some of the educational and informational materials are not so much a curriculum as links to the information, the site provides a considerable amount of information about still-image and multimedia data formats, reports, and other information from the National Digital Stewardship Alliance and standards used at LC.[105]

Finally, a group of northeast research libraries, led by the University of Massachusetts Medical School Library, was funded to create the "Frameworks for a Data Management Curriculum."[106] Differing from the previously cited curricula, the framework provides an outline of the necessary components to teach data management. "The curriculum [was] designed as a series of seven course modules in order to allow maximum flexibility for customizing instruction."[107] The modules can be used together as a complete course on data management or individually to target a particular learning need. Each module consists of lesson plans, reading lists, student exercises, research data management cases, and assessments. Each lesson plan consists of learning objectives, lecture outline, activities, assessment, and readings. While many of the linked resources are health care related, the extensive curriculum is discipline neutral and can be easily adapted to any subject area.

Many more resources are available in books, in journal articles, and on the web, which cover every aspect of data management, curation, and preservation. Information on each component of the topic could fill hundreds of gigabytes of space. The broad range of disciplines makes it difficult to discuss a topic from a single point of view. Fortunately, information about data management curation and preservation is available for many specific subject disciplines. The web linking system facilitates discovery of these resources and offers another reason for the move toward contextual linked data!

CONCLUSION

The dramatic and ongoing changes in higher education and academic libraries signal paradigm shifts for the operations in technical services departments. Pressure for greater accountability by education communities filters down to the faculty and staff. The faculty is asked to bring in more research grant money, and irrespective of funding, they are expected to conduct research and involve students in the process. Providing research data services to faculty and students is an excellent and highly visible way to demonstrate the library's integration into the research life of the institution and affords an assessable metric for accountability.

The vast amount of literature on research data management indicates the growing importance of data curation and data management planning. It seems likely that the number of agencies requiring data management plans and open access to data sets will only increase. Big science research projects rely on grant funds, and researchers must work to deadlines. Several authors cited in this chapter reported that data curation was not a high priority in terms of researcher time. If graduate students are assigned this task, they will need training in data management—an area where librarians excel. Carlson reminds us that the majority of research conducted campuswide is *small* research projects operating with little funding and a small number of staff; he conjectures that this is probably true for most universities. These small research projects could be the low-hanging fruit for launching research data services.

Much of the process of data management is a collaborative effort—one in which librarians in all sectors of technical services and beyond will have future roles. Librarians in acquisitions and collection development will collaborate with researchers on acquiring existing data sets through purchase or licensing. Knowledgeable catalogers will help organize research documentation, identify standard controlled vocabularies, and provide guidance and best practices for building new taxonomies and ontologies. Metadata specialists will identify appropriate metadata standards, modify existing schemes, and create APs. Scholarly communication librarians can assist with details of depositing data sets in institutional repositories and help locate existing subject repositories. Information technologists are needed to upgrade existing technology to accommodate digital data sets and install or build applications for new data services.

Collaboration must extend outside the technical services department to other areas of the library and campus. Archivists will work with metadata specialists on digital data archiving and preservation. Reference and instruction librarians are generally the most experienced at offering information literacy classes. Instruction will extend to data literacy, which will be taught collaboratively, with each module assigned to a library expert in that particular area. Adept at the reference interview, reference and liaison librarians will be assets for interviewing researchers to develop a data curation profile. Metadata specialists, catalogers, and others involved in data management and curation will participate in planning the data curation profile interview. And harking back to Wakimoto, collaboration between the library, research computing, and the research office is critical for the success of any research data services.

Finally, everyone will have to ramp up their knowledge and skills for the specific role they will play in research data services offered by the library. It will be critical for librarians to understand the research process in specific subject areas, the flow of the data life cycle, the process of developing a data management plan, and the use of standards and application profiles. Familiarity with the Semantic Web and the linked open data structure will be essential for future catalogers and metadata librarians alike. Of course, not everyone will be expert in all areas, but collaboration among members of the research data services team will cover all areas in depth.

Research data services will not have a meteoric implementation as a full-blown program overnight. Librarians must learn what local research services are needed, and what is already available. They must decide on the types and extent of services that can be realistically offered and identify the resources needed for the program to grow. Start small and plan for the future. According to the ACRL "Environmental Scan 2013," "There will likely be a substantial role for librarians in curating, managing, and preserving data. Many predict that professional opportunities will increasingly be centered in this area through the retraining, reorganizing, and repositioning of staff." Yes, research data services will be in the future of technical services, and it will be an interesting and stimulating future indeed.

NOTES

1. Association of College and Research Libraries Research Planning and Review Committee, "2012 Top Ten Trends in Academic Libraries: A Review of the Trends and Issues Affecting Academic Libraries in Higher Education," *College and Research Libraries News* 73, no. 6 (2012): 312, http://crln.acrl.org.

2. Becky Yoose and Jody Perkins, "The Linked Open Data Landscape in Libraries and Beyond," *Journal of Library Metadata* 13, nos. 2–3: 197–211, doi:10.1080/19386389.2013.826075.

3. Charles W. Bailey, "Research Data Curation Bibliography," version 3, June 17, 2013, http://digital-scholarship.org/rdcb/rdcb.htm. In this 2013 version, Bailey cites 235 books and articles on data curation alone.

4. Association of College and Research Libraries Research Planning and Review Committee, "Top Ten Trends in Academic Libraries: A Review of the Trends and Issues Affecting Academic Libraries in Higher Education," *College and Research Libraries News* 75, no. 6 (2014): 294–302.

5. Ibid., 294–95.

6. Library Information and Technology Association, "Top Tech Trends—Midwinter 2014," http://www.ala.org/lita/2014midwinter. Top Tech Trends is a LITA featured session at every ALA conference.

7. Tyler Walters and Katherine Skinner, *New Roles for New Times: Digital Curation Preservation, Report Prepared for the Association of Research Libraries* (Washington, DC: Association of Research Libraries, 2011), http://www.arl.org/storage/documents/publications/nrnt_digital_curation17mar11.pdf.

8. The policy was updated to a mandate in 2008. In February 2013 the Office of Science and Technology issued a memorandum outlining a new policy on "increasing access to the results of federally funded scientific data" that included digital data sets as well as peer-reviewed publications. See http://www.whitehouse.gov/sites/default/files/microsites/ostp/ostp_public_access_memo_2013.pdf.

9. The National Information Standards Association (NISO), *Recommended Practices for Online Supplemental Journal Article Materials*, January 2013, http://www.niso.org/apps/group_public/download.php/10055/RP-15-2013_Supplemental_Materials.pdf. The recommendation covers accompanying data sets, metadata, and metadata for objects stored in local repositories.

10. White House, "Executive Order: Making Open and Machine Readable the New Default for Government Information," press release, May 9, 2013, http://www.whitehouse.gov/the-press-office/2013/05/09/executive-order-making-open-and-machine-readable-new-default-government.

11. *Open Data Charter*, https://www.gov.uk/government/publications/open-data-charter. The five Principles are: (1) open data by default; (2) quality and quantity; (3) usable by all; (4) releasing data for improved governance; and (5) releasing data for innovation.

12. United States Government, *U.S. Open Data Action Plan*, May 9, 2014, http://www.whitehouse.gov/sites/default/files/microsites/ostp/us_open_data_action_plan.pdf.

13. Clifford A. Lynch and Joan K. Lippincott, "Institutional Repository Deployment in the United States as of Early 2005," *D-Lib Magazine* 11, no. 9 (September 2005): doi:10.1045/september2005-lynch.

14. Anna Gold, "Cyberinfrastructure, Data, and Libraries, Part 1: A Cyberinfrastructure Primer for Librarians," *D-Lib Magazine* 13, nos. 9–10 (2007), doi:10.1045/september2007-gold-pt1; "Cyberinfrastructure, Data, and Libraries, Part 2: Libraries and the Data Challenge: Roles and Actions for Libraries," *D-Lib Magazine* 13, nos. 9–10 (2007), doi:10.1045/september2007-gold-pt2.

15. Graham Pryor, ed., *Managing Research Data* (London: Facet Publishing, 2012), 2–3.

16. E. Deumens et al., "Research Data Lifecycle Management: Tools and Guidelines," June 17, 2011, http://ufdc.ufl.edu/IR00000570/00001.

17. Erin Bartolo and Jill Hurst-Wahl, "Curating Library Data, Big Data, Data Sets: Using Big Data for Library Advocacy," Syracuse University School of Information Studies, September 27, 2013, http://www.slideshare.net/jill_hw/curating-library-data-big-data-data-sets?qid=d0642ffe-dde6-447a-9b46-2c64646cc852&v=default&b=&from_search=1.

18. Kathryn Lage, Barbara Losoff, and Jack Maness, "Receptivity to Library Involvement in Scientific Data Curation: A Case Study at the University of Colorado Boulder," *portal: Libraries and the Academy* 11, no. 4 (2011): 915–37, doi:10.1353/pla.2011.0049.

19. Ibid.

20. Ibid., 922.

21. Gail Steinhart et al., "Prepared to Plan? A Snapshot of Researcher Readiness to Address Data Management Planning Requirements," *Journal of eScience Librarianship* 1, no. 2 (2012): 63–78, doi:10.7191/jeslib.2012.1008.

22. Ibid., 77.

23. Lori Jahnke, Andrew Asher, and Spencer D. C. Keralis, *The Problem of Data* (Washington, DC: Council on Library and Information Resources, 2012), 15.

24. Carol Tenopir, B. Birch, and S. Allard, "Academic Libraries and Research Data Services: Current Practices and Plans for the Future," white paper, Association of College & Research Libraries, June 2012, http://www.ala.org/acrl/sites/ala.org.acrl/files/content/publications/whitepapers/Tenopir_Birch_Allard.pdf.

25. Jina Choi Wakimoto, "Developing Research Data Management Services," *EDUCAUSE Review Online*, February 26, 2013, http://www.educause.edu/ero/article/developing-research-data-management-services.

26. Ibid.

27. Tenopir, Birch and Allard, "Academic Libraries and Research Data Services," 8.

28. ACRL Research Planning and Review Committee, "Environmental Scan 2013," April 2013, http://www.ala.org/acrl/sites/ala.org.acrl/files/content/publications/whitepapers/EnvironmentalScan13.pdf.

29. Of the 330 articles published between January 2005 and June 2014 on data curation that are cited in Bailey's "Bibliography," 73 percent were published between January 2011 and June 2014, a period of only three and a half years.

30. David Fearon Jr., Betsy Gunia, and Barbara E. Pralle, *SPEC Kit 334: Research Data Management Services* (Chicago: Association of Research Libraries, 2013).

31. University of California Curation Center, Data Management Planning Tool, https://dmp.cdlib.org/index.html.

32. Fearon, Gunia, and Pralle, *Spec Kit 334*, 12.

33. Tenopir, Birch, and Allard, "Academic Libraries and Research Data Services," 3.

34. Mark Dahl, "Data-Driven Liberal Arts: The Library Role," *Academic Commons: For the Liberal Education Community*, July 24, 2014, http://www.academiccommons.org/2014/07/24/data-driven-liberal-arts-the-library-role/; Megan Toups and Michael Hughes, "When Data Curation Isn't: A Redefinition for Liberal Arts Universities," *Journal of Library Administration* 53, no. 4, (2013): 223–33, doi:10.1080/01930826.2013.865386; Tenopir, Birch, and Allard, "Academic Libraries and Research Data Services," 3.

35. Katherine Goold Akers, "Looking Out for the Little Guy: Small Data Curation," *Bulletin of the American Society for Information Science and Technology* 39, no. 3 (2013): 58–59.

36. Jake R. Carlson, "Demystifying the Data Interview: Developing a Foundation for Reference Librarians to Talk with Researchers about Their Data," *Reference Services Review* 40, no. 1 (2012): 7–23.

37. Akers, "Looking Out for the Little Guy."

38. Toups and Hughes, "When Data Curation Isn't."

39. Jahnke, Asher, and Keralis, *The Problem of Data*, 8; Jessica Adamick, Rebecca C. Reznik-Zellen, and Matt Sheridan, "Data Management Training for Graduate Students at a Large Research University," *Journal of eScience Librarianship* 1, no. 3 (2012), dx.doi.org/10.7191/jeslib.2012.1022.

40. Angela Brew, "Understanding the Scope of Undergraduate Research: A Framework for Curricular and Pedagogical Decision-Making," *Higher Education* 66, no. 5 (2013): 603–18, dx.doi.org/10.1007/s10734-013-9624-x; Pete Smith and Chris Rust, "The Potential of Research-Based Learning for the Creation of Truly Inclusive Academic Communities of Practice," *Innovations in Education and Teaching International* 48, no. 2, (2011): 115–25, dx.doi.org/10.1080/14703297.2011.564005.

41. Council on Undergraduate Research (CUR), "Conferences and Events," http://www.cur.org/conferences_and_events/.

42. Dahl, "Data-Driven Liberal Arts."

43. Data Curation Centre, "DCC Charter and Statement of Principles," http://www.dcc.ac.uk/about-us/dcc-charter/dcc-charter-and-statement-principles.

44. Sarah L. Shreeves and Melissa H. Cragin, "Introduction: Institutional Repositories: Current State and Future," *Library Trends* 57, no. 2 (2008): 93, dx.doi.org/10.1353/lib.0.0037.

45. Gold, "Cyberinfrastructure, Data, and Libraries, Part 1."

46. Anna Gold, "Data Curation and Libraries: Short-Term Developments, Long-Term Prospects," Robert E. Kennedy Library, April 4, 2010, http://digitalcommons.calpoly.edu/lib_dean/27/.

47. Committee on Earth Observational Satellites Working Group on Information Systems and Services (WGISS), *Data Life Cycle Models and Concepts*, CEOS 1.2, Version 13.0, April 19, 2012, http://ceos.org/ourwork/workinggroups/wgiss/interest-groups/data-stewardship/.

48. John L. Faundeen et al., "The United States Geological Survey Science Data Lifecycle Model," U.S. Geological Survey, Open-File Report 2013–1265, 2013, dx.doi.org/10.3133/ofr20131265.

49. University of Virginia, Research Data Services, "Research Data Life Cycle," 2014, http://dmconsult.library.virginia.edu/.

50. Andrew Treloar, David Groenewegen, and Catherine Harboe-Ree, "The Data Curation Continuum: Managing Data Objects in Institutional Repositories," *D-Lib Magazine* 13, nos. 9–10 (2007), http://www.dlib.org/dlib/september07/treloar/09treloar.html.

51. Merinda McClure et al., "Data Curation: A Study of Researcher Practices and Needs," *portal: Libraries and the Academy* 14, no. 2 (2014): 151–52, dx.doi.org/10.1353/pla.2014.0009.

52. Melissa H. Cragin et al., "Data Sharing, Small Science and Institutional Repositories," *Philosophical Transactions of the Royal Society A* 368 (2010): 4023–38, doi:10.1098/rsta.2010.0165.

53. Ibid.

54. McClure et al., "Data Curation."

55. See the DataCite website at http://www.datacite.org/.

56. Force11, Data Citation Synthesis Working Group, "Joint Declaration of Data Citation Principles," https://www.force11.org/datacitation.

57. "DataCite Metadata Schema for the Publication and Citation of Research Data," version 3.0, July 2013, doi:10.5438/0008.

58. Jake Carlson, "Data Management Plan Self-Assessment Questionnaire," Purdue University Libraries, 2011, https://purr.purdue.edu/dmp/self-assessment.

59. Michael Witt et al., "Constructing Data Curation Profiles," *International Journal of Digital Curation* 4, no. 3 (December 2009): 93–103, dx.doi.org/10.2218/ijdc.v4i3.117.

60. Ibid., 93.

61. Ibid., 95.

62. Jake Carlson and D. Scott Brandt, *Data Curation Profiles Directory*, http://docs.lib.purdue.edu/dcp/.

63. Sherry L. Vellucci, "Knowledge Organization," in *Academic Library Research: Perspectives and Current Trends*, ed. Marie L. Radford and Pamela Snelson, 138–88 (Chicago: Association of College and Research Libraries, 2008).

64. Carlson, "Demystifying the Data Interview."

65. Jane Greenberg, "Metadata for Managing Scientific Research Data," presentation, NISO/DCMI Webinar, August 22, 2012, http://www.niso.org/news/events/2012/dcmi/scientific_data/.

66. Each of these types of metadata are described in detail and discussed in Steven J. Miller, *Metadata for Digital Collections: A How-to-Do-It Manual* (New York: Neal Schuman, 2011).

67. United States Environmental Protection Agency, "Data Standards: Fact Sheets," http://iaspub.epa.gov/sor_internet/registry/datastds/outreachandeducation/educationalresources/factsheets/.

68. International Standards Organization, "ISO 19115-1:2014, Geographic Information—Metadata—Part 1: Fundamentals," http://www.iso.org/iso/home/store/catalogue_tc/catalogue_detail.htm?csnumber=53798.

69. See the Data Documentation Initiative website at http://www.ddialliance.org/.

70. Digital Curation Centre, "Disciplinary Metadata," http://www.dcc.ac.uk/resources/metadata-standards.

71. JISC, "Putting Things in Order: A Directory of Metadata Schemas and Related Standards," http://www.jiscdigitalmedia.ac.uk/guide/putting-things-in-order-links-to-metadata-schemas-and-related-standards.

72. Society of American Archivists, "Metadata Directory," http://www2.archivists.org/groups/metadata-and-digital-object-roundtable/metadata-directory.

73. Jenn Riley, "Seeing Standards: A Visualization of the Metadata Universe," http://www.dlib.indiana.edu/~jenlrile/metadatamap/.

74. NASA, "Metadata Protocol and Standards," http://gcmd.nasa.gov/add/standards/index.html.

75. NOAA, National Geophysical Data Center, "U.S. ECS Project Data Management," http://www.ngdc.noaa.gov/mgg/ecs/metadata/.

76. EPA, "Metadata Standards," http://systemofregistries.supportportal.com/link/portal/23002/23017/ArticleFolder/1581/Metadata-Standards.

77. Springshare, LibGuides Community, http://libguides.com/community.php.

78. Miller, *Metadata for Digital Collections*, 260.

79. ANSI/NISO Z39.19-2005 (R2010), *Guidelines for the Construction, Format, and Management of Monolingual Controlled Vocabularies*, http://www.niso.org/apps/group_public/download.php/12059/z39-19-2005r2010.pdf.

80. Ibid.

81. NASA, *NASA Thesaurus, Volume 1: Hierarchical Listing with Definitions*, January 2012, http://www.sti.nasa.gov/thesvol1.pdf; and *Volume 2: Rotated Term Display*, January 2012, http://www.sti.nasa.gov/thesvol2.pdf.

82. Getty Research Institute, *Art & Architecture Thesaurus Online*, http://www.getty.edu/research/tools/vocabularies/aat/.

83. Lars Marius Garshol, "Metadata? Thesauri? Taxonomies? Topic Maps! Making Sense of It All," *Ontopia*, October 26, 2004.

84. Ibid.

85. Klaar Vanopstal et al., "Vocabularies and Retrieval Tools in Biomedicine: Disentangling the Terminological Knot," *Journal of Medical Systems* 35, no. 5 (2011): 527–43, dx.doi.org/10.1007/s10916-009-9389-z.

86. Ibid.

87. Thomas R. Gruber, "Toward Principles for the Design of Ontologies Used for Knowledge Sharing," *International Journal of Human-Computer Studies* 43, nos. 5–6 (1995): 907–28.

88. Vanopstal et al., "Vocabularies and Retrieval Tools," 533.

89. Steven J. Miller, "Introduction to Ontology Concepts and Terminology," DC-2013 Tutorial, September 2, 2013, http://dcevents.dublincore.org/IntConf/dc-2013/paper/view/140/105.

90. Dublin Core Metadata Initiative, "DCMI Abstract Model," http://dublincore.org/documents/2007/06/04/abstract-model/.

91. Dublin Core Metadata Initiative, "Guidelines for Dublin Core Application Profiles," http://dublincore.org/documents/profile-guidelines/#sect-1.

92. Miller, *Metadata for Digital Collections*.

93. Ibid.

94. Library of Congress, "LC Linked Data Services: Authorities and Vocabularies," http://id.loc.gov/.

95. Silvia B. Southwick and Cory K. Lampert, "Not Just for Geeks: A Practical Approach to Linked Data for Digital Collections Managers" Mountain West Digital Library, October 2013, http://digitalscholarship.unlv.edu/cgi/viewcontent.cgi?article=1116&context=libfacpresentation.

96. OCLC, "Linked Data Survey Results—1: Who's Doing It (Updated)," August 28, 2014, Hangingtogether.org, http://hangingtogether.org/?p=4137.

97. Pryor, *Managing Research Data*, 10.

98. See the LibGuides Community website at http://libguides.com/community.php?m=g.

99. Digital Curation Centre, "Roles," http://www.dcc.ac.uk/resources/roles.

100. DataOne, "Librarians Outreach Toolkit," https://www.dataone.org/for-librarians.

101. DataOne, "Investigator Toolkit," https://www.dataone.org/investigator-toolkit.

Sherry Vellucci

102. See the Inter-university Consortium for Political and Social Research website at http://www.icpsr.umich.edu/icpsrweb/landing.jsp.

103. Data Curation Profiles Toolkit, http://datacurationprofiles.org/.

104. MANTRA, Research Data Management Training, http://datalib.edina.ac.uk/mantra/.

105. Library of Congress, "Digital Preservation Outreach and Education," http://www.digitalpreservation.gov/education/curriculum.html.

106. "Frameworks for a Data Management Curriculum," http://library.umassmed.edu/data_management_frameworks.pdf.

107. Ibid., 2.

Chapter Seven

Skills for the Future of Technical Services

Erin E. Boyd and Elyssa Gould

When considering the skills needed for the future of library technical services, our thoughts turned to previous transitions in the field. What allowed technical services to succeed during past times of change? What can we learn from the past as we look to the future? How can we make sure that the future of technical services confirms or enhances our contribution toward the overall goal of connecting people to information via libraries?

Swan Hill raises an excellent point when she describes transformational change in libraries as having its roots in technical services.[1] Examples of significant change include the implementation of AACR and MARC in the 1960s; the introduction of online catalogs in the 1980s; and our current, ongoing struggle for how to best provide access to and description of electronic resources, which may or may not be resolved in part by the implementation of Resource Description and Access (RDA) (http://www.loc.gov/aba/rda/) and the Bibliographic Framework Initiative (BIBFRAME) (http://www.loc.gov/bibframe/). Each of these changes was prompted by a significant change in technical services workflows, which were required to handle the changing technologies and information resources of the time.

The web has significantly impacted librarianship. The Internet has changed how we communicate. It has also changed how we expect services to be delivered. Library services are constantly evolving as demands for the way we access and retrieve information progress.[2] As we shift from collections of predominately print materials to those increasingly populated with digital materials, we will be presented with more challenges, including licensing, copyright, printing permissions, and concurrent users, but the greatest is keeping pace with the rapid rate of these technological changes.

Technical services librarians are *already* change makers. They have previously encountered change and will continue to experience future changes. Our natural response to changing technologies and formats often makes us the "first responders" by initiating appropriate changes in technical services work. The abilities and tendencies we have to seek order, minimize unnecessary delays, and provide seamless transitions between metadata standards or new software programs serve us well when change occurs. We are already well positioned to respond to and lead change in the library community. As Calhoun notes, "People are the key to success, together with what they know, their attitudes and behaviors, how they choose to do their work, the tasks to which they are assigned, and the processes they use."[3]

As previously noted, technical services is currently in the midst of another period of transformational change. Technical services librarians are well equipped and adept at adapting to changes, creating consistency, and thinking about how our data will affect the future. Now is the time to think creatively about what the catalog *can* and *will* be, to consider our future universe and dream about what we can do *now* to prepare our data and ourselves for the future. What skills should be acquired and improved as the rest of technical services work is in flux?

SKILLS

The underlying thread of the ancient and modern library is that of learning. Above all else, the library is a place where learning occurs: through books, videos, electronic resources, workshops, group meetings, interactions with other library patrons, and more. Librarians typically enter the field to participate in this environment. Many people come to the library to be inspired by this atmosphere. Therefore, we should approach our jobs as technical services librarians with an attitude of and skill toward continual learning. The following are several ways to promote continual learning that the authors believe have proven helpful.

CREATIVITY

Learning on and for the job is very different than learning from a book. One way to avoid the rut of "book learning" is to think and learn with creativity. Learning creatively often emerges out of a need on the job. Creativity also emerges from collaboration. Chances are that you are on a committee or email discussion list where you can hear other voices and learn about experiences within libraries. Listen to your colleagues to discover problems or issues that they are currently experiencing. You may discover that they do not fully understand a situation, and your technical services knowledge can answer a question. Or you may find that while you do not know the answer to the problem, you have the skills to work together to find a solution.

Creativity emerges from interactions with coworkers. Simply getting to know coworkers on a personal level can create a positive rapport where the coworker feels comfortable approaching you with a problem or need. Casual conversations in and of themselves can also reveal problems or needs. Listening with a focus of serving a coworker or being attuned to ways that your skills can be used beyond your job description can provide a venue for creativity to emerge.

Northern Michigan University (NMU) in Marquette, Michigan, will be used to illustrate this point. NMU has a collection of over twenty thousand nonfiction and fiction juvenile materials to support their strong education program. The education liaison librarian mentioned a desire to provide reading level information in the bibliographic record for each title in the collection to enable preservice teachers to easily identify appropriate books to take with them to observations, placements, and student teaching. The metadata and cataloging services librarian and a cataloging assistant seized this idea and quickly enlisted the web services student assistant to provide technical expertise. The education liaison librarian worked with the teaching faculty in the Education Department to determine what kind of reading level would benefit their students. A system of "interest age levels," in which a range of appropriate ages were given, was identified. To identify the correct reading level information for such a large group of titles, the entire contents of the Scholastic online database were scanned and compared to NMU's holdings via an internally developed program. If two records matched with 90 percent or greater certainty, the program identified the appropriate reading level. If the certainty was less than 90 percent, the records were placed in a custom user interface where another student assistant manually matched the appropriate reading level to the catalog record. In total, almost seven thousand records for nonfiction and fiction juvenile materials now provide reading levels in NMU's library catalog. The education liaison librarian demonstrates how to find this information to students in education classes and in course guides. This is an example of how collaboration yields greater creativity to serve a need than one individual could accomplish alone.

INITIATIVE

Initiative is an important quality for continually learning, and also one of the most difficult to practice regularly. As noted in the previous topic of creativity, listening to coworkers with an attitude of serving positions one to detect opportunities to take initiative. The authors of this chapter suggest either volunteering in the moment or researching the topic and emailing your coworker to detail your thoughts and how you can help. Be proactive in scheduling a first meeting to discuss a project; be aware that you might need to schedule and run any future meetings. This is also a great opportunity to practice and hone your project management skills.

Initiative requires persistence. Important stakeholders, such as a supervisor or library director, may not respond enthusiastically to your initial solution to a problem. Follow up on any concerns for a project by re-envisioning the solution. Do not be surprised if more than one solution or step is required to adequately tackle a problem. If your solution is for a problem you foresee in the future rather than an existing problem, be prepared to explain why taking proactive steps will prevent future issues. For example, the future universe of BIBFRAME and linked data relies heavily on authority control. As NMU's library does not subscribe to a regular authority control service, the metadata and cataloging services librarian determined that it would be beneficial to enhance the library's catalog records to contain RDA-compatible authority headings with a one-time enhancement service from an authority control vendor. The library dean and department supervisor were supportive of this proposal, but persistence was required in arranging for the vendor's services, determining the parameters of the record enhancement, and effectively communicating the changes and outcomes to library staff. As the initiator of any project, it is your responsibility to lead and initiate conversations that will help your project succeed, both internally among library staff and externally to library patrons. Be persistent in your goals and communications, and also be responsive to questions and feedback as the process unfolds.

Initiative also takes humility. It is entirely possible that you may have proposed the wrong solution to a problem, were not aware of other variables to the issue, or could be duplicating a coworker's efforts. Be willing to drop your ego and collaborate to find a solution that resolves as many issues as possible. Much library work is collaborative, whether within your own department, in your library, or across campus or branches, and working with a focus on the end goal will enable you to truly focus on the task at hand.

COMMUNICATION

Communication skills are the most essential quality to develop to enhance continual learning. In librarianship, we are constantly communicating with colleagues, patrons, and vendors. Each interaction requires a different communication skill set, and we must learn the best way to work together to achieve common goals.

Collaboration with colleagues often aids in developing creative solutions to problems. In librarianship, collaboration between departments (and in some instances, branches) is crucial for the library's success. Librarians at

Troy University (where author Boyd was previously employed), a multi-branch library system, developed strong communication and collaboration skills between the technical services departments across the three campus libraries. Each library's collection had a slightly different focus and different patron base, yet there was a need to constantly stay connected to ensure the consistency of all procedures and policies for processing and cataloging materials. Because of this, they developed ways to keep the lines of communication open, including virtual meetings and the implementation of an internal wiki. Through this creative approach, lines of communication were always open to provide consistency and openness throughout the department.

Developing strong communication skills and having open conversations with colleagues can also directly impact vendor interactions. Questions that develop through these interactions in relation to external services can help when it is time to negotiate (or renegotiate) subscriptions and licensing agreements, implement new products, or troubleshoot ongoing issues. Working to develop strong lines of communication will help everyone achieve common goals.

ADVOCATING

Lastly, one of the greatest abilities a librarian can develop is advocacy. There should be a need and desire to advocate for the profession. What does advocating for technical services mean? What is the best way to advocate? To whom should one advocate? Much of our work is not understood outside of the profession or, in some cases, by our own colleagues who work in other departments in our libraries. For technical services professionals, we have indirect interactions with our patrons that further complicate this fact. Opening up a dialogue no matter the length will help us in educating individuals outside of libraries. Picture yourself as an ambassador for libraries, always at the ready to quickly explain why and how libraries matter. The above questions are a few points to consider in terms of advocacy efforts. These efforts can be on a small or larger scale, ranging from within an institution to the community to the state or nationally.

The authors define advocacy for technical services as supporting, recommending, or educating others about the various aspects of technical services work and how they impact the success of other library operations. Since technical services positions are most often behind the scenes, people do not understand the breadth of skills needed to perform the multiple tasks executed by a librarian serving in one of these positions. There is a great deal of overlap between technical services responsibilities, depending on the functions of one's job. For example, an individual working in acquisitions should have basic cataloging knowledge to determine the quality of a record for quick processing downloads. Advocating can mean educating another department within the library about the technical services workflow and who to approach with particular problems or issues. It can also mean that technical services staff members support other staff members' work throughout the library with cross-training or following established procedures.

What follows are some ways that one can advocate for technical services. First, determine how advocacy is defined and what it means to you. Second, develop an elevator or "parking lot" speech. An elevator or parking lot speech is a concise speech that lasts between 30 to 120 seconds that quickly demonstrates the value and importance of one's work. Participation in a professional organization can provide additional membership benefits related to advocacy. For example, the American Library Association (ALA) provides a wide variety of resources through its Office for Library Advocacy (http://ala.org/offices/ola). Additionally, the Association for Library Collections and Technical Services (ALCTS), a division of ALA, has developed a portal on their website dedicated to advocacy efforts for technical services professionals and support staff (http://www.ala.org/alcts/about/advocacy).

REQUIRED PROFESSIONAL COMPETENCIES

This section will explore the competencies needed to prepare for the future of technical services. It is essential to develop a combination of practical experience, professional networking, and professional development by devising a regime to continually update and refresh one's skills to keep pace with the constant change in the field.

Competencies Needed for the Digital World

A discussion of competencies needed for the future raises the rhetorical question: will professional technical services librarians be needed in the future? To the authors, the answer is a resounding *yes!* Despite that fact that librarians have the ability to automate many of our workflow processes, there is still the need for professionals capable of and able to evaluate new forms of resources and determine the appropriate course of action. The biggest area of growth in developing skills for technical services professionals is the ability to leverage the new technological environment in regard to new cataloging rules and initiatives. Our work environment has drastically changed in the last forty years with the wide variety of applications, platforms, and interfaces.[4] As we continue to add an increasing number of digital resources to our collections, there will be a need to develop skills related to these resources. Some of the skills needed for the digital field are a working knowledge of programming languages, as well as non-MARC metadata schemas. For instance, as the number and formats of electronic resources grow, more technical services librarians will need to learn negotiating and licensing skills, as well as handle formats such as research data, to have more individuals with this experience to handle the workload. Furthermore, with the promise of linked data and BIBFRAME on the horizon, authority control is increasing in importance. These areas listed above are well suited for a professional-level librarian.

Some of the core competencies needed now and for the future are a basic understanding of email functions, computer hardware, software and peripherals, mobile devices, the Internet, and word processing functions.[5] ALA and its divisions typically provide a set of "core competencies" that librarians can reference. As one progresses into specific types of technical services librarianship, more detailed skills should be developed. For instance, with the changing pace of formats cataloged on a regular basis, catalogers must change their orientation to think in terms of resource description. The changes in formats and access have considerably impacted how librarians evaluate materials in the cataloging process. Because of this, we must actively work to continually develop and refresh our skills. An in-depth knowledge of the entire technical services field can aid in strengthening one's knowledge. Knowing how an item proceeds through technical services from beginning to end will help to build strong investigative skills for improving processes or pinpointing which part of the process no longer functions correctly.

Developing a Professional Network

When developing professional skills, there is no better place than your professional network. A professional network consists of individuals with similar interests or backgrounds that you can seek for advice, counsel, or problem solving. We all have unique skill sets, and building and maintaining a diverse professional network should be a continual process throughout your career. The best way to start developing a professional network is in library school or through attending professional conferences. Many of these conferences include "101" sessions, which are geared to individuals who are newer to the profession or organization. Your professional network can also be cultivated through virtual or in-person interactions. With the changing pace of technologies, it is easy to build and maintain professional networks via email, telephone, and video conferencing programs. Dedicate time every month to reconnect with your network. Creating time devoted to these interactions will help you learn about the profession, discover new opportunities, or reenergize or discover new ways of performing common tasks at work.

Time Management

Of course, a willingness to learn is not the same as the ability to learn. The authors have found that removing ourselves from the "school learning" mindset and swapping in full-time employment, family, friends, and life in general greatly complicates the ability to learn. From personal experience, the biggest lessons we can impart is that one must *make* and *prioritize* the time to learn and network with your professional peers. An important aspect needed for continual learning is time management. As newer professionals, we often feel obligated to pursue every opportunity that comes our way. Because of this, new professionals can quickly enter into a burnout phase. Not only can burnout affect new learning opportunities, but it can also distract one from regular job responsibilities and can cause one to be ineffective. One way to help prevent or relieve burnout is to develop strong time management skills. We suggest devoting at least two hours a week to reading books, blogs, articles, emails, and the like that have accumulated during the week. This may not be possible to do during your workday, but making the time to read over several lunch breaks or evenings is a way to manage your time wisely and ensure that you are leaving time to learn about developments in technical services. It can even be inspirational—keep a notebook or electronic document on one of your devices with ideas you have seen and read about that are relevant to your workplace or enhance your understanding of the future of technical services. Making the time to learn continually will make technical services librarians more thoughtful, intentional librarians who are well equipped to face the future.

We encourage librarians to cultivate an environment of learning in the workplace. Consider forming an interest group, open forum, or casual lunch discussion group that will bring together individuals who want to share and learn together. This will be particularly effective if individuals outside of technical services participate and form an interdisciplinary group. Having reference librarians present, for example, will help technical services librarians explain new ideas and innovations in a way that is understandable to those outside of technical services. It can also help technical services librarians think creatively about *how* to explain exactly what linked data is and how it might or will affect access to library resources. By sharing with and learning from each other, we can avoid duplicating efforts and implement ideas and solutions that are comprehensible to all the stakeholders in the work environment.

CONTINUING EDUCATION AND PROFESSIONAL DEVELOPMENT

It is important to remember that professional development and continuing education are the key to preparing for the future. Professional development follows the entire length of one's career, and we must make a commitment to continual learning. We must actively develop and refresh our skills with each changing initiative or technology introduced in our profession, or we will fall behind and become ineffective. The willingness and ability to learn is an important component of having an attitude of continual learning. A willing attitude will benefit you tremendously when advancing your skills. Librarianship is influenced by many areas: technology, publishing, legislation, and libraries themselves, to name a few. New technologies and innovations come from all of these sources, often at an alarming rate. It is simply impossible to keep up with every source of information. Instead of becoming overwhelmed by the information sources, commit to learning the information itself. In this sense, willingness also refers to being proactive. Proactively subscribe to information sources that will push enough information your way to help determine what is relevant to you and what can be ignored.

The Internet makes it relatively easy to keep pace with current and emerging trends. There are a wide variety of sources of information that can be used to increase knowledge about technical services, both in learning the basics and preparing for the future of technical services. Our favorite sources of information areas are provided below:

- Books: This includes the basic texts used in library school and new publications. ALA Editions, Neal-Schumann, Taylor & Francis, Litwin Books, Libraries Unlimited, Rowman & Littlefield, and Taylor & Francis are publishers that typically publish library-related titles. Look for reviews in journals or online to help determine if a book will benefit you.
- Articles: These are often packed with research studies, fresh ideas, or new applications of old practices. Keeping up with journal articles through emails announcing the new issue's table of contents is a great way to learn about interesting and useful articles. It is also an effective means to weed out potentially irrelevant articles. We have found that articles contain especially useful ideas for how to test or implement ideas at your own institution.
- Discussion lists: Discussion lists provide a way to share information and resources quickly via email. They are another wonderful way to read and learn as time permits. Librarians are very helpful people, and a question to a list can generate many responses that include shared experiences, new solutions, or philosophical thoughts on an issue. We recommend setting up folders and automatic transfer rules for discussion list messages within

your email program to avoid becoming inundated by the conversations during the day. Discussion lists also provide the added benefits of advertising for professional conferences and opportunities, as well as forming professional relationships with librarians across the globe.

- Blogs: Blogs are an excellent way to stay on top of current topics both in librarianship and technical services. Subscribing to blog posts from specific blogs via email or RSS feeds can push information to you, while allowing you to read at your convenience.

- Social media: There are many avenues librarians can pursue using social media accounts on Facebook, Twitter, and Google+. Pages, groups, and hashtags have been created to aggregate all this information and allow an open forum for sharing problems, generating solutions, seeking guidance, and gaining support.

- Webinars: These are free or fee-based sessions that you can attend from anywhere, provided you have the needed technology to participate. Both professional associations and library vendors provide webinars on various topics related to technical services. Look for webinars on "how-to" topics, innovations in a specific subject, and enhancements to existing products or services.

- E-Forums: E-Forums are essentially discussion lists devoted to a specific moderated topic over specified time period (i.e., one or two days). These are excellent for discussing current topics with librarians across the world and often result in learning about new projects, solutions, and innovations on that topic.

- Professional associations and conferences: Professional associations require membership dues that frequently include benefits such as reduced conference attendance fees, journal subscriptions, and professional development opportunities. Becoming involved in an association provides access to a plethora of information through conferences attended, webinars, and the opportunity to network with other librarians. We highly recommend using this approach when learning, as it broadens your understanding of libraries beyond the one in which you work. Conferences include programs, poster sessions, networking events, and opportunities to speak with vendors. These activities can spark ideas for innovations, problem solving, and encouragement in learning skills to prepare you for the future of technical services. Being engaged in a professional association will reap far greater benefits than merely paying to belong to an organization and standing on the sidelines.

- Other forms of learning: This includes continuing education classes, white papers, newspaper articles, and more. Any source can provide a learning opportunity. The trick is how to balance finding relevant sources of information with the time required to read these resources. Focusing on skills that are valued in technology fields, such as computer programming, coding, project management, and data querying, are current skills listed on position announcements that might be worth acquiring.

CONCLUSION

We envision a future of technical services where these operations are more fully integrated into the workings of the entire library, instead of operating in a silo. Our field has already begun this transition by becoming more involved in digital projects, making local collections accessible, and implementing new discovery tools. A diagram of the "Transformation of Research Libraries" provides a visualization of the blurring of lines among all the departments in a library.[6] This does not just apply to research libraries, but all libraries. As we move into the future, we anticipate that collaborative and creative approaches to libraries will be essential to the success of libraries with decreased staff and funding, rapidly increasing technology, and lowered barriers between traditional technical services work and the work of the entire library.

Unfortunately, we do not possess the ability to predict the exact future of technical services and what specific skills will be most valuable in that future. Instead, we chose to focus on the characteristics that we believe will best serve all technical services librarians in *any* situation. We hope that this chapter provides a way forward in the changing environment of technical services. We strongly believe that the knowledge and discernment skills of technical services librarians will be essential to the future of librarianship and encourage you to gain the characteristics and skills outlined in this chapter. By cultivating such characteristics as creativity, initiative, willingness to learn, communication skills, and advocacy for yourself and your work, we believe that technical services will be better positioned to prepare for and proactively respond to the changes in technologies, libraries, publishing, and other industries to redefine and reposition libraries to connect people to information.

We have included below a list of competency sources that either compile existing competencies or link to distinct technical services competencies. We strongly recommend consulting these sources to discover specific areas where you can develop a skill set for the future of technical services.

- ALCTS Competencies and Education for a Career in Cataloging Interest Group: http://www.ala.org/alcts/mgrps/camms/grps/ats-ccsdgcomp.
- *Core Technology Competencies for Librarians and Library Staff: LITA Guide 15* (2009), edited by Susan M. Thompson.

- North American Serials Interest Group's Core Competencies (2014): http://www.nasig.org/site_page.cfm?pk_association_webpage_menu= 310&pk_association_webpage=1225.
- WebJunction's Competency Index for the library field (2014): http:// webjunction.org/content/dam/WebJunction/Documents/webJunction/ 2014-03/Competency-Index-2014.pdf.

NOTES

1. Janet Swan Hill, "Transcending Widgets: The Nature of Technical Services," *Library Collections, Acquisitions & Technical Services* 27, no. 4 (2003): 377–91.
2. Carlen Ruschoff, "Competencies for 21st Century Technical Services," *Technicalities* 27, no. 1 (2007): 14–16.
3. Karen Calhoun, "Technology, Productivity and Change in Library Technical Services," *Library Collections, Acquisitions & Technical Services* 27, no. 3 (2003): 288.
4. Swan Hill, "Transcending Widgets."
5. "Essential Library Competencies," from *Competency Index for the Library Field*, comp. WebJunction, http://webjunction.org/content/dam/WebJunction/Documents/webJunction/ 2014-03/Competency-Index-2014.pdf.
6. "The Transformation of Research Libraries," University of Chicago Library, 2013, http:/ /www.lib.uchicago.edu/about/LibraryTransformation_2page.pdf.

Chapter Eight

Breaking Up Is Hard to Do

The End of Technical Services? A Think Piece on the
Future of Technical Services

Amy K. Weiss

I was in the audience of a meeting of major players in the world of technical services. The conversation until that point had been insightful and creative until someone asked, "What do you see for technical services in five years?" There was a sudden, uncharacteristic silence. The truth of it was that no one at that time—about five years ago—was really sure what was going to happen with technical services. Technical services departments had been shrinking as more tasks became automated or outsourced; Resource Description and Access (RDA) was in what appeared to be endless planning stages; MARC (Machine Readable Cataloging) was clearly on its way out but did not have a successor. It was apparent that technical services in five years would be very different, but no one was sure what it would look like.

At that time, the trends were already in place that would disperse or make disappear many technical services functions. This paper will discuss trends in technical services that have been in play in some cases for as many as twenty years and will examine how those trends eventually have led to a diminution of traditional technical services functions and a new emphasis on outsourcing and automated processes.

CATALOGING THE WEB

The first graphical web interface was introduced in 1993,[1] followed by an explosion of web pages on every imaginable subject, and all of it free. Librarians were as swept away as any group of people—soon every library had its own web page and made its catalog available to be searched by anyone who stumbled across it.

The question soon arose: how should the web be cataloged, or should it be cataloged at all? After all, this was not information that had been vetted by authorities in most cases. On the other hand, for some very obscure subjects, a web page maintained by an enthusiast might represent the only information on that topic. As public services librarians discussed information literacy, catalogers discussed how best to make the web accessible.

A few optimists thought that the entire web could be cataloged. However, most catalogers (and public services librarians as well) thought that selected sites should be added to the library catalog. But even this could quickly become unmanageable because of the problem of hierarchical websites. The desired site or document might require several clicks to reach. The issue was whether all the layers should be cataloged, or just the individual page or document. The other problem, of course, was the capricious nature of the web. Today's website could be gone tomorrow; hence the widespread practice of dating web citations.

The experience of libraries with attempting to do traditional selection and cataloging is significant as this was the first time it was obvious that the universe of material to be cataloged vastly exceeded the ability of subject specialists and technical services librarians to make headway. For the most part, web resources are left to search engines to discover, and only occasionally is something cataloged to specifically call attention to it. In short, there was more material than could possibly be handled in the traditional technical services workflow.

AGGREGATORS/AGGRAVATORS

Commercial aggregators emerged at the same time as the web explosion and provided another example of a resource seemingly too large for conventional cataloging. While the aggregators each represented a finite amount of material, there was no information given as to what comprised all of the material. Aggregators tended to represent a subset of any given serials' content, but the rules for omission were not, and never have been, clear. Journal content was added or removed seemingly at random. Vendors made lists of titles available, but these were only marginally reliable. So even though the material, unlike the ever-expanding web, could be described, the amount of revision necessary to do so would quickly overwhelm any technical services department that would attempt it. Hence aggregators became known as "aggravators."

The other aspect of aggregators, unlike the web, was that they contained what was traditionally a library material. The journal content frequently overlapped with what was already held in print. This suggested that the aggregator's content should be cataloged, yet its mutability and fragmentary coverage made this seem an impossible task.

One library that attempted to catalog its own aggregated journal content is Hong Kong Baptist University. They cataloged stable aggregators in-house using a single-record approach and automated production of records for unstable aggregators. They relied on vendor lists and records, which they did not check for accuracy, and they admitted their process was expensive.[2] For most libraries, there were two possibilities for aggregated journal access. A library might use either or both. One is the A-to-Z list, and the other is purchasing records from a vendor.

An A-to-Z list for aggregated journals is an electronic throwback to an earlier era of journal access. Many libraries maintained lists of all of their journals in giant books held by the reference desk. By all accounts, these lists were loved by users and hated by librarians, who wanted users to use the catalog. Likewise, the electronic A-to-Z list is often easier to use than the catalog—provided, of course, that you know exactly what you are looking for and the title does not start with "Journal of." The early electronic A-to-Z lists were dependent on vendors to supply accurate and complete information about their holdings. In general, they did not. Nevertheless, A-to-Z lists remain popular for both journals and databases.

The other route was to purchase bibliographic records. Serials Solutions, which sold records for aggregators, was started by a librarian, Peter McCracken, in 2000.[3] Other vendors soon followed suit. Buying records for aggregator content has from the start been a mixed experience. Initially, the records provided were subminimal level and might not even contain holdings information. It could be difficult to remove outmoded records, and the information from the company supplying the records might be out of date by the time it was compiled and sent to the subscribing library. Contemporary purchased aggregator records are more complete and have more accurate holdings, but can be overwhelming as the same journal may be aggregated in numerous databases, leaving the user with several possible links that may display the same content in a dozen different ways.

For technical services departments, the ever-expanding web and the immense and complex aggregators were examples of where traditional technical services failed. No technical services department was large enough or sophisticated enough to derive the information necessary to adequately catalog the web, and most could not even handle a good-sized aggregator. As these materials became more important, the necessity of keeping a large technical services staff seemed less, and the need for a large systems department for loading files and making sure than the electronic materials were always accessible became greater. These were the first places where technical services began to splinter.

JSTOR: THE OTHER AGGREGATOR

JSTOR was in the planning phases in 1993–1995 and was released in 1995.[4] Per its name, its original intent was to assist large research libraries to create open shelf space by allowing electronic access to lengthy journal runs, which could then be placed in remote storage. However, it did several other things. One, it allowed smaller institutions to purchase large back files of journals to which they may not previously have had access. Additionally, storage is expensive. Soon JSTOR became a way for academic libraries to discard large runs of little-used journals without losing the content. JSTOR was very different from the aggregators: it was truly a complete representation of the journals, although it was not up to date. Because the content was stable and the information about the content was made available to subscribers, JSTOR journals were soon cataloged. JSTOR was important as it showed a workable model of what a stable aggregator could be and, as such, presented a challenge to commercial publishers and vendors to create more stable databases.

THE BIG DEAL

Serials publishers and vendors also saw opportunities for making their journals (and sometimes their back files) available electronically. The "Big Deal" was another super-sized conglomeration of materials. A Big Deal basically works in this way: a publisher offers a consortium a package of journals consisting of everything from that publisher to which everyone in the consortium subscribes, plus additional bonus content. In exchange, the consortium will agree to a three- to five-year contract where they will keep all the proffered content in exchange for an increasingly large sum of money, paid up front. Generally, for the first couple of years, the per-journal costs are lower, and everyone in the consortium, especially the smaller institutions, gets more content, hence the "The Big Deal." Content providers are willing to do this because it gives them guaranteed income in a time of mass serials cancellations. They also hope that the institutions will become hooked on the large quantity of journals available, and that there would be an uproar from users if the institutions attempted to walk away from the deal at the end of the contract.

Consortia jumped on these deals when they were first offered. They have since been having second thoughts. I have two articles in front of me as I write: one from 2003 entitled "Big Chill on the Big Deal?"[5] and another from 2013 entitled "Is the 'Big Deal' Dying?"[6] Apparently, the intervening ten years failed to kill off the practice despite the considerable problems associated with Big Deals. These included paying for large amounts of content that go entirely unused and high up-front costs that can break the budget of an institution in need of savings. Several institutions have broken their deals and lived to tell the tale, but it is generally agreed that versions of the Big Deal will remain.[7]

So, especially for serials, the web, the aggregators, and the Big Deals all contributed to a culture where individual work was needed less and, perhaps, less valued. Journals bought in large packages only need a single invoice to pay for scores of titles. Technology departments were as likely, if not more likely, to load the bibliographic records into the catalog. There was little regard for the quality of the records for highly volatile materials. There was little role for collection development since most resources came as part of a package constructed by a vendor or publisher. Everything in serials was "supersized" to the point where only commercial services would be able to provide the access desired by contemporary library users.

OUTSOURCING

The first institution to completely outsource its cataloging department was Wright State University in Dayton, Ohio. Wright State developed a backlog due to personnel issues and union rules. The technical services managers demonstrated that they would not only eliminate their arrearage but save money by outsourcing it to the then clunky OCLC TechPro (it was necessary at that time to send books physically to OCLC for cataloging). They then disbanded the cataloging department.[8]

For years afterward, Wright State was held up as the worst-case scenario in technical services (for the staff, not the administration) and also as a model (for the administration, not the staff). There was a period where one would hear conference presentations by pro-outsourcing managers where they rather sheepishly stated that the catalogers' time had been freed up to do more interesting tasks. Whether their staff was truly more engaged was left to the audiences' imagination.

Outsourcing, at this juncture, is one of the tools in any technical services department's toolkit. With fewer catalogers being hired at all levels of expertise, having adequate catalog records that can be quickly loaded and shelf-ready materials and books sent directly to the stacks after check-in is necessary in more libraries. It is not a philosophical choice so much as necessary evil. The quality of vendor records is an issue for many catalogers in libraries that outsource their materials. Vendor records may be incomplete or flatly wrong in many instances. While some libraries have the resources and personnel necessary to edit records at least in a cursory way, smaller institutions, in particular, simply have to accept what the vendor sends their way.

E-BOOKS

E-books, while sometimes sold individually, are more likely to be sold as part of a "library"—a group of books aimed at a specific audience in the academic universe. Without catalog records, access is confined to publishers' sites, which can be difficult for potential users to negotiate. A-to-Z lists do not appear to be frequently used for e-books. Fortunately, catalog records are frequently sold with the e-books.

Much has been written on the subject of e-books. Walters gives a good overview in his paper "E-Books in Academic Libraries: Challenges for Discovery and Access."[9] From a technical services standpoint, there are several problems with e-books: for example, it is easy to be overwhelmed by the amount of batchloading assuming that there are record sets available, whether to edit the records to be batchloaded, and the need to track what has been loaded in case relations with the publisher or vendor take a wrong turn.

E-books got off to a slow start with both librarians and users, partially owing to the intransience of publishers and vendors. Initially, e-books were bound by too many rules that discouraged their use: too few simultaneous users, too little printing, and short loan periods. These factors made e-books unattractive for classroom assignments. It has been assumed by librarians that if one was using a monograph for research, that one would want to read or print large portions of it. The restrictive rules of the e-book packages made this difficult. Initially, screen size and readability were also issues. However, perhaps because of the popularity of personal e-readers and some concessions by publishers with printing and circulation issues, e-books are more accepted by users. Librarians still have qualms over issues of ownership and potential effects on interlibrary loan (ILL) and archiving of materials. However, it now appears that e-book usage is similar to that of print books.[10]

Another issue surrounding e-books is the nature of vendor-supplied records. Quantity of records does not mean quality. The records made available for e-book batchloads may be of poor quality. For example, a unique identifier is necessary for loading. The records supplied by the vendor may lack a unique identifier. Incorrect identifiers, such as ISBNs for print versions or OCLC numbers for nonmatching records, may have been left in records that were derived from print records. Identifiers supplied by the publisher might be arbitrarily changed, so that it is necessary to remove earlier record sets and replace them with a new set (which hopefully will have a more stable identifier). Recently, the State University Libraries of Florida, which maintain a union catalog, have begun to place all OCLC numbers found in batchloaded records in a note field, recognizing that the OCLC number might be the correct number. For this reason, batchloaded records are never loaded based on an OCLC number match.

Catalog management issues with e-books may also be complicated by the uncertain rights and rules of e-book ownership. It is necessary to have a mechanism to identify books from batchloads so that they can be removed in case the publisher or distributor decides to remove a title. Perpetual access is frequently offered, but what this means in practice is not entirely clear since policies vary with vendors and there is no universal standard.

While e-books, like e-journals, can be purchased separately, the model set by e-books is the same as what has been presented by serials—big packages with thousands of titles. Despite the fact that many libraries are editing batchloaded records, the size of the e-book sets is similar to the aggregator problem—sheer numbers complicate making the records as complete and correct as individually cataloged print materials. Tools like MarcEdit (http://marcedit.reeset.net/) make certain kinds of corrections simple; more complex issues, principally the quality of access points, remain unresolved. Subject and authority work remain in the hands of the vendors. If the vendor has derived its record from a high-quality record, the e-record will be of acceptable quality. But vendors do not appear to be searching for the best available record, and some proprietary records are of very poor quality indeed. The presence of vendor records in a catalog may not destroy it, but they may do little to enhance it besides increasing its size.

The question for catalog librarians and their administrators becomes: are e-books receiving sufficient cataloging treatment? In many, if not most, technical services departments, the focus of cataloging remains on a shrinking quantity of print materials, despite the masses of e-books that are being added to catalogs. It is up to technical services librarians to make a case for a higher standard of bibliographic control for these materials, so that they are visible to catalog users.

PATRON-DRIVEN ACQUISITIONS

Patron-driven acquisitions (PDA) originated in interlibrary loan departments, when decisions were made to purchase requests rather than to borrow them on the grounds that there was a recognized need for the material from at least one patron. Now PDA (also known as demand-driven acquisitions, or DDA) is becoming increasingly important in academic libraries. Essentially, a package of e-books is offered to users as part of the PDA agreement. At first, these books are leased by the library. If a book is not used, it is more or less returned to the publisher (the record for it is deleted) and new books are then offered. If a book is used an agreed number of times, the library will pay for the book and it will own it indefinitely.

PDA affects technical services on several levels. First, it affects collection development. While PDA plans can be scoped to a certain group of users or confined to specific topics, the entire point of the plans is to offer more than would be selected by a bibliographer and to allow users to choose their books. While the decision to use a PDA plan may be made by collection development, it is one decision as opposed to the many small decisions that go into selecting books one at a time for firm orders.

The lack of firm orders, in turn, affects monographic acquisitions. Where there may have been a number of people placing orders, fewer are needed if a large quantity of the budget has gone into PDA plans and e-book packages. The work required to keep up with the purchases made via PDA appears to be less than with firm orders (in my personal observation). With fewer physical books to invoice, the need to be physically proximate to cataloging lessens. The actual physical unit of technical services becomes less of a necessity.

Cataloging of PDA titles shares many similarities with e-book cataloging. However, with an e-book package, the package is what is owned. Libraries have segregated PDA records within their databases or discovery layers and, as titles are purchased (or more precisely, receive the requisite number of uses), the e-books are "cataloged" by transferring them to the main catalog. Again, with the reduction of firm orders, there is less time needed for cataloging. Firm orders have traditionally been where the most difficult cataloging was required, so the need for professional catalogers may now be considered less important.

METADATA

Since the introduction of Dublin Core (DC), and subsequently other non-MARC metadata schemes, catalogers have felt that they should be involved with the creation of non-MARC metadata. However, the goals and construction of non-MARC metadata are very different from those of MARC. Non-MARC metadata records tend to be simple and, in the case of a collection, can be repetitive, where MARC records attempt to offer a highly detailed view of a manifestation. MARC records also can serve as surrogates for the resources they describe. The intellectual work in non-MARC metadata lies in choosing or creating a standard, determining what is important in the description of the collections, and choosing how the record will be marked up and displayed. With MARC, these decisions are all broadly made in advance by our cataloging standards, and the intellectual energy of a MARC record is in filling out the fields dictated by the conventions of the material being cataloged, following one of several established content standards.

Because of the emphasis on programming rather than the content, non-MARC metadata has found its way into technology and digitization departments more often than technical services departments. Admittedly, there is also a glamor factor, with the new, flexible metadata being seen as supplanting stodgy MARC and AACR2. At any rate, this was one of the splintering points for cataloging work—description, identification, and collocation of library materials done not just in cataloging but also in technology and digitization, special collections, and archives.

Interoperability needs to become a more pressing issue when new systems are brought online by libraries. Some next-generation integrated library systems are capable of storing records both in DC and MARC. Possibly even more flexible systems could be created using open-source software. This could organize the scattered records into a single system for search and display. Other alternatives would be an interface capable of searching multiple databases seamlessly. As long as more than one markup standard is being used, our tools must be constructed in such a way that users will be able to locate materials, regardless of the media or the department responsible for its upkeep. It is rather ironic that so many librarians are anxious to do description of materials in their units—just so long as the description is not being done by people called catalogers.

THE FUTURE OF CATALOGING

Three reports on the future of cataloging were released in 2005–2006. These reports galvanized the cataloging world. While the reports reflected trends that had been happening for some time, such as shrinking department size and outsourcing of routine cataloging, the appearance of the three reports together, all stating that handmade, one-at-a-time cataloging was essentially finished as a library activity, sent shock waves through the cataloging community.

The first report was from the University of California Bibliographic Services Task Force. Entitled *Rethinking How We Provide Bibliographic Services for the University of California*, it was the most forward looking of the reports because it emphasized catalogs as much as cataloging. The discussion of the single search box that would retrieve all of the libraries' materials[11] looked forward to the discovery layers that now envelop library catalogs along with aggregated journal articles. The most famous part of the report is the statement, "We must adapt and recognize that 'good enough is good enough,' we can no longer invest in 'perfect' bibliographic records for all materials."[12] The phrase "good enough cataloging" caught on and many a cataloging manager has since been told to produce "good enough cataloging" by senior management without any consensus of what "good enough" might mean. For the Task Force, they were willing to accept "skeletal" records in the catalog, but believed that "through iterative automated queries of metadata content,"[13] these skeletal records would be enhanced. So while administrators tended to stop with "good enough" on the assumption that their cataloging staff was spending too much time enhancing records for local use, the task force actually viewed a different kind of cataloging record, presumably outside the confines of MARC, which could accept data pulled from publishers' sites or contributed by users as well as rechecking OCLC for updated records. The infrastructure for doing this kind of work is not yet in the hands of catalogers, and there are no commercial products that can do this work. It remains to be seen if anyone will make the investment to do continuous improvement of catalog records.

In her paper sponsored by the Library of Congress (LC), entitled "The Changing Nature of the Catalog and Its Integration with Other Discovery Tools," Calhoun portrays the library catalog as dying and offers suggestions for its replacement or revitalization. Her premise, essentially, is that because users go first to the web for their research needs, there needs to be a catalog, preferably maintained by an organization other than the library, with expanded search capabilities so that the library catalog and web results will be delivered when it was searched. In this, as in the University of California report, she anticipates discovery layers, although current discovery layers do not search the open Internet. She also anticipates OCLC's foray into providing an OPAC and technical services. Her paper is based on business approaches. Calhoun's view is that catalogs are expensive to maintain and receive lower use than search engines and therefore need to be improved or eliminated. She suggests models for further development, including speculation on quick divestment.[14]

Calhoun's report is marred by her assumption of resistance from staff. She states, "Many research library readers, most staff members, and some university faculty are not ready for change of this magnitude."[15] Statements such as this are what made the paper controversial when it came out. When catalogers object to such statements, it is taken as further evidence of their inflexibility. There are several factors at play here. First, no one wants to do a job that is openly being declared as a waste of library resources. Second, technical services librarians and staff want to keep their library jobs and need to be reassured that they will have valuable work to do. Third, in many technical services departments the rate of change has been dizzyingly fast and constant since the dawn of the web, and a certain level of exhaustion has set in to some departments. If technical services librarians and staff are included in decision making and goal setting, much of this presumed resistance dissipates.

The Indiana University report, "A White Paper on the Future of Cataloging at Indiana University," takes a more conventional approach. The authors do not envision the end of catalogers or cataloging—merely changing tasks. It suggests the need for new and upgraded skills for catalogers and notes the pitfalls of searching the web for research rather than using the library catalog or the library's website. It places catalogers as information stewards on a broader scale, working with a variety of metadata schemas to provide information access to users. [16]

It is interesting that two of the three reports (University of California and Calhoun) advocate elimination of LCSH (Library of Congress Subject Headings). Assignment of subject headings is by no means the most time-consuming part of creating records. The University of California suggests changing to FAST (Faceted Application of Subject Headings), [17] but as of the time of writing, the FAST headings in OCLC appear to be cribbed from the LCSH headings already on the record. There still is not enough known about how people search to state that the keywords in subject headings are unnecessary where basic descriptive information, which is often of use to the bibliographer rather than the average user, is essential.

LIBRARY OF CONGRESS: ON THE RECORD

After the appearance of the three major reports in 2005–2006, LC decided that it also needed to conduct a more formal analysis of its cataloging operations. This was important, since most libraries still rely on high-quality LC cataloging to make their copy cataloging operations feasible. These are records that can generally be agreed upon not to need editing. However, LC has had to deal with a shrinking budget and the proliferation of materials in need of cataloging as much as any research library. In addition, LC is a major player (really *the* major player) in the creation of cataloging standards for the United States. [18]

The resultant paper is a well-thought-out analysis of what LC can do and what LC needs to leave to other libraries. The working group refers to this as "divestment." Divestment of this sort by LC has tremendous ramifications for libraries. Cataloging of commonly held works is among the practices considered for "sharing" with other libraries and with publishing communities. [19] It is unlikely in this age of tight budgets that more positions would be funneled into cataloging departments to make up the shortfall in cataloging copy. Publishers like Cataloging in Publication (CIP) data, but it seems unlikely that they would be willing to distribute free records if it required them to hire additional staff. It is much more likely that this work will fall to vendors, and libraries will be paying more for cataloging records of lower quality. As vendors gain more of the market, it is possible that cataloging could become prohibitively expensive, and that some libraries would discontinue cataloging. It is hoped that LC can continue to catalog, if only at a "good enough" level so that other cash-strapped libraries can keep their catalogs intact.

At the time of publication, the part of the report that raised the most eyebrows was the suggestion that work on RDA be discontinued.[20] Early drafts of RDA did not look promising to the U.S. cataloging community. RDA was hard to read and, seen in bits and pieces, seemed like it would be hard to use to catalog. This recommendation was not taken, but it did mean that LC, along with the National Library of Medicine and the National Agricultural Library, held a major trial of RDA before agreeing to implement it. RDA was implemented by LC on March 31, 2013.[21]

RDA: RESOURCE DESCRIPTION AND ACCESS

It would appear to be a strange time to be launching a new content standard. The previously discussed papers show how cataloging as a profession is under intense scrutiny if not outright attack. Because of the unfortunate timing of its appearance, RDA can seem like rearranging the deck chairs on the Titanic—a theoretical exercise in the midst of a catastrophic breakdown and attack. Having to train a department to work with a new set of descriptive rules would not seem to be a priority, even if, as can be admitted, the old rules were showing their age.

However, RDA has been a long time in the making. The roots of RDA extend back to 1997 with the International Conference on the Principles and Future Development of AACR.[22] In 2004 a draft of AACR3 was issued, which made no one happy.[23] The main objections were that it was too similar to AACR2 and failed to address the rapid changes in the types of materials that catalogers were expected to handle.

RDA has a solid theoretical background, taking its cues from FRBR (Functional Requirements for Bibliographic Records) and FRAD (Functional Requirements for Authority Data). This is both RDA's strength and its weakness. On one hand, there is tremendous potential in FRBRized displays for catalogs. However, the elements of the records are discussed where they fall logically and not necessarily where they would be found in a catalog record, which can make RDA hard to read and use. Admittedly, it was not intended to be read sequentially, but even though it is primarily available via the RDA Toolkit website rather than a monograph (RDA is available in print, but it lacks the functionality provided by the RDA Toolkit's hyperlinks to related rules, resources, etc.), at some point one has to read a series of concepts that interlock for it to make sense.

While using the RDA Toolkit and interpreting RDA's rules can be difficult because of the obscurity of much of its language, RDA records can be made simpler than AACR2 records if that is the desire of the institution. Complex punctuation and capitalization rules are gone. Publishers, distributors, and manufacturers can be separated from one another in successive statements, rather than having to follow one another according to a pattern. Fewer elements are required in an RDA record. A cataloging department can decide whether to continue with standard capitalization and ISBD (International Standard Bibliographic Description) punctuation (most libraries seem to have kept both, for now), and make determinations about whether to include more than the basic fields, set up a cheat sheet for the copy catalogers, and make the switch with little difficulty.

As to the question of whether RDA is good for cataloging or detrimental, after considerable grumbling, I would have to say the former. While it has many drawbacks, it is a better standard for these times of ambiguous and morphing formats. It is unfortunate if libraries do not switch to RDA because of fear of its complexity or because of administrative conservatism.

BIBFRAME

BIBFRAME (Bibliographic Framework) is the document markup that is currently being developed as MARC's replacement. Based on the RDF (Resource Description Framework) markup language (http://www.w3.org/RDF), it is hoped that BIBFRAME will be used beyond libraries by other cultural institutions such as museums and archives. It intends to use linked data to make library data more visible on the web and to improve traditional bibliographic searching. BIBFRAME makes use of "authorities" for access points, which are not like current authorities but are basically unique identifiers that can then link to other data, creating a web of bibliographic information. [24]

It is not clear how BIBFRAME will play out in practice. MARC is very old and collapsing under the weight of its welter of detail. However, I have had conversations with vendors, touting their next-generation integrated library systems, who have not heard of it, suggesting that implementation on a broad scale may be slow. It will undoubtedly be easier to use than MARC, since a template can be created to cover the RDF, which will alleviate the need for catalogers to remember dozens of codes and tags to do their work. This could have the result of further deprofessionalizing cataloging. However, BIBFRAME, like RDA, is FRBR-compliant, which means that there will be professional-level work to create work records and appropriately linking the various record levels. It is too soon to tell how BIBFRAME will affect us, but it is an important part of any dialogue on technical services in the future.

THE ONCE AND FUTURE TECHNICAL SERVICES LIBRARIAN

We have reached a critical juncture where traditional technical services exists only as a shadow of its former self in many institutions, if it exists at all. Based on an examination of the ALA JobLIST, there are still traditional technical services positions available, but they are few. Most require skills in metadata and electronic resources management in addition to traditional skills. It is increasingly common to find jobs that combine systems and technical services, with a systems job description including a single line such as "knowledge of MARC" to suggest that this person will manipulate catalog records at some level. The job loss has happened for technical services managers as well. As more technical services tasks are done in other divisions, fewer heads of cataloging or heads of technical services are being hired.

There are still books and journals requested by selectors, ordered by acquisitions, received and invoiced, sent to cataloging for a full record, sent to binding for a label, and finally delivered to circulation for shelving. These materials have become the minority. Other scenarios for the acquisition and cataloging of library materials include:

- A book is ordered by a selector in public services using a vendor's website. The book arrives in circulation shelf-ready and is shelved in the open stacks. At approximately the same time, a MARC record is sent to a cataloger, who uploads it to the catalog.
- A book is ordered using Amazon's one-day delivery option. The uncataloged book is given to a user who had requested it through ILL. When the book is returned, ILL sends it to cataloging to add to the collection.
- A book is requested by a professor. The professor is asked if an e-book is acceptable. He says yes. A vendor with an electronic version of the book is contacted, and access to the book, either rental or purchase, is procured. The book is purchased and the URL is sent to the professor for immediate use; the MARC record for the e-book will be delivered shortly thereafter to be uploaded.
- A student creates DC records for a collection of photographs in the Special Collections Department. She fills in a limited set of fields and assigns a single subject taken from a premade list.
- A total of 1,500 journals have been purchased from a single publisher. The invoice is paid, and the publisher sends the electronic resources librarian a link to their site where she can download the MARC records for the journals purchased.

In these scenarios, all based on examples from my home institution, Florida State University, technical services work has been dispersed to everyone from student workers to vendors and takes place in a variety of departments. Technical services is no longer a division within the library. Rather than vanishing, technical services work has melded into other parts of the library and beyond. In short, whether the traditional form of technical services departments hold up, the work remains vital to libraries. So the question becomes, what skill set is needed by technical services librarians in the future?

First, one must consider that a technical services librarian may be found in departments other than technical services. A technical services librarian could be working in special collections, access services, technology, or a hybrid department. The technical services librarian would be expected to gain knowledge of the goals and procedures of the department to which he or she belonged as well as technical services work. A technical services librarian must know RDA, MARC, AACR2, LCSH, and other standard cataloging tools and resources. Even if working in nontraditional circumstances, it may be necessary to manipulate legacy data, and to do that, one must understand the construction of the data.

Programming is becoming an increasingly useful tool for technical services librarians. Any way that you can learn more about manipulating your ILS system to produce reports, download and upload a variety of data, and create shortcuts in cataloging will be useful. One need not be a full-fledged computer scientist, but the more one can do without recourse to the technology and systems personnel, the better. Increasingly, technical services librarians are expected to be able to manage the ILS. One must know multiple types of metadata. It is not just MARC or even MARC and DC anymore.

Communication skills are essential for any technical services librarian. Technical services librarians, whether in a traditional technical services department or falling under another administrative unit, must be able to articulate clearly the needs and concerns of technical services to other librarians and library administrators. Without such communication, there may truly be an end to technical services.

NOTES

1. "World Wide Web," *Wikipedia*, last modified May 4, 2014, https://en.wikipedia.org/wiki/World_wide_web.

2. Yiu-On Li and Shirley W. Leung, "Computer Cataloging of Electronic Journals in Unstable Aggregator Databases: The Hong Kong Baptist University Library Experience," *Library Resources & Technical Services* 45, no. 4 (2001): 209–10.

3. Norman Oder, "Peter McCracken: Librarian as Entrepreneur," *Library Journal* 126, no. 13 (2001): 45.

4. Roger C. Shonfeld, "JSTOR: A Case History in the Recent History of Scholarly Communication and Information," *Program: Electronic Library & Information Systems* 39, no. 4 (2005): 337.

5. Lee Van Orsdel and Kathleen Born, "Is the Big Deal Dead? 43rd Annual Report, Periodicals Price Survey 2003," *Library Journal* 128, no. 7 (2003): 51.

6. Robert W. Boissy et al., "Is the 'Big Deal' Dying?," *Serials Review* 38 (2012): 36.

7. Boissy et al., "Is the 'Big Deal' Dying?," 45.

8. Barbara A. Winters, "Catalog Outsourcing at Wright State University: Implications for Acquisitions Managers," *Library Acquisitions: Practice & Theory* 16, no. 4 (1994): 367–73.

9. William H. Walters, "E-Books in Academic Libraries: Challenges for Discovery and Access," *Serials Review* 39, no. 2 (2013): 97–104.

10. Robert Slater, "E-Books or Print Books, 'Big Deals' or Local Selections—What Gets More Use?," *Library Collections, Acquisitions & Technical Services* 33, no. 1 (2009): 32.

11. University of California Libraries. Bibliographical Services Task Force, *Rethinking How We Provide Bibliographic Services for the University of California*, December 2005, http://libraries.universityofcalifornia.edu/groups/files/bstf/docs/Final.pdf.

12. Ibid., 25.

13. Ibid.

14. Karen Calhoun, "The Changing Nature of the Catalog and Its Integration with Other Discovery Tools," Library of Congress, March 17, 2006, http://www.loc.gov/catdir/calhoun-report-final.pdf.

15. Ibid., 9.

16. Jackie Byrd et al., "A White Paper on the Future of Cataloging at Indiana University," Indiana University, January 15, 2006, http://www.iub.edu/~libtserv/pub/Future_of_Cataloging_White_Paper.pdf.

17. University of California Libraries, *Rethinking How We Provide Bibliographic Services*.

18. Library of Congress Working Group on the Future of Bibliographic Control, "On the Record: Report of the Library of Congress Working Group on the Future of Bibliographic Control," January 9, 2008, 6, http://www.loc.gov/bibliographic-future/news/lcwg-ontherecord-jan08-final.pdf.

19. Ibid.

20. Ibid.

21. Library of Congress, "Library of Congress Announces Its Long-Range RDA Training Plan," March 3, 2012, http://www.loc.gov/catdir/cpso/news_rda_implementation_date.html.

22. Kathryn P. Glennan, "The Development of Resource Description & Access and Its Impact on Music Materials," *Notes* 68, no. 3 (2012): 526.

23. Ibid.

24. Library of Congress, "Bibliographic Framework as a Web of Data: Linked Data Model and Supporting Services," November 21, 2012, http://www.loc.gov/bibframe/pdf/marcld-report-11-21-2012.pdf.

Chapter Nine

Interviews and Feedback from the Profession

Mary Beth Weber

The following section consists of interviews with various people from technical services about the current state of technical services and the future of technical services. The people interviewed run the gamut from newer professionals to established professionals and are from a variety of types of libraries. The questions, which are provided below, do not necessarily support my personal beliefs, and some of them are intended to elicit a strong reaction.

INTERVIEW QUESTIONS

1. What's your technical services background/experience?
2. How do you define technical services? What does that term mean to you?
3. In your opinion, what do you believe is the most important development that's taken place in technical services in the last five years? Ten years?
4. Has technical services been deprofessionalized? Why or why not? If it has, what do you think has contributed to this change?
5. In your opinion, should cataloging and other technical services courses be required to earn an MLS? Why or why not?
6. Is there value for library and information science programs in offering a technical services concentration? Why or why not?
7. What advice might you give to recent MLS graduates or those considering a career in technical services?
8. Do you think cataloging as it's been known will become a thing of the past? Why or why not?

9. In your opinion, will RDA deliver? Will it meet its own expectations, as outlined in the Joint Steering Committee's prospectus? Does it meet the needs of library users?

10. Should established technical services work be automated or out-sourced to vendors to free up librarians' time to tackle new initiatives such as research data and open access?

11. What skills will be needed for technical services work in the future?

12. What changes or trends do you predict will take place in technical services in the next five years? Ten years?

13. Respond to the following statements:

   • Metadata trumps MARC cataloging.
   • RDA isn't the answer.
   • Vendor-supplied services can replace costly positions, reduce re-dundancies, and increase efficiencies in technical services.
   • PDA/DDA is the answer for acquisitions, collection development, and collection management. Let the users choose!
   • Preservation is necessary only for digital resources to ensure access to them well into the future.
   • Technical services is dead.

INTERVIEW RESPONSES

Norm Medeiros, Associate Librarian and Coordinator for Collection Man-agement and Metadata Services, Magill Library, Haverford College, Haver-ford, Pennsylvania

What's your technical services background/experience?

While still an undergraduate at UMass Dartmouth, I was trained in serials cataloging using OCLC. By the time I completed my library degree at the University of Rhode Island, I was well prepared as a cataloger and started my first professional position days after earning my MLIS. As I progressed through my career, I gained experience and responsibility for web design, electronic resource management, acquisitions and licensing, budgeting, and collection development. In my current position, I oversee collection develop-ment and technical services.

How do you define technical services? What does that term mean to you?

Technical services has expanded since I came into the profession twenty years ago. It includes a larger array of activities beyond the foundational ones of acquisitions, serials management, and cataloging. Metadata services for repository systems, scholarly communications, and discovery services are all relatively new responsibilities that are managed by technical services staff in many libraries. It's really an exciting time to be involved in technical services.

In your opinion, what do you believe is the most important development that's taken place in technical services in the last five years? Ten years?

The emergence of repository functions situated in technical services has been hugely important. As I think of the future of my technical services unit, I look to the digital curation function we serve for the campus as among the most important. It places on us responsibility for the description, discovery, and long-term preservation of digital objects of enduring value to the institution. Working collaboratively with faculty, administrative offices, and student groups pushes out our services, and reminds the campus of our value. We'll always acquire and catalog materials, but it's this outward-facing work, the customized one-on-one services we provide, that has the greatest return.

Has technical services been deprofessionalized? Why or why not? If it has, what do you think has contributed to this change?

I don't think so, though nonexempt staff are increasingly performing tasks that were formerly the domain of professionals. This is the case in my library, but not because we're deprofessionalizing technical services, but rather that we need to deploy librarians to other projects. For example, there are practically limitless opportunities to apply metadata expertise across digital projects, not just within the library, but on campus. This is the kind of work in which we need to engage.

In your opinion, should cataloging and other technical services courses be required to earn an MLS? Why or why not?

Absolutely! Irrespective of one's desire to work in a particular area of librarianship, understanding the core that underlies the business processes of a library is valuable. In terms of cataloging, there's been a renaissance of sorts in maintaining rich and valid MARC, as enhanced catalogs can provide robust faceting by leveraging quality bibliographic records. Public services librarians with some knowledge of cataloging and the way MARC manifests in catalogs are better equipped to work with technical services librarians to optimize discovery, and to assist patrons with their searches.

Is there value for library and information science programs in offering a technical services concentration? Why or why not?

Possibly. I guess I'd like to see the curriculum for such a concentration before weighing in. It's certainly an idea worthy of discussion.

What advice might you give to recent MLS graduates or those considering a career in technical services?

I think it's incredibly important for recent graduates to gain practical experience, even if it's unpaid. Such experience will demonstrate responsibility, and to some degree aptitude. It tells potential employers that the graduate brings some tangible skills to the table. When hired for the first time, new librarians need to be flexible and enthusiastic. The position won't likely be their dream job, but they need to recognize that it's a necessary step to something better. The best libraries—and by extension the best technical services departments—constantly adjust to meet new challenges and take advantage of new opportunities. New recruits should be the kind of team player that is consistently positive, and one that volunteers regularly. Not only will this endear them to their colleagues, it will further fill out their portfolio, thereby making them more marketable when the time comes for that next position. Above all, they should join and contribute to ALCTS. The Association for Collections and Technical Services, a division of ALA, is the professional home of technical services librarians, and is a network that opens doors and provides numerous opportunities for professional growth.

Do you think cataloging as it's been known will become a thing of the past? Why or why not?

Certainly the way cataloging was performed in the prior decades will—I think largely already has—become a relic. Libraries are loading records en masse, and using scripting languages to manipulate them. We're more reliant on third parties for such records, to the point where as long as a vendor supplies any sort of record for large sets of items, we're generally satisfied. This generalization is perhaps overstated, but what's clear is the practice of record-level review, except for a library's "special" materials, is no longer feasible. I think if a library has the staff resources to perform cataloging today as it did in the past, that library isn't appropriating its catalogers' time on the right stuff.

In your opinion, will RDA deliver? Will it meet its own expectations, as outlined in the Joint Steering Committee's prospectus? Does it meet the needs of library users?

RDA was overly ambitious and too late to achieve many of the goals originally conceived. The idea that RDA could serve as a code for nonlibrary communities was inspired yet unreasonable, as there was no way to simultaneously dumb down the code sufficiently for adoption by these other communities, while maintaining the rigor desired by libraries. And while FRBR is an intelligent concept, the emergence of discovery systems seems to me to provide FRBR-like benefits to patrons, without the need to apply a new cataloging code. In talking with colleagues at larger libraries where introduction of RDA will be more onerous and expensive than at Haverford, I get the strong sense that RDA just isn't worth it.

Should established technical services work be automated or outsourced to vendors to free up librarians' time to tackle new initiatives such as research data and open access?

That horse has left the barn, but I don't think it's entirely a bad thing. It used to be the sole purpose of technical services to acquire, catalog, and physically process materials for users whose chief interest in libraries was the consumption of said materials. Technical services and libraries more generally do *so much more* today, directly supporting faculty and student work, whether that is through maintaining OA repositories, assisting with data management plans, publishing student journals, collaborating on digital scholarship projects, and so forth. There simply isn't time to conduct business as we once did. Again, I don't think this a problem, but rather an opportunity.

What skills will be needed for technical services work in the future?

A combination of hard and soft skills will be necessary. The nature of library organizations is changing, as is the work, and having the capacity to collaborate in teams, and to work across divisions and university departments, is important. I think programming and similar technical skills will be increasingly useful. I think proficiency with statistical software will be valuable, particularly in collection development, as evidence-based decisions will become more prevalent. Fluency with several metadata schemes will be expected of catalog/metadata librarians, as will the ability to provide consultation and project management to assist clients with projects. Flexibility, enthusiasm, dependability, and good judgment will continue to be critically important traits, as they are today.

What changes or trends do you predict will take place in technical services in the next five years? Ten years?

I'm interested to see the effect of article- and chapter-level purchases on publishers, specifically how the erosion of guaranteed revenues affects the industry or causes it to rethink the profitability of providing pay-per-view services. I'm eager to see whether e-book DDA is a fad or a revolution in collection development, and whether print-on-demand services gain traction in libraries. There's a large role for libraries to play regarding the "openness" mandates coming out of the federal government, and I think technical services can and should be serving their institutions in this regard. On a related note, I'm anxious to see whether the recent favorable fair-use court decisions lead to legislative action. I'm also eager to see if linked data lives up to the hype. I'm interested to see how more forward-facing technical services work transforms the institutional identity of these librarians, many of whom are pejoratively classed as "backroom staff."

Respond to the following statements:

Metadata trumps MARC cataloging.

MARC is like the Hulk. You can't kill it. The more you try, the more powerful it gets. Metadata is like Tony Stark. Slick, but unpredictable. Given the immense investment in MARC records and rendering systems, I can't see an exit plan for it. I think MARC/AACR/RDA and varieties of metadata schemes can coexist in harmony. They have for some time now.

RDA isn't the answer.

I suppose it depends on the question, but for the questions I would pose, RDA isn't the answer.

Vendor-supplied services can replace costly positions, reduce redundancies, and increase efficiencies in technical services.

I don't see vendor-supplied services as replacing positions, but rather as releasing positions to focus on other, higher-value work.

PDA/DDA is the answer for acquisitions, collection development, and collection management. Let the users choose!

Like most things in life, moderation is the key. We can't predict all user needs; this is why interlibrary loan services were developed. In my library, DDA serves niche areas not attended to by our approval plan. We rely far more heavily on the expertise of subject librarians to build collections. Each library is unique, so I don't believe there's an optimal DDA approach.

Preservation is necessary only for digital resources to ensure access to them well into the future.

Certainly *not* true. We need to care for our analog collections equally if not more so.

Technical services is dead.

To the contrary, I think this is the most exciting time to be involved in technical services.

Sarah Peterson, Technical Services Manager, Tulsa City-County Library System, Tulsa, Oklahoma

What's your technical services background/experience?

We used to be able to specialize a lot more than we do now—I started out as a copy cataloger for adult nonfiction with Library of Congress copy—detoured into Interlibrary Loan before becoming a cataloging supervisor who also cataloged—adult nonfiction, serials, and electronic resources, and am now technical services manager, overseeing cataloging, acquisitions, and physical processing.

How do you define technical services? What does that term mean to you?

To me, technical services provides access to everything we have. We're the people that build the catalog so that you can find what you want, and we get materials ready to go on the shelf or get accessed by customers in whatever way they're available. These two pieces both have different demands, and go hand in hand. The stickers on the books need to get the items to the same place it says they'll be in the catalog. The catalog needs to provide as much access as possible in as many ways as we think people will look for things, and for electronic materials, the links need to be accurate and reliable. The processing needs to mean that items go out in a way that customers will both find them *and* be willing to take them home, because they're in good condition and processed to hold up to substantial library use over time.

In your opinion, what do you believe is the most important development that's taken place in technical services in the last five years?

Thinking about how to use new technology to connect people to our materials. I'm not sure how far we've gotten, but I know it is the thing that is either leading us forward or getting us off track—RDA, linked data, BIB-FRAME, the proliferation of metadata schemas, the attempts to move our data out into the larger world. I still don't know enough about it to know if it's necessary, useful, overly optimistic, or exactly the road we need to be traveling.

Ten years?

Deprofessionalization and outsourcing seem to me to be the biggest changes over the last ten years. As budgets have been cut, technical services has borne more than our fair share of that cut while at the same time having to learn new technologies, build new processes, and accomplish more than ever with less staff than ever. At the same time, outsourcing especially to the shelf-ready level has been moving us toward an acceptance of items and catalog records that may not be providing the access or information our users need, but no one left behind has the time to do the research and put together the evidence of what we have lost and continue to lose.

Has technical services been deprofessionalized? Why or why not? If it has, what do you think has contributed to this change?

I can't help but think that's the case, because I know too many instances, especially in public libraries, where positions that used to require an MLIS just don't anymore. I don't know that I'll get to hire any more professional librarians as catalogers when positions open up. I would hope that isn't true, but I know there is a definite trend away from that. In addition, some cataloging work is being shifted toward acquisitions, outsourcing to the point of shelf-ready materials is increasing, and people aren't being replaced, which means even those professionals who are left don't have the time to provide the complete and thoughtful access that we used to be able to provide. It seems as if administrators think that bibliographic copy just exists, but all of that copy is created by someone—if every library decides to rely on copy cataloging, we will soon be left with vendor records, and I don't think anyone who understands what that means will want that to happen. There have always been libraries that have borne more than their share of record contribution, but how much more can they shoulder as more and more libraries opt out of doing our part? What we lose with deprofessionalization is the time and thoughtfulness that keeps us finding new and better ways to provide access to our materials. Without professional catalogers, the move to BIB-FRAME, to other types of metadata, to finding ways to push our information out into the larger world will just not be manageable.

In your opinion, should cataloging and other technical services courses be required to earn an MLS? Why or why not?

I definitely think cataloging courses should be required, even if they're focused more toward "here's what you need to know about cataloging and the catalog in order to better serve your customers." I've always said that a cataloging class directed at the rules and actual cataloging would be much more valuable after you've actually cataloged for a while. However, not understanding anything about cataloging and how the catalog is built can seriously hamper any librarian's ability to help customers find materials. Understanding the catalog of the library in which you work—what's in and what isn't in it—is also absolutely necessary. Until that magical day when we get everything integrated, librarians need to know that different types of materials need to be searched for in different interfaces, and be able to explain them clearly to customers. I know when we have public service staff rotate through technical services, they always learn something that helps them do their job better. However, if you're only going to have one or two courses, you might as well target the public service staff—they can learn what they need to learn to be more successful at their jobs without having to know how to traverse the RDA Toolkit. I'm not yet convinced that I need to know how to do that.

Is there value for library and information science programs in offering a technical services concentration? Why or why not?

Absolutely, I would strongly recommend this. I took a whole bunch of library school classes that weren't helpful to my career, and there were almost no offerings for those of us interested in the technical services side. As you can tell from the variety of professional development opportunities offered by ALA and elsewhere, there's a great need for training in the technical services side of things—from selection to acquisitions to cataloging to processing. Right now, that all has to be learned on the job, making the library school experience a fairly frustrating one. I would have loved to learn about book jobbers and EDI invoicing and metadata schemas and discovery platforms and how they work with the catalog and things like that instead of reading all those children's books. And if there were a whole concentration, cataloging could be taught in a much friendlier manner—starting with concepts and leading up to finding, understanding, and applying the rules, rather than trying to cram all of that into one semester.

What advice might you give to recent MLS graduates or those considering a career in technical services?

I think I would say that it's an amazingly interesting time to get involved in technical services, but also a confusing one because everything is still kind of shaking out. We're trying to get rid of MARC, but we have all that legacy data and no money. We're creating metadata for electronic items using other encoding systems and other software. We want to take advantage of the technology being developed to connect our materials with users all over, but still need to be able to let our customers look up a book and find out which library it's in and get it sent to their library. The catalog may not be the best place for discovery, but it's hooked up to the cataloging systems that allow our users to place holds and renew items online, and we can't let go of that functionality or make it more complicated. If you're willing to get in there and figure out how to make things work, and are interested in what technology may have to offer the library world, this is an absolutely brilliant time to get involved in tech services, because there are so many opportunities—and in many cases, those opportunities may allow you to be a part of creating the future of libraries and library technology.

Do you think cataloging as it's been known will become a thing of the past? Why or why not?

I do think cataloging has changed and will continue to change, but cataloging or something like it will remain. We still need to know who has what, at varying levels of specificity, and we need to be able to tell people where they can find it or how they can get it. I do think we will need to reexamine our processes in much more depth than we have thus far. I think we'll do less pointing people to records about materials and more of connecting them to the materials themselves, and that will mean big changes for the catalog or for how we do what we do. But with the proliferation of materials both physical and electronic, the need for assistance in finding and accessing it just continues to grow. I hope our organizations will allow that need to continue to be met by libraries, because I don't think anyone else will do it as well or with purer intentions than we do.

In your opinion, will RDA deliver? Will it meet its own expectations, as outlined in the Joint Steering Committee's prospectus? Does it meet the needs of library users?

Some days, I really think RDA was just the warning shot that we really do need to realize that we need to think about what we're doing and how we're doing it. I don't think RDA goes nearly far enough, and making sure that it worked with legacy MARC records certainly hampered its ability to make big and probably necessary changes. For all it accomplished, we could have had AACR3 and poured our energies into creating a completely new solution free from MARC, focused on how the world, library and otherwise, can use data and technology to connect people to resources. It seems to me that it fails both as AACR3 and as a new and different methodology—the Toolkit isn't easy to use, and I'm not convinced it has made our data any more useful outside our catalogs. And the terminology used seems insane to me in some cases. I would really like to be able to tell people in a bib record that the item in hand is a music CD, in exactly those terms. I hope the technical and specific terms are helpful to some libraries—we'll just reinsert the GMDs and suppress the 3XX fields until we can find a use for them. I have to admit that it doesn't seem worth the time, trouble, and expense for what we're getting from it. We need bigger change than this, but if it can get us started down that road, that's something anyway. As far as meeting the needs of library users, I haven't even been able to come up with training to demonstrate any additional benefits to our public service staff, much less to our customers. I've been to a number of training sessions on talking to public service staff about RDA, and honestly, even at the most basic level, most of the things they have been including in those training sessions are not things public service staff really seem to need to know. They didn't mind the abbreviations in the records, but they're not going to mind things not being abbreviated. We're keeping the GMDs, so nothing to tell them there. The 33X fields are too technical and have strange enough language that we're not even displaying them.

Should established technical services work be automated or outsourced to vendors to free up librarians' time to tackle new initiatives such as research data and open access?

I'd love to think that's what would happen if we continue to automate and outsource, but that certainly won't be the case in the public library world. Automating and outsourcing will likely largely mean the end for a technical services, a potential end to authority control, and an end to local control and the ability to modify the catalog and catalog records to meet the needs of our customers. And vendors aren't doing a particularly good job at what we do. If they can do what we do better and cheaper, that would be fine, but it just doesn't seem to be the case. We recently insourced much of what we had outsourced because we can do it better and cheaper. So, sure, automate what makes sense, I'm all for that—and we've worked really hard to make our processes efficient and effective. We always will get bestsellers shelf-ready from the vendors so they can go out the day they appear in the bookstores. However, any reduction in a need for personnel has just resulted in, well, less personnel, not redirecting those personnel to doing more interesting or professional-level tasks. I'd love to believe that things will be different in the academic world, but I haven't seen much evidence of that either.

What skills will be needed for technical services work in the future?

That is the million-dollar question, isn't it? I'm not sure that, at least in the short term, the demands for acquisitions staff and processors will be changing that much, but wow, for cataloging, it's so hard to know! A willingness and ability to deal with technology and its accoutrements will be vital. You won't know what metadata schemas you'll be using, how much programming stuff you'll need to know, how many systems you'll have to convince to play nice with each other. The link between tech services and IT seems to me to be getting fuzzier every year, maybe every month. In the future, we'll probably need to be the ones who are really engaged in figuring out how to make the most of the data and access we have using technology we haven't even imagined yet. So anything that gets you farther down the road of being comfortable in that world is going to be helpful—be able to carry on an intelligent conversation about linked data and why the library world is interested in it, know what BIBFRAME is and keep an eye on its progress, learn to code in some way—lots of interesting online opportunities there—learn about various metadata schemas and why libraries choose one over the other for various purposes, learn about how the commercial world is using data or access or information similar to ours, and keep an eye on the library bloggers and others who are trying to find ways to do similar or completely different but extremely cool things.

What changes or trends do you predict will take place in technical services in the next five years? Ten years?

I honestly have no idea. I'm not sure the jobs of the people on my staff will change that much in the next five years—not because they shouldn't, but because change is slow in coming, business cases for big changes aren't being stated clearly, and we still have a lot of stuff that needs to get ordered, cataloged, processed, and out on the shelves. I think the changes will be more incremental over that time frame—we'll be continuing to put more of our energies toward figuring out how to better manage electronic resources, how to change our processes to reflect different quantities of different types of materials, and how to continue getting work out as staff don't get replaced. We just insourced a lot of work, but if too many people leave, it will likely take the work right back to the vendors, which brings up another whole set of questions because vendor work is just different than local work.

Over ten years, we could have immense change, but only if someone finds a way to make it seem necessary, doable, and affordable. A library world free of MARC is fine with me as long as our customers can still check out all the materials we cataloged that way, and we won't have enough people with the skills to write crosswalks to new data formats or to figure out how to combine that data with new types of data and still ensure good search that will give useful and complete results. We'll have to rely on vendors to make massive changes, and those vendors will have to be affordable. Maybe Gates will change their mind and just retarget their library funds to making the changes that need to happen to join our resources to the world and make them widely available instead of trapping them in local pockets. And while academic libraries can focus more on sharing electronic materials and how to make that happen, public libraries still need to get picture books to kids and series titles to, well, everyone, and to provide the broad collections we need to serve our communities with less money and a proliferation of formats. So, I don't know, I think the biggest possibilities for change in the next ten years will come in the opportunities to share our electronic resources with the wider world, but we need to figure out how to do that in a way that grabs people's attention and shows the value added by library services.

Respond to the following statements:

Metadata trumps MARC cataloging.

MARC is another form of metadata in very many ways, and it isn't metadata that plays nice with newer technologies, so it is time to admit that, over the long haul, it isn't a solution, and we will need to figure out what comes next and who can do that and how we're going to pay for it. Libraries are already choosing multiple metadata schemes for various types of materials, and figuring out how to make those choices and then how to make those choices work in harmony for our customers is the real issue. The thing libraries will need to focus on is making the right metadata choices—asking the right questions, not just choosing a scheme because someone at the institution understands it, and taking full advantage of the benefits of the schemes they choose to demonstrate library value.

RDA isn't the answer.

If it is the answer, I think someone asked a really weird question. RDA is a step down a road that says our data has to play nicer with new technology if we're going to be able to use it and present it to the world in any useful, cool, or meaningful ways going forward. A business case that would demonstrate benefits to users or libraries would certainly be a useful thing to have, since the process of moving to RDA is expensive in staff time and training, and the immediate benefits, if any, aren't easily obvious. It also isn't clear that future benefits will rely not just on a full implementation of RDA but also on a lot of other changes as well—some of which may leave RDA behind, potentially. RDA may be a better question than an answer—it certainly begins to suggest the ways that we need to change our thinking about how we share our data and resources with the world.

Vendor-supplied services can replace costly positions, reduce redundancies, and increase efficiencies in technical services.

That's very true—we can reduce staff, get rid of useful local additions and information, and increase efficiencies by simply opening boxes and putting them on the shelves however they come in. I can see the appeal to administration, until they see the quality of what comes in those boxes. If outsourcing is used carefully to address specific needs, it can be a very valuable part of the technical services process. However, using outsourcing carefully means building and then updating complete profiles to meet local needs, carefully selecting the types of materials that benefit the most from quick and efficient processes, and making sure there is some sort of quality control process in place when the materials are received. The catalog records received from vendors range from thorough and complete and correct down to almost no information including the wrong title and authors' names appearing in formats that render them unsearchable in our catalogs. We've worked very hard over many years to streamline our work and our processes, reduce redundant steps and activities, and focus on only adding information or steps that obviously increase value for our users. Our cost studies suggest that we cost less than vendors and can still get materials out in about the same amount of time it takes to receive shelf-ready material from the vendor, with the notable exception of bestsellers. Those we buy the number we want shelf-ready and lease the rest. We were outsourcing juvenile fiction, picture books, and readers, but when it came right down to it, we found we could incorporate them back into our workflow for less money and without a noticeable loss of turnaround. We'll be redoing all of those cost and time studies regularly to make sure that remains the case.

PDA/DDA is the answer for acquisitions, collection development, and collection management. Let the users choose!

If we relied on PDA for everything, we'd have a delightful romance and erotica collection, but possibly not a collection that would be of overall value to our community—at least that's what happened when we ventured into PDA for e-books, and we ended up needing to pull back on the allowed number of requests to make sure there was money for other types of materials. Unless we can find a way to engage the whole community in expressing their needs to us, PDA just caters to the needs of those people who like to do that kind of thing. We're working to improve our "suggest a purchase" processes so that it's easier to make requests, and to make sure you get holds on materials we end up purchasing. And while there's a real place for patron suggestions or choices, we also suddenly have a lot more data that library staff can use to target their choices better as well. Our collection management department is also working hard to get and use data that suggests the materials our community will really use. From Decision Center software that tracks usage and relates it to expenditures, to other community data gathered for us by Orangeboy, we're trying to get better and better at making collection decisions based on actual data about how the people in our community use our resources, and what issues and topics and materials are important to them. PDA does tend to skew the collection in the direction of the customers who enjoy making those requests.

Preservation is necessary only for digital resources to ensure access to them well into the future.

Well, preservation is definitely necessary for digital resources—as technology changes so quickly, it's no longer uncommon to lose access to digital material that's no longer upwardly compatible with the new versions of software. The truth of the matter is that preservation is necessary for anything we want to ensure access to well into the future. Probably the biggest question in front of us is exactly *what* stuff will that be. We're binding many less print periodicals; we assume paperback books will disappear within a year or so. However, our unique collections—for us, that's mostly oil, gas, geology, that kind of thing—have always needed to be cared for to ensure continuous access. The same is very true for digital resources, and people don't always realize just how much work it is going to be—either keeping older versions of software working on older versions of hardware or finding ways to move that data into new software on an ongoing basis. And since it can be so easy to store vast amounts of electronic data, it means we need to devote time to maintaining accessibility, as well as making some interesting choices about what we will and will not preserve for the future. There are some who would argue that organizational emails are one of the most valuable ways of understanding what's really happening at that organization, but the sheer volume of email, much of which should never have been sent in the first place, creates a problem that is quite a large one. It's kind of funny to me that microfilm is still the longest-lasting, most reliable preservation method because the film is stable, the machines used for it are relatively easy to maintain, and new versions of film readers seem more than able to work easily with old microfilm. The same can't be said for the digital formats of the many things we want to save. So put the books in digital format if you don't want to keep buildings filled with them, but we also need to be prepared to continually manage those books to keep them available.

Technical services is dead.

Do you think everyone will respond with, "Technical services is dead, long live technical services"? The services we provide will not become less necessary, and I suspect if we move in a direction where we (or outsourcers) provide them in less useful ways, the pendulum will swing again when people realize that they're losing access to information they want or need because they haven't been willing to pay to make it findable. While we have competition in overall information provision, there aren't companies waiting to take over our work—especially public libraries and institutions—because it can't be monetized—that's kind of the point of why we're here. A business plan that involves hiring staff, buying technology, building buildings, offering programs, and sharing materials with people without making them pay for it other than through taxes isn't going to gather a great deal of attention from vendors who need to pay their shareholders regularly. Then again, who knows, if we can throw in a bunch of ads to generate revenue, maybe the big boys will come calling. I don't think we should hold our breath for that to happen. We need to make a better case for why what we do is so important, and we need to focus on providing and demonstrating the value we bring to our organizations and the community. Without advocacy, traditional tech services, even as it is evolving, will go away, and the communities we serve may not even understand what they have lost when that happens.

Melissa De Fino, Special Collections Cataloging and Acquisitions Librarian, Rutgers, the State University of New Jersey, Piscataway, New Jersey

What's your technical services background/experience?

I've cataloged special collections materials for ten years and overseen acquisitions of special collections materials for four years. I've also been responsible for the cataloging and acquisitions of e-books, and have managed metadata for digital projects.

How do you define technical services? What does that term mean to you?

To me, technical services encompass all cataloging, acquisitions, metadata, and preservation activities within the library.

In your opinion, what do you believe is the most important development that's taken place in technical services in the last five years? Ten years?

In the past five years, the development of e-resources. In the past ten years, the growth of institutional repositories. Our work looked very different before and after each of these two changes. We went from working mainly with print resources to digital. Both innovations improved access. Our materials are reaching a wider population of users.

Has technical services been deprofessionalized? Why or why not? If it has, what do you think has contributed to this change?

No, I think quite the opposite has happened. I became a technical services librarian ten years ago. When I started, I still saw some need for paraprofessionals doing things like copy cataloging and end processing. I've been told that in the past we had many more paraprofessionals responsible for typing catalog cards and searching the catalogs. What I see now is the need for more professionals in technical services. Our work is changing so quickly and becoming so complex that we no longer have unskilled work. Copy cataloging and end processing are often outsourced. What's left is original cataloging of our most rare and valuable materials, as well as metadata and digital work that requires creative and adaptable librarians with strong technical skills.

In your opinion, should cataloging and other technical services courses be required to earn an MLS? Why or why not?

Yes, absolutely. An understanding of cataloging, metadata, and acquisitions is very important for reference and collection development librarians. Likewise, I think all technical services librarians should be educated in public services. I've always tried to catalog with the end user in mind. I try to imagine how our patrons will use the metadata I'm creating, rather than following cataloging rules just because they're "the rules." In my institution, my only connection to the public is through our public services librarians. I try to always ask them for feedback on my work, from themselves as well as from their users. The easiest librarians to work with are those who already have an understanding of the catalog and what it can and can't do.

Is there value for library and information science programs in offering a technical services concentration? Why or why not?

Yes, definitely. My library school did not offer a technical services concentration, and I feel like I really missed out. I was fortunate enough to have a part-time job with a very experienced cataloger who taught me everything I know, but not everyone can be so lucky.

What advice might you give to recent MLS graduates or those considering a career in technical services?

I try to steer new librarians away from library school because I think we've overloaded the market at the moment. There are just too many new graduates and too few entry-level positions. But for those who really are determined, I'd say that they should learn a little bit about everything and learn one thing really well. Learn cataloging in as many formats as you can. Learn preservation. Learn acquisitions. Learn metadata. If you can, learn programming. Then find your niche and really develop your skills in an area that isn't very popular. Find ways to make yourself stand out.

Do you think cataloging as it's been known will become a thing of the past? Why or why not?

In some ways, yes; in some ways, no. I think we're evolving rather than facing extinction. The Library of Congress is no longer the gold standard for cataloging. Their subject headings are an outdated relic, and the sooner they go the better. MARC has a lot more flexibility than most people want to admit, but it's so unpopular that I think it's going to have to go. I think we're going to see fewer standards in the future, and more local policies and practices set up to meet our changing local needs.

In your opinion, will RDA deliver? Will it meet its own expectations, as outlined in the Joint Steering Committee's prospectus? Does it meet the needs of library users?

I don't understand what problems the Joint Steering Committee thought they were going to solve with RDA. The controlled vocabulary selected for the new 3XX fields doesn't mean anything to anyone. How many of us can say we love to curl up by the fire with a nice unmediated carrier, rock out to a great audio disc, or rent a movie on videodisc? The world is becoming more gender neutral, but RDA says we need to start assigning genders to everyone. The English language is making more use of acronyms and abbreviations, but RDA is eliminating them. And what public or academic libraries have the time or money to spare on training for these new rules? How does any of this benefit our users? I'm surprised RDA has gotten this far. Like I said about the previous question, I think we're going to move toward fewer standards in the future, and RDA will likely slip away forgotten. Maybe that's just optimism on my part!

Should established technical services work be automated or outsourced to vendors to free up librarians' time to tackle new initiatives such as research data and open access?

Copy cataloging and end processing can be outsourced, but I don't see how that would happen for professional work like original cataloging and preservation of rare materials. And we wouldn't trust research data and open access to copy catalogers. There's just an overall need for more professionals in technical services, and fewer unskilled workers.

What skills will be needed for technical services work in the future?

We need creativity, adaptability, technical skills, strong education in the humanities (because librarians do still need to be well read!), people skills (because technical services librarians are working with the public more and more), and a strong service mentality.

What changes or trends do you predict will take place in technical services in the next five years? Ten years?

I hate fortune telling, but again I'll say that I do see us moving toward less standardization and more creative local policies that make the most sense for our own individual users. There are probably new formats of material coming down the line that we can't even imagine yet, and we're going to have to find ways to acquire and provide access to them. But there's no point in guessing what these resources will look like.

Respond to the following statements:

Metadata trumps MARC cataloging.

Right now, I think MARC trumps metadata. But people hate MARC, so I think eventually metadata will improve to surpass MARC. Who knows how long that will take!

RDA isn't the answer.

Amen! A better use of our time would have been revising the LCSH to meet current cultural and academic needs.

Vendor-supplied services can replace costly positions, reduce redundancies, and increase efficiencies in technical services.

I think vendor-supplied services can replace our lowest-cost positions, like copy cataloging. The work that requires the most skill is changing too much and becoming too complex to outsource effectively.

PDA/DDA is the answer for acquisitions, collection development, and collection management. Let the users choose!

I think this is right, to some extent. We can't survive on PDA/DDA alone. But I have seen it work successfully, when done correctly.

Preservation is necessary only for digital resources to ensure access to them well into the future.
This is absolutely false. Digitization may preserve the text, but it doesn't preserve the artifact. It's our responsibility as librarians to preserve our cultural heritage.

Technical services is dead.
Technical services is evolving. Years from now we may only see subtle reminders of technical services as we used to know it, but it will still be there.

Anonymous, Assistant Professor, Library Science Program

What's your technical services background/experience?
I worked in cataloging as a cataloging librarian for three years at an academic library (2002–2005), and I worked in cataloging (and as a department liaison) for two years (2005–2007) in an academic library in New Jersey. I've been teaching/co-teaching cataloging on and off since 2004 (have taught in various locations in the United States and worldwide); I taught Information Technology in 2003; I've taught Organization of Information (2010–present, once per academic year); I've also taught Metadata a few times.

How do you define technical services? What does that term mean to you?
The definition of technical services varies from library to library, so this is a tricky question. A somewhat oversimplified approach might be to think of technical services as the work carried out behind the scenes in libraries (for example, inputting catalog records, digitizing collections, working with vendors), but that doesn't necessarily include the maintenance of computer systems like the ILS. Lines are easily blurred when behind-the-scenes library work supports frontline services.

When I was in library school in 2001, it was generally understood that reference or public services work was sexy—a word I heard over and over. With post-Web advances in technology and the reliance of services upon backroom products, I can't imagine anyone saying nowadays that technical services isn't the sexy part of the library.

In your opinion, what do you believe is the most important development that's taken place in technical services in the last five years? Ten years?
Last five: Our maturity as a profession has allowed us in the last five years to commit to engaging with the computer age. Collection development

is no longer concerned that PDA didn't work in the 1980s. Cataloging is no longer wedded to MARC and is interested in future web architectures. The web has changed things fundamentally, and we are ready to get the training and look to the future.

Last ten: The general agreement that metadata is not "cataloging for men"—it's a fundamental aspect of access in digital environments.

Has technical services been deprofessionalized? Why or why not? If it has, what do you think has contributed to this change?

I admit that I'm very intrigued by this question. In one place where I worked, TS was almost completely deprofessionalized—it was a hard pill to swallow for me, too, since as I mentioned, I can't think of anything sexy that happens in librarianship that doesn't pass through technical services.

TS is a very expensive part of the library payroll, but one that hasn't always been able to advocate well for itself. When jokes circulate about the difference between a terrorist and a cataloging librarian, and the punch line describes the ability to negotiate with a terrorist (and not with a cataloger), that's a problem.

In your opinion, should cataloging and other technical services courses be required to earn an MLS? Why or why not?

I believe they should, though I really struggle with the nature of those classes. I strongly feel they should be theoretical, yet employers expect students who've taken Cataloging, for example, to be able to build a basic MARC record. But shouldn't they understand Dublin Core too? And what about the content standards and the myriad controlled vocabularies that go into a single cataloging record, not to mention all of the systems that are in use in standard cataloging agencies?

Why? Libraries do not corner the market on information. They do, however, excel at organizing it—going well beyond the Amazons of the world in description and access. The big picture of that access along with the practice that's developed and the theory that supports that practice need to be understood as libraries move forward. When librarians only focus on the skills and not the theory, that deprofessionalizes the work we do.

Addendum: I think *all* library programs should require a practicum—practica in TS should be a way for prospective employers to see that students are truly ready to make the leap to professional TS work (and this should alleviate some of my concerns about the overloaded curriculum in cataloging, for example).

Is there value for library and information science programs in offering a technical services concentration? Why or why not?

I believe there's value, but I'm not sure that employers would recognize it. At my school, it would be hard to implement, as I'm the only faculty member with any TS library experience.

What advice might you give to recent MLS graduates or those considering a career in technical services?

Do a practicum. Take Metadata. Take Cataloging. Take the Digital Libraries course and a few courses focusing on systems. Take the copyright class (everyone should take that). Plan to work in an academic library, so (1) take Academic Libraries and (2) understand that you'll need to do research as an academic librarian, and take Research Methods too.

Start grooming your CV now—prepare your skill set. Look at job ads and start learning skills/programming languages/and other things that aren't taught in library school but that you need to know based on what employers want.

Do you think cataloging as it's been known will become a thing of the past? Why or why not?

Probably, though I suppose we could argue it already has. Understanding library data and making sure it's interoperable, however, will not become a thing of the past any time soon.

In your opinion, will RDA deliver? Will it meet its own expectations, as outlined in the Joint Steering Committee's prospectus? Does it meet the needs of library users?

RDA is a step in the right direction. I understand that practically speaking, it's very difficult to do updates to systems and that we are the stewards of a lot of valuable library data. I'm not sure, however, why it's so *difficult* as professionals to learn a new standard—in some ways, that seems to be the real challenge. Didn't we all end up learning HTML at some point? And the new interface for Office products over the years? Why is change when it comes to content standards so difficult?

In short, I think the important thing that RDA did was to show cataloging librarians that it's very possible to adapt to new standards and to think about their work actively. I assume that new and evolving standards will be the way of the future, so the skill of learning new skills (such as content standards) is an important one to master.

Should established technical services work be automated or outsourced to vendors to free up librarians' time to tackle new initiatives such as research data and open access?

It's compelling, isn't it? The danger is that in outsourcing our skilled professional work no one in the library understands the systems anymore.

That's probably not always a bad thing, but it does imply that local concerns cannot be managed or implemented, or at the very least explained.

In the post–Web 2.0 era, advances in systems and advances in practice are increasingly grassroots, participative initiatives; top-down initiatives like the ones from the JSC are going to be fewer and farther between. To remain at the cutting edge, libraries will need skilled staff who understand library perspectives.

What skills will be needed for technical services work in the future?

Great question! There's so much of an emphasis on the technical aspects at present, but I'm not sure that means all TS librarians will need to be programmers. An understanding of systems will help though.

TS librarians will need to be curious and inquisitive—always looking for the next system. They'll need soft skills including communication and teamwork. They'll need project management skills.

The ability to understand the importance of standards and to implement them will be important. They'll need to be curious, to want to understand their users and to make products that will appeal to their users.

What changes or trends do you predict will take place in technical services in the next five years? Ten years?

Ten years: Content standards in cataloging will be a grassroots initiative based on best practices developed in library metadata projects; the JSC will be phased out and working TS librarians along with researchers will codify descriptive practice. Same with encoding standards. BIBFRAME will die.

Five years: Repetitive tasks will be done by nonlibrarian staff while professionals focus increasingly on big-picture issues and documentation/training and so on. The definition of TS will broaden/change as all of the work done behind the scene using technology will be the basis for services to patrons. TS librarians will continue to work in the back of the house, but the most successful TS librarians will turn their attention at the same time to the end users and the communities supporting access to their work through patron services.

Respond to the following statements:

Metadata trumps MARC cataloging.

MARC cataloging has its place, and will continue to have a place until a better solution for managing data about library materials comes along. At present, metadata works in different systems for different reasons. MARC does the job for now; it's exciting to think about what might replace it and how it might work in other metadata environments!

RDA isn't the answer.

And neither is EAD. And neither was AACR2. RDA is a content standard that provides an agreed-upon solution to the problem of standardized description. It will be replaced in time, and that's fine. It's a means to an end.

Vendor-supplied services can replace costly positions, reduce redundancies, and increase efficiencies in technical services.

This is true, especially for small institutions that lack expertise or budget. I can't imagine it would work across the board though.

PDA/DDA is the answer for acquisitions, collection development, and collection management. Let the users choose!

Helping patrons to (1) save money and (2) think the library is their ally in information seeking does not preclude libraries from having a collection development strategy, last copy networks, and so on.

Preservation is necessary only for digital resources to ensure access to them well into the future.

Paper and realia also still deserve to be preserved. Digital preservation has made great strides in the past ten years, but it's not infallible.

Technical services is dead.

If you think TS is sitting in the basement typing up MARC records one at a time or checking in serials, then, yes, it's pretty dead. If you think TS is anything done in the back of the house using technology to support patron services, then TS is alive and well and is outpacing all other parts of library operations.

Erica Findley, Cataloging/Metadata Librarian, Multnomah County Library, Portland, Oregon

What's your technical services background/experience?

I earned my MLS in 2008 and wanted to be a cataloger even before I knew what cataloging was. I concentrated on technical services in my course of studies, even though it wasn't a big part of the program. My first position was as a temporary staff member at Pacific University, and I did copy cataloging and related work. I also supervised cataloging and acquisitions work. I was essentially the head of technical services. I began my current position at Multnomah County Library in December of 2013. My current position is cataloging/metadata librarian; half of my work is spent on creating metadata for digitization projects, and the other half is spent digitizing resources for projects.

How do you define technical services? What does that term mean to you?

Traditional acquisitions, cataloging, and serials, but more and more it includes other types of work. Technical services differs by library. I see different functions provided in other locations in the Multnomah County system, such as selectors who are part of technical services.

In your opinion, what do you believe is the most important development that's taken place in technical services in the last five years? Ten years?

I haven't been in the profession long enough to comment on the last ten years. We're struggling with how to best manage electronic resources and to provide access to them. I feel that there's so much out there that we're not able to share with our patrons.

Has technical services been deprofessionalized? Why or why not? If it has, what do you think has contributed to this change?

No, I don't think it's been deprofessionalized. I see people discussing this topic on discussion lists. I haven't been in the profession long enough to see whether this has happened. Much depends on the institution and its priorities. When I worked at Pacific University, I was the only cataloger and needed help. I trained students to do copy cataloging.

In your opinion, should cataloging and other technical services courses be required to earn an MLS? Why or why not?

Yes. I always tell people to take cataloging classes. As long as we have MARC, there will be a need to understand the structure and its limitations. I'm not familiar with other types of technical services courses. It would have been helpful if I'd been able to take a course on selection since knowing the principles helps to understand selectors who are on the front lines.

Is there value for library and information science programs in offering a technical services concentration? Why or why not?

Yes, but not for everyone. Certainly if it could be offered, it would be extremely helpful. I'm not sure how many people know what they want to do when they enter library school. Those who take cataloging classes often end up being catalogers since they've gained an understanding of that work.

What advice might you give to recent MLS graduates or those considering a career in technical services?

Volunteer! Find a job to get by and also volunteer. Don't wait for opportunities to come to you in technical services. The program director in a library science program may be able to find opportunities for students. I did my own work to find opportunities and called libraries and did internships.

Get experience through a practicum or some other means. You need to get more exposure than what you get from a class.

Do you think cataloging as it's been known will become a thing of the past? Why or why not?

Not for a long time! I don't know when the article "MARC Must Die" was written. BIBFRAME is a promise we have that there will be something that we can transition to after MARC. There will still be legacy MARC records, and five years is an ambitious timeline that will require a completely different set of skills.

In your opinion, will RDA deliver? Will it meet its own expectations, as outlined in the Joint Steering Committee's prospectus? Does it meet the needs of library users?

Our users won't know the difference until we move from MARC and it's not an RDA problem. What our systems now do with new information is only to display it to show relationships more powerfully than MARC. Until their [users'] experience changes, RDA will be more an internal change for staff.

Should established technical services work be automated or outsourced to vendors to free up librarians' time to tackle new initiatives such as research data and open access?

Why not? You need to determine your library's priorities when determining other projects. Outsourcing isn't the only option. ORBIS Cascade's shared cataloging will contribute records to all members. Cooperation will free up time to do more. My library is developing a new position that will be devoted full-time to digitization.

What skills will be needed for technical services work in the future?

We've already been doing this and it also depends on what people are encouraged to do at their libraries. People will look more to their communities to bring in, describe, and make accessible unique materials and those of local interest. When we have become better at resource sharing, we will outsource other work to concentrate on local resources. Patrons will value this. Outreach and marketing skills will be needed in technical services.

What changes or trends do you predict will take place in technical services in the next five years? Ten years?

I'm already seeing some changes. Local projects and cooperative regional projects are being brought into the library framework to collect, describe, expose. Linked data could really change the landscape, especially with vendors.

Respond to the following statements:

Metadata trumps MARC cataloging.
    MARC is part of metadata.

RDA isn't the answer.
    Not yet. I've been working with RDA at Multnomah. I was hesitant to implement it at my last position.

Vendor-supplied services can replace costly positions, reduce redundancies, and increase efficiencies in technical services.
    Yes, they can. Definitely. It's what you have available at your institution or through cooperation. ORBIS Cascade is already sharing language expertise. It's not always necessary to pay a vendor for cooperation.

PDA/DDA is the answer for acquisitions, collection development, and collection management. Let the users choose!
    This is another tool that I'm very excited about, even from a cataloging and access perspective. We're giving people more access. People may not know what they need, and we need to try to anticipate as much as possible to determine their needs. PDA may not be the answer for places with a heavy research component.

Preservation is necessary only for digital resources to ensure access to them well into the future.
    I don't completely agree. It's necessary to digitize resources. Doing so will enable you to place them in a more stable physical environment, so whatever you can do is good. My library is digitizing 50 percent of our resources. We're never able to say what we'll have access to in ten years. We have the cloud, but things are changing so much. We're keeping physical objects even if we don't provide access to them.

Technical services is dead.
    Not at all! This is where it all starts! I don't know who else could do it. Technical services might be decentralized and frontline people might end up doing the work at some places. This could absolutely happen.

Karen E. K. Brown, Preservation Librarian, University at Albany, SUNY, Albany, New York

What's your technical services background/experience?

I'm a preservation librarian and my department is part of collection development. I work closely with technical services. It's politically important to keep preservation aligned with collection development.

How do you define technical services? What does that term mean to you?
Behind the scenes for most libraries. The primary job description is to work with acquisitions, collections, purchasing, linking information organizationally.

In your opinion, what do you believe is the most important development that's taken place in technical services in the last five years? Ten years?
Being able to manage serials better. Being able to work with vendors and batchload into the catalog without any manual intervention. We're bringing in enormous amounts of data. RDA is up there, and the jury is still out in terms of the impact. This has been a big step for our profession.
JSTOR and weeding print. Making the transition has been a challenge. Coping with the big shift to digital, especially with respect to journals. Dealing with vendors and the costs of doing so.

Has technical services been deprofessionalized? Why or why not? If it has, what do you think has contributed to this change?
There was a feeling at one point at my institution that a head of cataloging wasn't needed. A head of cataloging was hired in the last five years, and later promoted to an academic line. There had been a belief that this work has become more technology driven. However, we do still need leadership and someone to guide others in terms of technology. It was thought that we'd need less staffing in technical services with technology. With the recession, we've considered hiring a lower-level position to manage this work.

In your opinion, should cataloging and other technical services courses be required to earn an MLS? Why or why not?
Yes. When I earned my degree, I enjoyed cataloging. In my first year, I did a project on the history of cataloging and classification schemes for a class. The second year of studies was too theoretical.

Is there value for library and information science programs in offering a technical services concentration? Why or why not?
It would provide an opportunity to see how work is done, and original cataloging and other technical services work could be explained by experts.

What advice might you give to recent MLS graduates or those considering a career in technical services?

I work with students a lot and advise them not to aim so high in their first jobs. Very young graduates will need to aim lower until they have more experience. They're not ready for academic jobs right after they've earned their degree. Get as much experience as possible as students. They need to know what they want. Consider first taking a staff job and learning the ropes. Be open-minded about the first three to five years as a librarian. Try as much as possible to determine what you like to do.

Do you think cataloging as it's been known will become a thing of the past? Why or why not?

It's not for everyone. There will always be a need for catalogers, and you should know the tools. Small libraries might not be able to justify having catalogers on staff.

In your opinion, will RDA deliver? Will it meet its own expectations, as outlined in the Joint Steering Committee's prospectus? Does it meet the needs of library users?

I'm not sure and not able to answer this. RDA hasn't been out long enough for me to determine whether it's made an impact.

Should established technical services work be automated or outsourced to vendors to free up librarians' time to tackle new initiatives such as research data and open access?

Sure, why not, if that model works for you, as long as it doesn't mean getting rid of librarians? When I can vend out services, I can do other things. It's more likely that libraries will start doing more collaborative cataloging within consortia.

What skills will be needed for technical services work in the future?

Dealing with metadata. It will be our biggest challenge, especially with crosswalks between information. More programming skills will be needed, plus the ability to manage metadata, controlled vocabularies, and the ability to describe electronic resources.

What changes or trends do you predict will take place in technical services in the next five years? Ten years?

There will be more collaboration. This is where SUNY is going. There will be fewer librarians but more cooperative work and dealing with publishers.

Respond to the following statements:

Metadata trumps MARC cataloging.

Only for electronic resources.

RDA isn't the answer.
Probably not.

Vendor-supplied services can replace costly positions, reduce redundancies, and increase efficiencies in technical services.
This is very possible.

PDA/DDA is the answer for acquisitions, collection development, and collection management. Let the users choose!
I disagree. This is just one more piece of equipment in our arsenal for effective collecting.

Preservation is necessary only for digital resources to ensure access to them well into the future.
I disagree. We're in a hybrid environment where legacy collections demand physical support. I don't see it changing. Special, unique collections will take priority. Digital preservation is very different from traditional preservation. One involves working with your hands, and the other requires knowing how to work with programs. Less time will be spent on general collections with multiple copies. Digitization doesn't undo the need for traditional skills.

Technical services is dead.
I disagree. Technical services is the backbone of the library and is absolutely essential. Public services needs to work in technical services to gain an idea of what we do. We're needed to organize and provide access to our information. When resources are described correctly, people can find them. Journal titles are the biggest challenge, and only recently have we had the ability to look for them in just one place.

Index

About the Editor and Contributors

Mary Beth Weber is head of Central Technical Services at Rutgers University Libraries, where she has previously served in a variety of positions, including special formats catalog librarian and head of Cataloging and Metadata Services. Her research interests include MARC and non-MARC metadata, and she chairs Rutgers' Metadata Interest Group. Weber has published books on cataloging and RDA and has served as an associate editor for the international journal *LIBRES*. She is an active member of the Association for Library Collections and Technical Services (ALCTS) and served for six years as the editor of the association's online newsletter. She is currently the editor of *Library Resources & Technical Services*, ALCTS's official journal, which is also one of the top-ranked scholarly journals for technical services research.

* * *

Erin E. Boyd is Technical Services Supervisor at the Irving Public Library in the Dallas/Fort Worth, Texas, area. Her expertise is in cataloging music, audiovisual materials, and electronic resources. Erin's research interests are mentoring, social media in libraries, long-distance collaboration, and collection management.

Alice Crosetto is the coordinator for collection development and acquisitions librarian for the University of Toledo Libraries. In this capacity, she oversees monographs and media purchases, determines the disposition of gift items, and coordinates the library liaison program and the participation of selectors in collection development. Alice also provides collection development for Mathematics, Religious Studies, and the Middle East/Islamic Studies programs.

Elyssa Gould is an assistant librarian at the University of Michigan Law Library, where she oversees electronic resources. She is an active ALCTS member and serves as the co-chair of the New Members Interest Group. Elyssa is also the book review editor for *Library Resources & Technical Services*.

Sylvia Hall-Ellis is currently the director of grants and resource development at the Colorado Community College System. Her previous professional positions include associate professor in the Morgridge College of Education, University of Denver, and serving as an adjunct faculty member for San Jose State University. Sylvia is a respected technical services educator, and her research interests include competencies for catalog and technical services librarians, library and information science, and Resource Description and Access (RDA).

Michael Luesebrink is the collection assessment librarian within the Collections Division, University Libraries, Florida State University. He earned a BA in Biology from the University of California, San Cruz; an MLS from San Jose State University; and a PhD in Information Science from Florida State University. Michael's library experience is varied and includes serving as an archivist at San Simeon in California, as a corporate librarian for a pharmaceutical company, and most recently in acquisitions.

Julie Renee Moore is the catalog librarian for special collections and special formats, California State University, Fresno, and has over twenty-five years of experience as a professional cataloger in academic and special libraries. She is an active member of Online Audiovisual Catalogers (OLAC), the Association for Library Collections and Technical Services (ALCTS), and the California Library Association's Technical Services Interest Group (CLA/TSIG). In 2010, she received both the Nancy B. Olson Award from OLAC and the CLA/TSIG Award of Achievement.

Sherry L. Vellucci is a professor and metadata services librarian at the University of New Hampshire. She is recognized internationally for her extensive knowledge of cataloging, metadata, and music cataloging. Sherry was awarded the Edward Swanson Memorial Best of *LRTS* Award in 2001 for her research paper "Metadata and Authority Control."

James L. Weinheimer has had a wide variety of library experience, plus extensive international library experience. A significant portion of his career has been devoted to open-source software development. Jim and his wife moved to Italy in 2001, where he has held a variety of library positions, and currently works in the Statistics Division of the Food and Agriculture Organization of the United Nations in Rome.

Amy K. Weiss is the head of description and cataloging in the Cataloging and Description Department at Florida State University Libraries in Tallahassee. She is known for her extensive knowledge of cataloging and technical services, including a strong record of scholarship. Amy was recognized for her expertise in 2004 when she was awarded the Edward Swanson Memorial Best of *LRTS* Award for her research paper "Proliferating Guidelines: A History and Analysis of the Cataloging of Electronic Resources."